Sport for Our Neighbours

A PRIDE AND PREJUDICE VARIATION

MELISSA ANNE

Copyright © 2025 by Melissa Anne

All rights reserved.

No part of this book may be reproduced in any form or by any electronic or mechanical means, including information storage and retrieval systems, without written permission from the author, except for the use of brief quotations in a book review.

This novel is entirely a work of fiction. The names, characters and incidents portrayed in it are the work of the author's imagination. Any resemblance to actual persons, living or dead, events or localities is entirely coincidental.

This is a work of fiction based on the characters created by Jane Austen in Pride and Prejudice. Ms. Austen created these characters, but like many others, I enjoy placing them in alternate circumstances and situations.

For my Family.

Contents

Preface	vii
1. Visitors to Longbourn	1
2. Impressions	9
3. Changes Abound	17
4. A Few Years Later	27
5. Reflections	37
6. A Gentleman's Agreement	45
7. Chance Meetings	51
8. Reintroductions	61
9. Confessions	73
10. A Threat	83
11. Arrival at Netherfield	93
12. Early Morning Encounter	101
13. The Set Down	109
14. The Assembly	115
15. First Dances	123
16. Revelations	131
17. A Private Meeting	137
18. Letters	145
19. Getting to Know You	153
20. New Arrivals at Netherfield	159
21. The Countess Arrives	169
22. Plotting	183
23. Visiting Longbourn	195
24. Confessions	203
25. A Tentative Understanding	213
26. Realisations	225
27. Meeting Wickham	235
28. Discoveries	245
29. A Confrontation	253
30. Defensive Tactics	261
31. Sweet Williams	271
32. Further Discussions	281
33. A Dinner Party at Netherfield	289
34. Caroline Bingley Plots	301

35. Countermeasures	309
36. The Confrontation	317
37. Bingley Finds Out	325
38. Decisions and Another Confrontation	335
39. Preparations Begin	345
40. Mr. Collins Intrudes	355
41. A Wedding	361
42. Travelling to London	367
43. Confronting the Earl	375
44. Many Happy Returns	383
45. Epilogue	393
Acknowledgments	399
About the Author	401
Also by Melissa Anne	403
Coming Soon	405

Preface

"For what do we live, but to make sport for our neighbours, and laugh at them in our turn?"

MR. BENNET, PRIDE AND PREJUDICE, CHAPTER 57

CHAPTER 1

Visitors to Longbourn

JUNE 1806

For much of the last decade and a half, Thomas Bennet had found enjoyment in laughing at his increasingly ridiculous wife and his silly daughters. The eldest two, Jane and Lizzy, had flourished under the influence of their grandmother, his mother, but the youngest three had not been old enough to benefit from her wisdom and example before she died. He regretted it, but he was powerless to do anything to change the situation. After all, they were all daughters, and despite Lizzy's quickness and love of learning, he had little to do with their upbringing. Had there been a son, he would have paid more attention to them all, but when the last babe came—another girl—he had turned to his books for comfort.

He listened to the noise descending the stairs. His two most sensible daughters were presently in London. Elizabeth was soon to turn fifteen, and Mrs. Bennet had insisted she and Jane visit their aunt and uncle to purchase a few new dresses to prepare for Elizabeth's entry into their local society. When Jane turned fifteen, Mrs. Bennet had insisted she be "out" and had decided that when each child attained that age, she would follow. Unwilling to argue since there were few men in the local area with whom to concern himself, he had given in to her pronouncement.

Bennet believed the extravagance of new dresses from London to be unnecessary; still, he permitted them to go to Edward Gardiner, his wife's younger brother. Where the sister was nervous and silly, the brother was confident and sensible. A genial man—a helpful trait for a tradesman to have—the man had a knack for investing that left him rather well off. His warehouses were full to bursting. His wife, the daughter of a clergyman, was well able to assist Jane and Elizabeth in choosing suitable gowns according to their tastes while providing a genteel example for the girls.

Frequently, Gardiner encouraged his brother Bennet to invest with him. However, other than turning over one hundred pounds for each daughter at their birth, Bennet had not availed himself of the offer. He was, by nature, an indolent man, and to do more would mean limiting his own purchase of books or else dealing with the fuss his wife was sure to create if he suggested she restrain her spending. Since he had little desire to do either, he opted to do nothing and pray that others would be there to care for his daughters and wife in the event of his death.

However, today he was to enjoy the company of friends, two gentlemen from his university days. They were to come for a brief visit, stopping at Longbourn as they travelled north from London. His wife and youngest daughters were above stairs; he could hear his wife's shrill voice even behind the closed door of his study.

The younger girls were still full young to be in company: Mary was thirteen, Kitty, as she was known in the family, had recently turned eleven, and Lydia was nine. Before her death, his mother had encouraged him to take the younger girls in hand, but he had not, and soon the money that might have been used for this purpose was claimed by his wife for some reason or another.

He considered them as silly and ignorant as other girls, taking after his wife. The youngest girls, Kitty and Lydia, had few interests outside of fashion. The idea of flirting and courtship intrigued them already because Mrs. Bennet had filled their heads that the ultimate goal of their lives was to capture a wealthy husband. *Her* primary concern in life was to ensure all her daughters married well so they could care for her. Mary attempted to appear as more, studying the scripture and other religious texts with a tendency to moralise.

To Bennet, however, all of this was a source of amusement. He neglected his wife and daughters, preferring to sit in his study with his books as company. He did enough on the estate to ensure that their income did not decline and spent some time training his second daughter to assist him. This was done more to free up his own time for his reading since Lizzy enjoyed walking and talking to the tenants; however, he did not allow her to implement any of her suggestions for improving the estate.

In the midst of these musings, his friends were announced. "Mr. George Darcy, Mr. Fitzwilliam Darcy, and Mr. James Livesay are here to see you, sir," the housekeeper said as she showed the gentlemen in.

"Darcy, Livesay, how pleased I am to see you! Darcy, is this young man your son? It is hard to believe either of us is old enough to have already raised a child to adulthood."

Bennet invited his guests to take a seat wherever they could find one amid the chaos of his study.

For the next several minutes, the three old school chums caught up, while the younger Darcy sat quietly, observing and listening. Although they exchanged letters with some regularity—Darcy and Livesay far more often than Bennet—there was still much to discuss: their estates, their children, and the politics of the day.

As the conversation wound on, George Darcy glanced around, laughing inwardly at the stacks of books strewn about his library. "It seems little has changed, Bennet. You still fill every available surface with your books. Now that Fitzwilliam is grown, he will begin to assume some of the responsibility for the estate. That will give me more time for reading. But you, Bennet, you have daughters, no son, so how do you find the time to read all these?"

Bennet chuckled at his friend. "I may not have a son, but my Lizzy is quite adept at visiting the tenants and learning their concerns. While she may not be able to do all your son does, she is of much assistance to me."

"I thought your oldest daughter was Jane," Livesay said, confusion evident on his brow.

"Jane is the eldest at seventeen. She and Lizzy are in London to purchase new dresses with my sister by marriage. Lizzy will soon celebrate her fifteenth birthday, and my wife has decreed that all the girls will be out at that age. She is eager for them to capture gentlemen to marry."

He laughed and did not notice the frowns that crossed the faces of all three of his guests. "Surely, Bennet, you are not encouraging this behaviour in your wife!" Darcy cried. "Do you recall how you felt when you were 'captured' against your will? You married a woman who is not a gentlewoman, and I knew your mother well enough to know she would have attempted to guide and teach her. And you, Bennet, you are too intelligent to allow such frivolous behaviour in your wife, even one who might have been unwanted."

Bennet scowled at the evident disapproval from his friend. "It is the business of women to train daughters. The eldest two, Jane and Lizzy, had the benefit of my mother's instruction prior to her death and have spent time in London with my brother and his wife. You know the Gardiners, do you not, George? Madeline once lived in Lambton. Her father had the living there."

Darcy nodded. "I do know Gardiner and have invested some funds with him. He told me he has tried to convince you to do so as well, but you refuse. Bennet, I know your estate is entailed along the male line, so what are you doing to prepare for your daughters' futures? It may be none of my business, but I know you, my friend, and you were always one to bury your head in the sand instead of facing what was coming."

Scowling again, Bennet went on the defensive. "My grandfather put an entail on this estate, and the woman who trapped me into marriage has borne five daughters. Five! None of whom can inherit due to that blasted entail. What am I supposed to do? The cousin who will inherit is a fool!"

"Ensure they are well provided for and properly trained so they might make decent matches," Livesay answered, his voice demonstrating their lack of empathy for his friend in this situation. He and Darcy had discussed what they expected to find when they arrived and, to his disappointment, it was worse than they had expected. "Do what any loving father would do for their daughters, regardless of how many he has or the status of his estate. Or even of his feelings towards his wife. None of those reasons should have a bearing on your duty to your family."

Bennet scoffed. "You each have a son to ensure your legacy continues. I do not. As I said, a fool will inherit in my stead, and, from what I know of my cousin, he will run the estate into the ground."

George Darcy stepped forward, his voice sharp and unyielding. "And we each have daughters to raise without their mothers. Do not act as though you are the only one who has endured loss or difficulties. I lost my Anne five years ago, and every day I wrestle with how to best raise Georgiana who is near the age of your youngest daughter. I have done everything possible to ensure her support, supplying her with a nurse and governess, yet I still worry about whether it is enough. Livesay here—" he gestured towards him— "lost his wife more than a decade ago and has since raised his two sons and three daughters on his own. You are not alone in your suffering."

Darcy's tone grew harsher as he continued, his gaze fixed intently on Bennet. "Tell me, do you ever leave your study? This daughter who aids you—you said she is fourteen? How much of her childhood have you sacrificed because you refuse to face the world beyond these walls?" He reproached his friend in a deliberate attempt to jolt his friend out of his obvious despondency.

"She is nearly fifteen," Bennet defended himself, refusing to meet his friends' eyes.

Darcy's eyes narrowed, his voice cutting like frost. "She aids you with your estate? Pray, tell me, Bennet, how does a fourteen-year-old girl manage to assist with the responsibilities of an estate such as yours? What tasks have you placed upon her young shoulders? Is she, practically still a child, left to handle all that you cannot be bothered to do yourself? Even Fitzwilliam here has had my support as he learnt, and he is a university graduate and a man. In addition, unlike you, we have competent stewards to assist us with our duties."

Darcy leant forward, his words laced with both incredulity and disdain. "When your father was alive, you boasted that this estate brought in three thousand a year. Is that still true, or has your neglect eroded even that?"

Bennet frowned, his tone sour. "It is less. Last year, the estate brought in only two thousand. It has brought in that amount for the last several years."

Livesay's expression darkened, his voice sharp. "How have you lost a third of the estate's income? A poor season or two I could understand, but last year should have been a prosperous one. I must echo my friend's question—when was the last time you stepped out of your study to see to your responsibilities?"

Bennet leant back in his chair, the weight of the conversation pressing down on him. "Not as often as I should," he admitted grudgingly. "Lizzy manages most of the visits to the tenants now and tells me what they say."

"Who accompanies her if you do not go and there is not a steward?" Mr. Darcy asked pointedly.

"She has traipsed through these fields since she was a child and likely knows them better than many of our servants and tenants," Bennet said, waving the question away.

The younger Darcy, who had been quietly observing the exchange between the older gentlemen, suddenly looked aghast. "She visits the tenants alone?" he blurted out, his voice filled with disbelief. "Does she not have a steward or at least a footman to accompany her when she visits your tenants? Even at Pemberley, where I know every tenant and servant personally, I would never encourage Georgiana to visit them alone. My mother certainly would never have attempted such a thing."

The elder Darcy fixed Bennet with a hard gaze. "You place her in a dangerous position, Bennet. Do you not care for your daughter's safety?"

"Longbourn is not Pemberley," Bennet snapped at the younger man. "Our estate is smaller, and I know my tenants well. None of them would harm her or allow her to be injured. Besides, Lizzy is fiercely independent and has roamed these fields since she was a mere toddler. Were I to restrict her to the house, she would sneak out a window."

When the younger Darcy bristled at this, his father placed his hand on his arm and turned to his friend. "My son was raised understanding a gentleman's duty to the women in his life. You are correct: Pemberley is not Longbourn, and the tenants there are spread further apart. The countryside is also different, but still, I am astounded that the daughter you claim as your favourite is allowed to roam freely. Even at Pemberley, safe as it is, there have been an instance or two of someone from outside who came in intending to do harm."

"Enough, gentlemen. Surely you did not come only to lambaste me for my poor parenting and stewardship." He cast a wary glance at the two men, their apparent disapproval pressing heavily upon him. Although he had not seen either of them in years and their communication had been limited to letters, he had long admired their character and principles—making their reproach all the more stinging.

Sensing the tension, the gentlemen allowed the conversation to meander into safer waters, discussing news of mutual acquaintances and exchanging light hearted anecdotes. Yet it was not long before the topic turned back to the estate.

"Come, Bennet," Darcy said with an encouraging smile. "We have much to catch up on, but it would do us all some good to stretch our legs before we spend the next few days confined to a carriage. Fitzwilliam and I are bound for Pemberley, and from there, Livesay has another day or two before reaching Greenfield Manor in Lancashire."

Bennet nodded though his enthusiasm seemed muted. "Ah, yes, Greenfield Manor. My Lizzy is enamoured with the idea of travel and would revel in seeing either of your estates. Alas, I can no longer abide long journeys in a carriage."

"You know you would always be welcome," Livesay replied. The invitation had been extended many times over the years without the other man's acceptance. A brief look passed between the three men; each understood Bennet would never leave Longbourn for such a visit, regardless of how often they asked.

Bennet cleared his throat and gestured towards the door. "Well then, let us prepare for our ride. I will have Hill show you to your rooms so you might change into something more suitable for riding. I shall do the same." He paused, glancing between the two men. "I assume you brought your own horses?"

"Of course," Darcy said, standing. "I have been eager to see the state of your lands, Bennet. The fresh air and ride will do us good."

CHAPTER 2

Impressions

Hill escorted the men to their rooms, where their trunks had been neatly placed and were awaiting them. Each man retreated to prepare for the ride. Fitzwilliam Darcy, the youngest of the group, was quick to change, but found his curiosity piqued as he surveyed the space assigned to him.

While arranged neatly and all the personal items stored away, the room still bore the faint traces of its usual occupant. A delicate scent of lavender lingered in the air, and subtle touches betrayed a feminine hand.

In particular, the bookshelves drew his attention. They were filled with well-worn volumes, ranging from novels to poetry, the spines bearing evidence of frequent handling. A glance at the desk revealed a few sheets of paper with faint imprints on them as though notes had recently been written and removed.

It struck him that this must be the room of one of the absent Bennet daughters, likely pressed into service to accommodate the unexpected visitors. *Which one?* he wondered.

Jane, the eldest—whom her father described as a beauty but said little else about? Or perhaps the second, Elizabeth, who, from the little he had heard, seemed to possess a lively wit and keen intelligence? It was unlikely to belong to the younger girls who were still in the school-room and at home.

His gaze lingered on a book left on the nightstand—*A Midsummer Night's Dream*. Its placement seemed deliberate as if the owner had only just set it aside. He smiled faintly, wondering whether the one who read it preferred the mischievous Puck or Titania for her nobility.

The thought warmed him, even while he reminded himself again of the impracticality of such musings. His father would never approve of a match with a young lady so far beneath their social station, would he?

Fitzwilliam shook his head, clearing it from such fanciful thoughts. *Why would I even contemplate such a thing?* he asked himself. *It is likely this room belongs to a young lady, nearly a child still, and I certainly am too young to consider marriage right now.*

Soon, all four men gathered again downstairs. They heard a shrill cry somewhere in the house followed by the sound of multiple feet coming down the stairs. "Mr. Bennet, you neglected to mention that your guests had arrived."

Mrs. Bennet turned to look at them, not bothering to acknowledge her daughters behind her, immediately honing in on the youngest of the group. Two of the girls were giggling loudly while the third merely looked on.

"Oh, which one of you gentlemen brought your son with you? It is a shame my dear Jane is in London, for she is ever so beautiful. Are you going to London now?" she asked, her voice grating to Fitzwilliam Darcy's ears.

"No, madam, we are bound for the north when we leave here," George Darcy said. "I thank you for allowing us to stay the night in your home before we continue. Bennet, will you introduce us to your family?"

Bennet complied with his friend's request, introducing his wife and the three youngest daughters to their guests. Almost at once, Lydia—the youngest of the group—sidled up to Fitzwilliam Darcy with a giggle and a flutter of her lashes, eager to practise what she had overheard her mother advising her older sisters was the proper way to catch a husband.

Fitzwilliam stiffened, his discomfort plain as he took a step back, putting distance between himself and the girl. His eyes flicked to the others in the room, silently pleading for intervention from the child's parents—but none came. When he looked back at Lydia, his expression had hardened into a mix of disapproval and unease.

He glared at her for a moment before turning his back fully, his displeasure unmistakable—even to Lydia, who responded with a sulky pout. Fitzwilliam glanced towards his father, hoping for some guidance or an end to the awkward encounter, but George Darcy merely watched, his expression unreadable, leaving his son to handle the moment alone.

His hand brushed the edge of a nearby chair, as though seeking something to steady himself. He had not expected such forwardness, especially from someone so young, and the impropriety of it all made his skin crawl. The behaviour only seemed to underscore a troubling lack of guidance in the household—a thought that deepened his unease.

However, Bennet only laughed, clearly unbothered by his youngest's behaviour. "Pay her no mind, young Darcy. Lydia is her mother's daughter, and *she* has decided our daughters do not need a governess."

He spoke with such casualness that he failed to notice the expressions of the three gentlemen who exchanged glances of surprise and concern. Had he observed their reactions, he might have been less surprised by the pointed remarks that would come from his friend during their ride.

After they had ridden for some time, the elder Darcy slowed his horse to a walk and urged Bennet to do the same. They lapsed into a silence that stretched for several minutes before Darcy finally spoke.

"Bennet," he began, his voice steady but firm, "you know I value our friendship. But I can remain silent no longer on this matter. You must take an interest in your daughters' lives. Your neglect is doing them no favours."

Bennet remained silent, his lips set in a firm line, and Darcy pressed on. "The man I knew at Cambridge was idealistic and intelligent, but through your letters, I have watched you allow your bitterness over your choice of wife being taken from you turn into someone else entirely. If you do not act soon, all your daughters will be nearly unmarriageable—not through any fault of their own, but by the actions of your wife and youngest daughter. They are already disadvantaged, but did you not see the look of disgust that crossed my son's face when your youngest daughter rubbed against him and tried to flirt with him? She's a child, Bennet! Do you not see anything wrong with a nine-year-old thinking it appropriate to flirt with a man twice her age?"

Darcy's tone grew more urgent as he continued. "Bennet, wake up and take a look at your family. Do something—anything—but stop hiding away in your study and allowing your second child to manage the estate because you will not."

When Bennet finally spoke, he was scowling at his friend. "Lydia is a foolish child, just like the rest of them. "Why should I bother to do anything?" he asked, his bitterness obvious as he continued. "It is not as though any of them could inherit."

Darcy just shook his head. "If you truly ask that, my friend, I am afraid I do not know you as well as I once thought. The man I believed I knew was, perhaps, equally interested in books, but not content to sit back and passively let life pass him by. You were once better than the man I have met today. That man would have never allowed bitterness to consume him as you have." With that, Darcy spurred his horse to catch up with the others, leaving his friend behind, unwilling to hear his retort. Little was said during the remainder of the ride as Bennet lagged behind the others.

When the men returned to the estate, they all retreated to their rooms for a rest before dressing for dinner. Feeling all the awkwardness of their earlier encounters, all four men waited until the last possible moment to return downstairs.

Bennet was quiet throughout the meal. His friends seemed to recognise his need for reflection and so attempted to speak amongst themselves. However, Mrs. Bennet and the two youngest daughters frequently interrupted their conversation by asking questions about the men's estates and houses in town and other equally grasping questions.

Despite his lack of participation in the conversation, Bennet was keenly aware of it and, as the evening wore on, a deep sense of shame settled over him. Among other things, it became painfully clear that his youngest daughters should not have been in company that evening. Their behaviour was crude, and their lack of proper instruction was evident. Regardless of their ages, they should have known how to conduct themselves with more restraint. Lydia's constant interruptions and her glaring ignorance were impossible to disregard, prompting frequent, disapproving glances from all three men, even the younger Darcy, which were often followed by pointed looks at Bennet.

When the ladies left the table, after much prompting from Bennet towards his wife, Bennet finally addressed his friends. "Darcy," he began, taking a deep breath and blowing it out slowly, "do you think you might know someone who can help me find a governess for the girls? One who is wise enough that she might take my daughters in hand while also helping my wife learn proper behaviour. I think you will find me writing far more often in the future since I need to do something to save for their dowries. Perhaps I will even send the two youngest to school. Watching them, it seems possible that Kitty will improve more quickly if she is separated from Lydia."

The two older men nodded in agreement while Fitzwilliam Darcy subtly distanced himself from the conversation. He was much younger than the others and had little to contribute, but he also did not want his father's friend to feel hesitant to speak because of his presence. As he listened, his thoughts drifted to the two older Bennet daughters. The fact that one daughter, just fourteen and soon to be "out," had been trained by her father to manage the estate—and was evidently doing a competent job of it—particularly intrigued him.

As he thought about it and the limited regard he held for most women he had met in society, Darcy briefly wondered if perhaps he should marry a country girl—someone practical, capable, and less concerned with the superficialities that often dominated society, which already made him uncomfortable.

He chuckled to himself, causing his father to look in his direction. At his father's questioning look, the younger Darcy shook his head.

Later, when everyone had retired for the night, George Darcy made his way to his son's room. "What was so amusing after dinner?" he asked, settling into a chair near the fire and looking around at the well-appointed room, his eyes scanning the bookshelves just as his son had done earlier.

"Merely an idle thought, Father," Fitzwilliam replied after a moment. "I was thinking about Mr. Bennet's fourteen-year-old daughter practically running the estate. I was certain she must have had *some* assistance from her father, but during our ride, the gentleman admitted she is largely responsible for much of what happens. Here I am, twenty-one with a university education, and yet I do not feel prepared to manage an estate the size of Longbourn, much less Pemberley. That led me to consider seeking a wife from the country rather than from the *ton*. I chuckled because I cannot imagine you ever approving of such a choice as my bride."

George Darcy sighed heavily. "Actually, Fitzwilliam, I would have no objection to you marrying a country miss in a few years, particularly if you find one similar to Miss Elizabeth Bennet. Neither of us has met her, but from what her father has said about her, I think you might find her interesting despite her age. Of course, you are far too young right now to consider marriage, and so is she. The Darcys are sufficiently wealthy that you could easily afford to marry a woman with no dowry. We have ample connections; I should think you would say we have too many."

"But would my marrying a 'country miss' injure Georgiana's chances of marrying well?" Fitzwilliam asked.

"Georgiana has a dowry of thirty thousand pounds, and she is the granddaughter of the Earl of Matlock, in addition to being a Darcy. I have no worries that she will not be pursued; the bigger challenge will be finding a suitor who is acceptable. But just as I hope for you, son, I want Georgiana to find a man to marry who will love her for who she is and not for the dowry she will bring. Fitzwilliam, I married your mother for love. It was to my advantage that she happened to be an earl's daughter. When it comes time for you to make a choice, concern yourself less with wealth and connections; choose a young lady based on character and affection. I do not want you trapped in a miserable marriage made solely for material reasons."

George Darcy paused for a moment, his gaze steady as he placed a reassuring hand on his son's shoulder. "When the time comes for you to manage Pemberley, son, I have no doubt you will do well. I sincerely hope that day is still many years off; still, I am confident you will be an excellent overseer. You have worked alongside me every summer and during each holiday when you are home and, over the years, you have gained a keen understanding of the estate, its operations, and our various investments. Your ability to grasp the complexities of the estate has always impressed me, from managing our lands to understanding the financial intricacies of our holdings. In many regards, you know nearly as much about it as I do, and you will only continue to grow in knowledge and experience over the coming years."

He gave his son's shoulder a gentle squeeze, his voice softening. "I have always been proud of you, Fitzwilliam. You have an intelligent mind and a strong sense of duty, both of which will serve you well when the time comes and I am gone. In the matter of taking a wife, I trust you will do so in your own time with all the wisdom and caution I know you possess."

Darcy was momentarily at a loss for words in response to his father's praise, but he nodded his quiet acknowledgment. A surge of pride swelled within him, knowing that his father held such a high opinion of his abilities.

The two men continued conversing for a short time though George Darcy, observing his son's thoughtful silence, could tell that Fitzwilliam was reflecting on their discussion. After a few more exchanges, the conversation naturally wound down, and in the morning, the three gentlemen set off for the north to continue their journey.

CHAPTER 3

Changes Abound

After nearly a fortnight of reflection—and considerable argument with himself—Bennet came to the uncomfortable realization that his neglect had only worsened his family's situation. Although he had been inclined to dismiss his friends' concerns, he could no longer deny the truth they had forced him to confront. By the time Jane and Elizabeth returned from London, he had already begun implementing the reforms he believed necessary for his family's future. Chief among his priorities was the education and refinement of his daughters, whose upbringing he now acknowledged as woefully inadequate for their station in life.

Letters had been exchanged between London and Longbourn, and a Miss Sutton accompanied Jane and Elizabeth home. She was engaged to oversee the academic and behavioural instruction of the three youngest girls—Mary, Kitty, and Lydia. Her no-nonsense attitude left a swift impression on all three girls.

Mary, whose natural inclination for learning and order had often gone unnoticed within the family before this, flourished under Miss Sutton's strict structure and guidance. Kitty, spirited but biddable, adapted with a bit of effort and quickly found enjoyment not only in learning but also in the praise she received for a job well done.

Lydia, however, proved a constant challenge. Even at nine years of age, her impetuous nature seemed to resist every attempt to check her, testing Miss Sutton's considerable patience with her heedlessness and growing tendency to seek attention through pert remarks and exaggerated charm. When thwarted, she turned to dramatic tantrums and fits of anger, showing little regard for decorum or discipline. No sooner would she be corrected on one piece of unseemly behaviour than she would invent another, more troublesome than the last.

For Jane and Elizabeth, a different arrangement was made. Recognizing their greater maturity and sense, Bennet hired a companion, Mrs. Graham—a genteel widow recommended by Mrs. Gardiner—to oversee their social and moral development. Under her tutelage, both girls expanded their accomplishments to include more of the skills expected of young ladies of their station in life.

Jane embraced these lessons with her usual quiet grace, applying herself without complaint. She joined Elizabeth in those subjects she found of interest, especially enjoying discussing current events with her father. Already seventeen, Jane remained "out" in their local society, and Mrs. Graham attended social events with her to provide additional chaperonage. Bennet also began attending gatherings, and he strove to curtail some of his wife's gossipy tendencies.

Determined to ensure Elizabeth's preparation was equally thorough, Bennet postponed her official "coming out" until her seventeenth birthday. Mrs. Bennet had protested at first, but Bennet had held firm in his decree. The idea that her husband's friends had disapproved of her daughters had been enough to convince her initially, and as she spent time with Mrs. Graham—ostensibly supervising the girls' education—she came to a greater understanding of what was expected.

While all the girls were taught the typical lessons of a gentleman's daughter, Elizabeth's studies were broadened to include history and current events, along with mathematics, languages, music, and literature. When Elizabeth's aptitude soon surpassed what Mrs. Graham could teach, tutors were engaged in subjects in which she desired further instruction.

To further refine his daughters' accomplishments, now that the estate was more profitable and the excessive expenses curtailed, Bennet was able to engage music and language masters, and, upon discovering that Jane and Catherine displayed an interest in art, hired a drawing master as well. Elizabeth attempted to learn, but she soon abandoned drawing in favour of her other studies. Mary, ever drawn to theological and moral pursuits, showed little interest in painting, while Lydia openly scoffed at the lessons, preferring instead to sneak away at every opportunity.

Beyond the girls' education, Bennet became a more active participant in the management of Longbourn. To the surprise of the tenants and household servants, he began overseeing estate affairs more closely, eventually hiring a steward recommended to him by Livesay.

Elizabeth, long her father's confidante, continued assisting him, particularly in maintaining positive relations with the tenants, something that her sisters now assisted her with. Although her days were filled with studies and lessons, she still found time to accompany him on estate visits, learning firsthand the practical skills needed to run a country property.

For Elizabeth, life soon settled into a satisfying rhythm with these changes. At times, she missed the unstructured hours once spent roaming the fields and woods, but she gladly embraced the greater purpose she found in her new studies and responsibilities. She discovered a particular aptitude for languages—excelling in French and Italian—and practiced her music with passion, if not quite with the diligence it required.

Beyond her lessons, Elizabeth continued to seek solace in the outdoors, walking whenever possible. Her father, newly mindful of her safety, insisted she be accompanied by a sister or a footman on these outings.

Initially, Elizabeth chafed at these restrictions. Her independent spirit rebelled against the limitations, and it took several stern reprimands—and the threat of severe punishment—before she grudgingly complied with her father's demands for someone to accompany her.

Early on in the process, unable to contain her frustration at the new limitations placed upon her, Elizabeth confronted her father one afternoon when a footman followed her without a word when she left the house.

"Papa, truly, must I have a shadow at my heel every time I wish to breathe fresh air?" she cried, arms folded tightly across her chest when she returned, barging into his study without bothering to knock.

Bennet, seated with a book in hand, arched a brow at her entry. "Given your penchant for solitary wandering and the alarming potential of a daughter being misplaced when not properly supervised, I think it prudent, Lizzy."

She huffed in irritation. "I have no desire to run off with a traveling tinker," she retorted. "You confuse me with Lydia."

"A relief to us all," he replied drily. "Nonetheless, you will take a companion. That is final."

By demonstrating her reliability, she gradually earned greater freedom, which allowed her to expand her assistance in tenant visits and estate matters. She enjoyed these, for it granted her the opportunity to be of use to her father and to escape the drawing room where she was forced to sit quietly and sew. While she did not mind sewing, it was the enforced stillness and the constant interruptions that plagued her.

Along with the other accomplishments they were taught, all five Bennet daughters were also required to master the basics of riding sidesaddle. Two additional horses were purchased to support these lessons and to provide gentle mounts for them to learn on. Lydia, naturally athletic, enjoyed riding but, true to form, her unwillingness to submit to Miss Sutton's authority prevented her from practicing as often as she might have done otherwise.

In time, only Elizabeth rode regularly. As a reward for her diligence, and for her increasing contributions to the estate's affairs, Bennet sold two of the older horses and purchased Elizabeth a mare of her own.

Bennet's reforms extended beyond education to household management. Under his orders, Mrs. Graham instructed all five daughters—and their mother—in the tasks necessary to run Longbourn effectively. From supervising the housekeeper and kitchen staff to understanding the intricacies of managing estate accounts, the girls received a thorough education in the practicalities of genteel life, including how to live within a set budget.

As with all these endeavours, some took to this more than the others. Mrs. Bennet initially resisted, bristling at the notion of submitting to the same standards of propriety and decorum imposed upon her daughters, not to mention the restrictions to her spending in order to pay for these changes.

"Manage the household accounts?" she exclaimed one morning, waving the steward's ledger away as if it might bite her. "As if I do not already have enough to do, Mr. Bennet! Five daughters to marry off, dinners to plan, callers to entertain—and now you expect me to play housekeeper as well?"

Bennet, leaning against the mantel, raised an eyebrow. "You are not being asked to scour the floors, madam, only to understand how those who do it are paid for the task and to learn how to minimise your expenses so you might live within the new budget I have given you.

You fear the hedgerows after my death; this is what it will take to ensure you have somewhere better than that to live."

Mrs. Bennet huffed and fanned herself dramatically at such a declaration. "If I had wanted to live like a tradesman's wife, I might have married that dreadful Mr. Elkins after all. I married a gentleman and wish to live as a gentlewoman ought to do."

"You forget, Mrs. Bennet, how frequently my mother spent time on this very same task," Bennet replied tersely, recalling the battles with his mother in the early days of his marriage. How he wished he had put his foot down all those years ago. Things would be different now.

Mrs. Bennet continued to glare at him, and their standoff might have continued indefinitely had it not been interrupted by the sound of rapid footsteps—and a loud crash.

"Miss Lydia!" came Miss Sutton's sharp voice from the stairwell.

A moment later, Lydia burst into the room, her gown smeared with dirt and grass stains, her hair tumbling down her back. In one grubby hand she clutched a torn piece of paper, ink smudged across its surface.

"I don't like Miss Sutton!" Lydia cried before anyone could speak. "She said I must write about 'obedience'—and I said obedience is stupid! I hate that I am no longer permitted to do as I wish."

Mrs. Bennet gasped, pressing a hand to her chest. "Oh, my poor lamb! Forced to endure such dreadful treatment—"

Behind Lydia, Miss Sutton entered the room, calm as ever, holding another sheet of paper.

"Miss Lydia, despite her opinions," said Miss Sutton coolly, "will write her sentences five times properly as punishment for her refusal to listen to or participate in lessons, and for her attempted escape from the school room through the third floor window by climbing down a tree."

Fluttering her handkerchief, Mrs. Bennet exclaimed over her daughter's actions, but further effusions were cut off by Miss Sutton's continued explanation.

"If she does not do as I have asked, she will copy a passage from Fordyce's Sermons until dinner which will be porridge served in the nursery. She will do it legibly, or she will repeat it until it is. The windows in the schoolroom will be locked from this point forward and perhaps barred if it proves necessary." This last was said with a pointed look at Lydia, who only glared back at her.

Lydia pouted furiously. "That's unfair!"

"Life often is," Miss Sutton said serenely. "Come along, child."

With that, she ushered Lydia back towards the schoolroom. Lydia grumbled the entire way, but she went.

The door closed behind them.

Mrs. Bennet stood silent, staring after her youngest daughter. Slowly, her gaze drifted back to the ledger resting on the table.

"She is more than ten now," she murmured, "and still runs wild like a stable boy. I suppose Miss Sutton has done well with her, considering she listens to hardly anyone—least of all her sisters or her mother. I gave her too much freedom before, did I not?"

Bennet said nothing. He merely waited.

Mrs. Bennet straightened her cap with trembling fingers.

"You think this is my fault," she finally said.

"I think," Bennet replied, "that we have both indulged too long in what was easiest, rather than what was wisest. All our children have suffered for it, but Lydia most of all."

She pressed her lips together, struggling with her emotions. At last, she let out a heavy sigh.

"Very well," she muttered. "I will meet with the housekeeper this afternoon to take a look at the books. But do not expect me to count poultry or to try my hand in the kitchen."

"Your sacrifice is noted, madam," Bennet replied drily.

From that day forward, Mrs. Bennet attended the household meetings—sometimes with a grimace, but with growing understanding. Although she never grew fond of ledgers, she soon developed a keen eye for household accounts and an even keener one for expenses she deemed "quite unnecessary."

As the months turned into years, the transformation at Longbourn became increasingly apparent. Neighbours frequently remarked upon the improved demeanour of the family. Jane's natural grace became more refined; Elizabeth's sharp wit was tempered by the wisdom gained through broader studies. Mary, with newfound confidence, contributed thoughtfully to conversation, while structured lessons gradually moderated Kitty's once flighty spirits.

However, not all the girls adjusted as well. Two years after the events of that fateful summer, Bennet called his wife into the study. Earlier that afternoon, Lydia had been discovered boldly flirting with a visiting groom—laughing and tossing her hair in a manner wholly unbecoming of a young lady.

"This behaviour must stop," he said curtly, closing the door behind them. "If she continues in this unchecked manner, none of your daughters shall have any reputation left to preserve."

Mrs. Bennet, unusually subdued, fanned herself in agitation. "But she is only a child, Mr. Bennet."

"A child who already knows how to behave like a woman of no sense or virtue," he replied sharply. "She must go where there is firmer discipline, or I fear for what her future may become. We have tried to teach her at home, but she has continued as she has always done.

Something must change, for I will not allow one daughter to ruin the chances of the rest of them."

Faced with this evidence of Lydia's increasing waywardness, Mrs. Bennet could offer no serious objection. Thus, at eleven, Lydia was sent away to school, where it was hoped that a stricter environment might accomplish what Longbourn's gentler efforts had failed to achieve. Not long after Lydia departed for school, the family's governess left as well, and Mrs. Graham assumed the role of companion to the four remaining girls.

In the years since his friends' visit, Bennet had changed greatly. The estate prospered, and Bennet found he had more time for his preferred pursuits than he would once have believed possible.

The residents of Longbourn were also happier. His daughters—at least four of them—assisted with the house and the estate as they were able and, although Elizabeth remained his favourite, all of them benefited from his increased presence and influence.

Mary, in particular, had taken to spending more time with their father, taking delight in deep discussions over books and essays. Catherine had shown a newfound aptitude for managing household affairs, regularly assisting both her parents and Mrs. Hill with the accounts. Her maturity had not gone unnoticed. In recognition of the change, most now addressed her as Catherine, although a few family members still occasionally slipped, out of long habit more than intent.

Mrs. Bennet, too, had changed. With the reassurance that she would not be left destitute upon her husband's death and comforted by the steps he had taken to secure her future, she grew calmer. Although she remained eager to see all her daughters married, she no longer felt the urgency and desperation she once had.

Like her husband, she had her favourites. Jane, still the most beautiful of her daughters, was never spared her mother's open praise; Mrs. Bennet fully expected her to marry well. Despite Lydia's persistent intransigence, she also remained a favourite, if only because she most resembled her mother.

CHAPTER 4

A Few Years Later

3 SEPTEMBER 1811

Under Bennet's guidance, Longbourn flourished. The estate became a symbol of growth and stability—a marked contrast to its former neglect. Over the past five years, Bennet had taken steps to safeguard his family's future, setting aside small sums annually for each of his daughters. Beyond financial preparations, he made significant improvements at Longbourn and even purchased additional properties outside the entail. These investments were intended to ensure continued income for his widow and any daughters who remained unmarried, providing them with security despite the limitations imposed by the estate's inheritance structure.

After his brother, Mr. Philips, a country attorney, had ensured the entail granted Mrs. Bennet the right to reside there rent-free for the duration of her life, the dower house was refurbished for this purpose. Other steps, including naming the girls' uncles as their guardians, had been taken to guarantee that the heir of Longbourn could seize none of the funds intended for Bennet's unmarried daughters, ensuring that they were held in separate accounts from the estate's funds. These were invested with Mr. Gardiner and earning well over the four per cent per year guaranteed in the funds.

In addition, Bennet had struck an agreement with the owner of Netherfield to share the rents, provided his family assisted in managing the tenants. This responsibility fell primarily to Elizabeth. Jane and Mary had gradually taken on more of the obligations for the Longbourn tenants to allow Elizabeth greater focus on those at Netherfield. With Lydia away at school, Catherine made an effort to be of some assistance in these matters; but having never fully recovered from a severe illness in childhood, her health remained delicate, and she was often obliged to remain near home.

Although her father had taken on much of the management of Longbourn, Elizabeth remained his assistant and shared in his estate duties. In this role, she was often in her father's confidence, and he had confessed to her that morning that he received a letter from the heir to Longbourn informing him of his intention to visit. It was this she was contemplating as she rode.

The letter made it clear that the writer was something of an oddity. He appeared to be apologising for his eventual role in displacing the Bennet daughters from Longbourn, an inevitability given the entail. His gesture of reconciliation came in the form of an "olive branch," which Elizabeth quickly deduced to mean he intended to marry one of them. When she shared her conclusion with her father, he agreed but reassured her that he would never force any of his daughters into a marriage they did not desire. Recalling the disagreement that had resulted in Bennet and Collins breaking ties all those years ago, Bennet did not want to depend on that man to do anything for his family upon his death.

Elizabeth's mind was whirling with all that her father had revealed that morning. It was difficult at times to be the one her father turned to in matters like these. The position rightfully belonged to his wife but, despite the improvements in the family, Mrs. Bennet remained flighty. Instead, Bennet continued to turn to his second daughter to provide the intellectual companionship his wife did not.

That morning, Elizabeth had attempted to persuade her father to inform her mother of their impending guest. Although Mr. Collins was not expected for more than two months, she believed it wise to give her mother ample notice. Bennet, however, disagreed—preferring a shorter warning to limit his exposure to her inevitable complaints. He remained undecided whether to encourage the visit at all or to write and suggest a delay in his cousin's journey.

Lost in these thoughts, she found herself rather startled at the sound of hoofbeats near her. She jerked her head around and saw three riders approaching. Recognising one of the gentlemen, she waved.

Mr. Morris, Netherfield's steward, called to the lady in greeting, "Miss Elizabeth, I am glad to see you about this morning. Are you going to call upon the tenants of Netherfield today?"

Although the gentlemen dismounted, Elizabeth did not. "I am. Mrs. Johnson is close to her confinement, and I intended to check on her this morning." She did not speak to the other gentlemen, but looked at them with interest. "There are a few others who need some attention as well, but she is my primary concern."

"Miss Elizabeth Bennet?" the taller of the two gentlemen blurted out as he stepped nearer, surprising both men who accompanied him. At her nod, he continued. "I visited Longbourn with my father several years ago and have continued corresponding with your father these last several years. I hoped to call on him while I was in the neighbourhood today. Will he be available?"

Elizabeth turned her attention towards the speaker. "Are you Mr. Darcy?" she asked, taking a moment to examine the gentleman. He was the tallest of the three and rather well favoured. Attempting to hide the blush caused by this thoughts, she spoke again quickly. "My father has spoken of you occasionally, well, nearly every time he received a letter from you, I suppose. I know it has been several years, but still, I would offer my condolences on the loss of your father."

By this time, Darcy was standing near Elizabeth and asked if he could assist her from the horse. She nodded in agreement and felt surprised by the jolt of energy she experienced when he briefly touched her to help her down. Their eyes locked for a moment, but Elizabeth swiftly looked down, feeling her cheeks heat again and hoping to hide her discomposure from him.

Darcy, too, found himself affected by the young lady.

Although they had not met during his previous visit, her father's letters had spoken of her often enough to pique his interest. He had not expected to see her in person, and her sudden appearance momentarily stole his breath. The brief sensation of her touch lingered, stirring something within him, and the sight of her blush delighted him more than he cared to admit. He had never before been aware a woman's blush—but now that he had, he found himself wanting to make it happen again.

Unlike his memories of the lady's mother, her hair was dark. She was, naturally, shorter than he, the top of her head reaching just to his chin, and her figure was undeniably pleasing. Although not the classical beauty so prized by the ton, she was lovely—and then she looked at him.

Her eyes, a vivid emerald green, flashed with intelligence and humour. They drew him in completely, transforming her from merely lovely into something far more captivating.

He stepped away as he acknowledged her words. "I thank you, Miss Bennet. He passed away not long after our visit here, but he was pleased to have seen his old friend again. He mentioned it several times in the months after our visit, and after he became ill, he hoped I would maintain the correspondence between Longbourn and Pemberley."

"Although he was saddened by his friend's death, my father was pleased that you maintained the connection," Elizabeth affirmed, then looked up at him with an impish grin. "You were of immeasurable help when I attempted to convince him to modernise at Longbourn. Often, you espoused the method I was attempting to persuade him to implement. Having your support, even without your knowing it, enabled Longbourn to prosper."

Darcy burst forth with a laugh at this statement surprising nearly everyone present. Elizabeth smiled broadly at her success, not knowing how rare it was for Darcy to laugh, but his friend merely stared wide-eyed at him. Mr. Morris was less surprised at Elizabeth's wit, having become accustomed to it, but was a little surprised that the stern man apparently did possess a sense of humour. That Elizabeth Bennet was the one to make him display it did not shock the steward whatsoever.

"I am glad to have done some good. I did not know that my input would have such an effect, but am infinitely pleased to have been of use. Tell me, what improvements did I champion?" Darcy asked as he contained his laughter.

Before Elizabeth could reply, Mr. Morris stepped forward to perform the introductions. "Miss Elizabeth, it is clear that you already know Mr. Darcy, or at least have heard of him, but allow me to introduce Mr. Charles Bingley as well. Mr. Bingley is considering taking the lease of Netherfield, and he and Mr. Darcy have ridden from London to examine it before making a decision."

Elizabeth acknowledged the introduction, speaking for a moment to Mr. Bingley before turning again to Mr. Darcy to answer his question. "Father was reluctant to modernise the tenants' cottages and replace the thatch roofing with slate. It was an expensive endeavour, but soon after I suggested it, you mentioned in one of your letters about doing the same. He was finally convinced when you extolled the benefits of it several times over the next few months."

The two spoke for several minutes as Elizabeth intelligently described some changes made at Longbourn over the last few years. Mr. Morris occasionally contributed to the discussion, while Mr. Bingley merely looked on. He had never seen his friend engage in any conversation with a female and was surprised at his holding a prolonged discussion about farming practices in the middle of a field with a young lady of marriageable age. She was a rather pretty young lady as well, Bingley considered as he listened to them.

Eventually, a noise from the horses seemed to make the pair aware of how long they had been speaking. Elizabeth's cheeks heated when she realised she had been conversing for some time with a relative stranger, or one who ought to have been a stranger.

Yes, they had a tenuous connection through her father, but despite Mr. Morris's participation, Elizabeth suddenly considered the possible impropriety of this entire exchange.

"Forgive me, gentlemen, for keeping you from your responsibilities. It is growing late in the morning, and I am expected home before too much longer," she said, ducking her head again in embarrassment.

Darcy looked at the position of the sun in the sky. "As much as I have enjoyed our conversation, Miss Elizabeth, I suspect you are correct about how long we have been here. If we are to return to London today, we will need to leave the area soon. You also had an errand to complete, if I recall. Did I understand you will visit one of Netherfield's tenants?"

Elizabeth offered a nod, briefly explaining the agreement between the masters of the two estates. After a moment of silence, she again indicated her need to depart.

Taking her meaning, Darcy stepped forward to assist her.

Flushing prettily, she hesitated for only a moment before agreeing, and Darcy gently placed his hands on her waist to help her into the saddle. As soon as they touched, they both felt that same jolt of energy pass between them, their eyes meeting again. However, this time, Elizabeth held his gaze for a moment longer.

Her cheeks warmed, but she smiled at him, her expression softening as she said, "Thank you, sir. I believe my father would enjoy a visit from you before your departure from our neighbourhood."

Darcy nodded in acknowledgement, and then he watched her leave, the groom a short distance behind her, before mounting his horse a moment behind the other two gentlemen. They made their way back to the manor house with the steward, finishing their business with him, before receiving directions to Longbourn.

Their visit was brief—only Bennet was at home to visitors, and he had a meeting scheduled shortly after their arrival. Darcy introduced his friend to Bennet, and again, Bingley had little to contribute to the conversation, which centred mainly around Netherfield and what having someone lease it might mean for the estate. However, the conversation was short, and Darcy promised to pay a longer call when he returned near Michaelmas with his friend. Soon the two men began their trek back to London.

They were well on their way towards town when Bingley sidled his horse up beside Darcy and punched him in the arm.

"Darcy, you have been holding out on me! You spoke as though you have known Miss Elizabeth Bennet for years and I have been wondering for hours why you have never mentioned her to me. This is simply priceless. No one will believe me!" Bingley smirked, clearly delighted with the incident. "I demand to know the details. How do you know her, and exactly what is the relationship between the two of you?"

Darcy gave him a flat look. "We have not met before today," he replied curtly, his tone clipped with irritation. "And it has scarcely been 'hours' since the encounter, Bingley."

Bingley, unable to suppress his surprise, blinked in disbelief. "You met the lady only today?" he asked, raising an eyebrow and remaining quiet for a moment as he reflected on the meeting. "But you were not even properly introduced. How did you know who she was?"

Darcy flushed, surprising his friend. "I met Mr. Bennet five years ago. He and my father attended Cambridge together and kept up the acquaintance through letters. Miss Elizabeth Bennet was in London when I visited, so today was the first time we met. After my father's death, I continued writing to Mr. Bennet; I suppose her father has shared something about me from my letters. Likewise, I have heard much of her from his own letters, so I feel as though I know her better than I actually do. Perhaps she felt the same."

For several moments, Bingley considered his friend's words. Finally, he spoke again. "Do you think Miss Darcy might want to join us when we return so that she can meet the Misses Bennet? I know you did not originally intend to have her accompany you, but perhaps now you will reconsider the matter. You have often said she needs the company of ladies her own age."

Bingley was again surprised when his friend's face darkened. "I do not believe Georgiana will want to come to Hertfordshire. She is staying with my aunt at Matlock and will remain there at present."

"Is all well with her?" Bingley asked.

Darcy considered what he had said, wondering if he had somehow revealed more intended. He shook his head.

"No, she is well enough, just…" he sighed. "I suppose this is a difficult time for any girl. She is not a child, yet not quite a woman. She is stuck in between. At her age, I was away at school, surrounded by young men my own age. Georgiana attended school for a year, but she did not seem to fit in there. I hope my aunt might be able to help her find her place in society."

"She has always been rather quiet," Bingley offered.

Darcy nodded, thinking back over the events of that summer. After the attempted elopement with George Wickham and her realisation that she had been manipulated by those she trusted, including her companion, Georgiana had become even more withdrawn. Darcy was concerned about her and had confided in his Aunt Matlock, who offered to spend some time with her to see what could be done. No one else knew of this, other than his cousin Richard, and Darcy was determined to keep it this way.

A new companion, a Mrs. Annesley, had been hired for Georgiana, and Lady Matlock insisted that Darcy spend time away from his sister. To say that he had been unhappy about this was an understatement. He argued with his aunt, but she finally persuaded him that his overbearing behaviour was the last thing his sister needed.

CHAPTER 5

Reflections

Arriving back in London, Darcy went directly to his study. Bingley had chatted most of the way back from Meryton, preventing his mind from wandering as he had wished.

Foremost in his thoughts was Georgiana. In one of their conversations after the attempted elopement, Georgiana confessed she was frequently lonely at school. More often than not, the girls who sought out a friendship with Georgiana had done so only for an introduction to her older brother. Georgiana was too shy to put herself forward and had spent most of her time on her own.

While her new companion was far better than the previous one, Georgiana still needed a friend. Could Elizabeth Bennet be the friend she needed? She was intelligent and appeared kind. She had several sisters herself although he could not remember their ages; surely she could find a way to relate to his timid sister. However, to bring Georgiana into Miss Elizabeth's company would require her to reside at Netherfield with Caroline Bingley, Bingley's sister.

Miss Bingley was probably worse than the girls at Georgiana's school. Under the guise of friendship, she constantly talked down to Georgiana and attempted to influence her to behave as she herself did. Since Darcy did not think well of Miss Bingley's behaviour towards others, she was not someone he wanted his sister to emulate. He told Mrs. Annesley, Georgiana's companion, as much and had a frank conversation with his sister about the matter as well. One benefit to the incident last summer was that the brother and sister were speaking to each other more openly.

Georgiana had been genuinely surprised to learn that her brother held no regard for his friend's sister. Much of her confusion stemmed from Miss Bingley's own behaviour, for she often spoke to Georgiana in a manner that implied a far closer relationship with Mr. Darcy than truly existed. Darcy suspected that Miss Bingley deliberately encouraged this misconception, hoping that, through repeated insinuations, she might persuade Georgiana to advocate on her behalf—and perhaps prompt him towards an offer of marriage.

It was largely for this reason that Darcy hesitated to invite Georgiana to join him at Netherfield. For the present, she remained with their aunt, Lady Matlock, with whom she was getting on very well, but Darcy knew that his sister, still so young, needed the company of girls nearer her own age.

This line of thought turned his mind once again to Longbourn. While Bennet had evidently made considerable improvements to his estate, Darcy could not help but wonder whether his younger daughters had likewise benefitted—or if any of them still resembled the brash, silly girls he had encountered five years before.

Miss Elizabeth, of course, was clearly very different, but she had not been among the girls he met that day. From Bennet's letters, he knew that the youngest daughter had since been sent away to school, and he could only suppose that similar improvements had been made in the others as well.

With this in mind, Darcy concluded that his wisest course would be to first speak with his sister and hear her thoughts on the matter. If

Georgiana was willing to endure Miss Bingley's cloying attentions for a time, then perhaps she could join him at Netherfield—but only after he had met the other Misses Bennet and determined for himself whether they would prove acceptable companions.

Nearly as soon as he came to this conclusion, his cousin Colonel Richard Fitzwilliam entered his study, interrupting his musings. "Darcy, how was your trip with that puppy you call a friend?"

Darcy laughed. "I have never understood what started you calling Bingley a puppy, but I admit, there are moments where being in his company is exhausting."

"He is easily excitable and enthusiastic without cause," Fitzwilliam replied with a wry smile. "One day, perhaps, someone will come along with the fortitude to temper those traits, but it will take a woman of considerable strength. As it stands, his sister has him well in hand, leading him about as if he were tethered to a leash of her own making."

"Why are you here, Richard?" Darcy asked, choosing to ignore the comment and pouring both of them a drink. "Be forewarned; I will be joining Bingley in Meryton for a brief visit as he learns to manage the estate he has leased. My father's old friend, Mr. Bennet, lives near there, and I would like to see him again. Father and I visited him a few months before his death. The estate was not well run at the time, but he has since made significant improvements to it."

"How do you know that?"

"We have corresponded since Father's death. He saw the notice in the London paper and wrote to express his condolences. It was a difficult time for me, and I appreciated his words of advice and support. Our letters gradually changed in tone, and we soon began discussing matters related to our individual estates. As my father did, I encouraged him as he sought to make changes, and he did the same for me," Darcy admitted.

"And Georgiana will remain with my mother during your visit?" Fitzwilliam asked.

Darcy let out a slow breath. "Mr. Bennet has five daughters, some of whom are near Georgiana's age. I think their company could do Georgiana good, but I am concerned about having her in close proximity to Miss Bingley for an extended period. Your mother reports that she is doing well with Mrs. Annesley, but…" Darcy trailed off, uncertain how to finish the statement.

"What if I were to accompany you?" Fitzwilliam offered. "Mother could come as well. You know that Miss Bingley would preen at the idea of hosting a countess, and Mother would have no difficulty slapping her down when she gets out of control. She will not like that there is competition for your attention in a country hamlet."

Darcy raised his brow at his cousin in question. "What do you mean?" he asked.

Fitzwilliam laughed. "You are willingly speaking of introducing your sister to a family of young ladies. The only reason you would do that is because one of them has caught your attention in some way. Given your inclination towards avoiding most ladies, that you are even considering introducing your sister to several at once is out of character for you. Your friendship, or rather, your father's friendship with the gentleman is not sufficient motivation."

Darcy's only response was to flush slightly. To say Fitzwilliam was surprised by Darcy's reaction was an understatement. Fitzwilliam had only been teasing his cousin; he had not expected his words to hit their target in this way. His mouth dropped open for several moments as he gaped at Darcy.

"One of the ladies *has* caught your notice?" Fitzwilliam asked. "Tell me, which country girl has captured your attention?"

Darcy blew out a breath and raked his fingers through his hair. "The second daughter, Miss Elizabeth Bennet, is around nineteen or twenty years of age. Her father has written of her frequently, and I met her yesterday while Bingley and I rode the estate he was considering leasing. She is a lovely girl; perhaps not what the *ton* deems as classically beautiful, but I found her captivating."

He paused, allowing himself to think about the young lady again before he continued. "However, her primary attraction is not her appearance, but her intelligence. In the few short minutes we were together, we spoke of estate management and her visits to the tenants on a neighbouring estate. The young lady has assisted her father in managing his estate for a number of years, and she has aided him in increasing the estate's revenue from around two thousand per annum to, I believe, a little under four now. When we visited, Mr. Bennet confessed that his lack of involvement and refusal to modernise had caused the income to decrease, but together, Miss Elizabeth and her father have been able to make considerable changes.

"As I said, her father often mentioned Miss Elizabeth in his correspondence at first, but then I noticed that the handwriting appeared different. Initially, I thought he had hired someone to assist him, but something in one letter not long after made me suspect that Miss Bennet was the author. Mr. Bennet wrote to me directly when I enquired and admitted that his daughter often acted as his secretary. However, he realised that she had been interjecting some of her personality into his letters to me which had given it away."

Fitzwilliam grinned. "What did you do when you learnt this? I imagine you being angry at first, but that obviously did not last long."

"For nearly half an hour, I raged at the temerity of the girl to risk both our reputations in this manner," Darcy admitted ruefully. "However, I soon realised that I was being a fool. The letters were signed with her father's name, and should anyone learn of it, they would assume, as I had, that they were dictated by Mr. Bennet. As I enjoyed the letters written by Miss Elizabeth more than those from her father, and that they were much prompter and more detailed when coming from the young lady, I found I could not complain in earnest. She began to include a line or two from her, and in that way, we have become… friendly, I suppose."

"And now that you have seen her?" Fitzwilliam asked.

Darcy did not speak for a moment, and Fitzwilliam wondered if he would ignore the question entirely. However, Darcy finally chuckled. "When I met Mr. Bennet, I was shocked that he would allow his fourteen-year-old daughter to act as his steward. However, the more I heard him speak of her on that visit, I considered what it would be like to marry a country miss instead of one of the haughty women I had met in the *ton*."

He paused again, and several moments passed before he continued, "Father laughed when I told him what I was thinking. Instead of confirming my duty, as your own father has done so often, he encouraged me to marry a woman whom I could love and not to worry about material concerns like her connections or even the size of her dowry. I think he approved of Miss Elizabeth, and, honestly, now that I have seen her, I admit that I would like to learn more about her."

"So, the young lady intrigues you?" Fitzwilliam prodded his cousin further. "Now I know I will need to join you in Hertfordshire, for I need to see your attempts at courting. You are so used to women fawning over you that you will not know how to win a lady's affection. Although, if you do manage it, you will win her by speaking of estate management and animal husbandry, for a woman who could not speak of such things would not interest you one whit."

He roared with laughter at his jest, guffawing even harder when he noticed the scowl on his cousin's face. "Oh, come now, Darcy, you know it is true. You avoid females and entanglements of all sorts, and frankly, I am astonished at you willingly putting yourself so near to Caroline Bingley at all."

Darcy grimaced. "I had hoped Bingley would be persuaded to leave her in London with her sister, but he mentioned needing a hostess. The man needs a wife, but I am afraid he will not be ready to settle down for several years yet, what with all his fluttering about every lovely lady he meets."

"Hence, my referring to him as a puppy," Fitzwilliam replied. "A young lady pays him the slightest bit of attention, and he will fall all over himself flirting with her for an evening or two, and then just as quickly he loses interest once she is no longer in his sight. I worry about that sister of his and how she leads him about by the nose. I am not certain your sense of honour would allow you to leave her to her ruin should she compromise you in some public way here in town. However, I think perhaps you will be safer in a small country village. Yes, Darcy, I will write to my mother immediately and insist that she and Georgiana join us at Netherfield."

"You do not wish to wait for an invitation?" Darcy asked drily.

Fitzwilliam chucked. "Do you truly believe a social climber such as Miss Bingley would turn a countess and the son of an earl from her door? She wants Georgiana for her brother, and you for herself, so she would not dream of insulting your relations even if we turned up uninvited," he replied drolly. "However, I will do things properly. When will you see Bingley next?"

"We are to meet at my club tomorrow at half-past one," Darcy answered.

"Then I will be there with you, and within a half hour, will have persuaded the lad to issue an invitation," Fitzwilliam said. "Would you care to place a wager on it?"

"No, I would not," Darcy remarked, his face and voice impassive, but his eyes were twinkling with mirth. Darcy had bet against his cousin only a few times, and rarely had he come out the winner. No, he knew better than to take that bet.

CHAPTER 6

A Gentleman's Agreement

4 SEPTEMBER 1811

The next day, Darcy arrived at White's just as his cousin was walking towards the door. Without waiting for the footman, he opened the carriage door and stepped down, not waiting for the step to be placed. His cousin, having observed Darcy arrive, awaited him.

"Darcy," Fitzwilliam said in greeting. "How long do you think we will wait for your friend to arrive?"

Darcy sighed and shook his head in an exaggerated fashion. "His sister is not with him, so it is likely he will arrive within a quarter hour of the appointed time. However, even without her accompanying him, it is possible she will cause him to be delayed. While we wait, let us have a drink and see who else is here."

The two entered, and, as Darcy had predicted, Bingley arrived a short time later.

"Forgive me, Darcy," he said in greeting. He paused for a moment at seeing the colonel beside him, turning to that man and greeting him as well. Once that was done, he continued as he had intended upon arriving. Letting out a slow breath, he began. "Caroline is upset that I have leased a home in such an 'unfashionable' country village. She would have preferred I lease an estate nearer to Pemberley, although I have tried to convince her that she will be happier nearer to London."

"I have been through Meryton, and the village there is somewhat larger than Lambton," Fitzwilliam said. "Its location, as you mentioned, provides easy access to the goods unobtainable elsewhere, being less than a morning's ride from London. As much as my mother loves her home at Matlock, there are luxuries she wishes she could have at home that would not survive the several days' journey."

"I know that, Colonel, but my sister cannot be convinced otherwise," Bingley replied, raking his fingers through his shock of bright red hair before turning towards his friend. "She was delighted to hear that you are planning to accompany us, Darcy, and is convinced that you are coming as a mark of your interest in her. I cannot stop her cries of joy, even as she complains about the location I have selected."

At Darcy's audible scoff at the suggestion, Bingley continued somewhat dejectedly. "I know, Darcy, I know. I have told her time and time again that you are not interested in her, but she will not hear me. If you prefer not to join us, I will understand."

Darcy drew in a breath through his nose, which he slowly released as he debated how to respond. However, before he could speak, his cousin did. "I have a suggestion, Bingley. Instead of Darcy cancelling his visit, I could accompany him. Even better, my mother and Georgiana could join us, and my mother will ensure Miss Bingley knows she has no chance of ever marrying Darcy. Surely, she cannot refuse to hear it when a countess tells her."

"Please do join us," Bingley replied. "Do you think your mother could be persuaded to stay at the home of a tradesman's son? I know I am not in her social class, regardless of what my sister may attempt to claim."

Darcy struggled not to release the chuckle that nearly overwhelmed him at his cousin's blatant manoeuvring for an invitation. However, he listened as Fitzwilliam assured Bingley that his mother would readily spend a few weeks at Netherfield, and they made more definite plans. Bingley was set to take possession of Netherfield just before Michaelmas—still nearly a month away—but in the meantime, arrangements would need to be made.

It was agreed they would ride to Hertfordshire within the week to meet with the solicitor once more and confirm that all was in order. Darcy promised to write to Bennet to arrange a meeting, and Bingley, with casual enthusiasm, suggested that perhaps Bennet might even host them for a night or two while they became better acquainted with the neighbourhood.

"I have met Miss Elizabeth Bennet," Bingley added, "and the steward mentioned that the elder sister is even more lovely than she. I look forward to meeting the rest of the family."

Darcy responded with a noncommittal murmur at the mention of the young lady's name. Although he would not be averse to spending more time in Miss Elizabeth's company, he remained uneasy about imposing upon Bennet—his father's friend or not—without invitation.

"Perhaps it would be best," Fitzwilliam lightly teased, "if we did not stay in a house full of five young women—six, if one includes their mother."

Bingley laughed aloud, clearly unbothered by the thought. Soon after, the three parted ways. Darcy and Fitzwilliam watched as Bingley boarded his carriage, then turned and began walking together through the streets of Mayfair, having dismissed their own in favour of returning to Darcy House on foot.

"You told me," Fitzwilliam continued, glancing sideways at his cousin, "that during your father's last visit, Mrs. Bennet and the youngest daughter behaved with a complete disregard for propriety. Are you quite certain we will be safe under their roof?"

His tone was clearly teasing, but Darcy still shot him a sharp look from the corner of his eye.

"That daughter, Miss Lydia, was sent away to school," Darcy replied steadily, not rising to his cousin's bait. "I am uncertain if she is at home at present, but all the girls have had lessons since then, and a governess and a companion were hired to assist with their upbringing. Mr. Bennet's letters only rarely mentioned Mrs. Bennet, but I believe the companion has managed to calm her significantly. He confessed to my father that much of what made her so…so frantic was her worry for her future with the estate entailed. As I understand it, Mr. Bennet has made arrangements for her continued care, and that has done much for her constitution."

Fitzwilliam nodded. "I have known of other women who fretted over an entail, particularly if there were no sons and their husbands were lackadaisical in ensuring their futures. It is hard to blame a woman for fearing genteel poverty."

"It is," Darcy agreed. "I recall Father being angry with Bennet over his dismissal of his wife's legitimate concerns about this, particularly how he was handling his estate, or, more accurately, what he was not doing to manage it. However, things seem to be better now, and we have corresponded often since then. Frankly, I am more concerned about Bingley than I am of the Bennets."

"In what way?" Fitzwilliam asked.

"Bingley will not stand up to his sister," Darcy said darkly. "He knows full well what she is, yet he refuses to restrain her. If Georgiana ever pursued a man with such forwardness as Miss Bingley shows me, I would not hesitate to speak to her in the strongest terms. I would withhold her allowance if necessary. If she still refused to listen—if she persisted in throwing herself at some gentleman who clearly wanted nothing to do with her—I would send her away until she learnt her lesson or find her a suitable husband without delay."

He paused, his expression hardening.

"Of course, I understand that the relationship is different; Bingley is only a year or two older than his sister, and their positions are not the same as Georgiana's and mine. But even so, he has the authority—and the duty—to correct her. That he refuses to exercise it is to his shame."

"Do you think she will attempt to compromise you?"

"If she did, she would ruin only herself," Darcy retorted. "A woman who compromises a man is a fool. Bingley has nothing over me that would force me to wed his sister in such a case, and no one in society would look down on me for refusing to marry her in those circumstances. Many are aware of her pursuit of me and do not think well of her for her ambition."

"Mother will put a stop to any antics she might try within the *ton*," Fitzwilliam said. "I have already written to my mother, asking that she join us, but I have waited to send it until I was certain of our invitation."

"Bring it to me this evening, and I will send it with my own letter to Georgiana," Darcy said. "My messenger is leaving in the morning for Pemberley, and he can easily travel to first to Matlock. It will not be too much of a delay, and my business is not urgent."

"Very well, Darcy," Fitzwilliam said with a slight smile. "Let us make our own plans, apart from your obliging friend. Even if you refuse to impose upon Mr. Bennet for lodgings, I confess I am curious to meet this Miss Elizabeth."

Darcy narrowed his eyes slightly, but he said nothing, and Fitzwilliam, undeterred, added with a grin, "Perhaps Bennet might at least be prevailed upon to offer us a meal while we are in the neighbourhood?"

Grimacing, Darcy hesitated slightly before inclining his head in agreement. With that, the two men parted ways, agreeing to meet again at Darcy House soon.

As Fitzwilliam disappeared from his view, Darcy lingered where he stood for a moment, a faint frown pulling at his brow.

Over the last five years he had often recalled his father's words on the idea of marrying a woman like Elizabeth Bennet. His father had approved of the match—at least in theory—even without having met her, judging her worth from what little he knew of her character and upbringing. Still, Darcy supposed her prospects were somewhat greater now than they had been. His father's advice, however, was in direct contrast to what he frequently heard from his relatives on his mother's side of the family who believed he had a duty to marry to increase the family's wealth and connections.

He dismissed the thought with a slight shake of his head. He had exchanged only a few words with Miss Elizabeth two days before, and while he had found himself more at ease in her company than with any other lady he had yet encountered, he told himself it did not signify. There was nothing remarkable in taking notice of a young lady with uncommon wit and sense.

Despite the Bard's assertion that "whoever loved that loved not at first sight," Darcy was far too logical to put stock in such romantic nonsense. Perhaps he had spoken of Miss Elizabeth more often than he realised since returning from Hertfordshire. He was intrigued by a young lady who was interested in estate management, and that was all it was.

CHAPTER 7

Chance Meetings

12 SEPTEMBER 1811

As agreed, Darcy and Fitzwilliam joined Bingley a week later when he returned to Hertfordshire. The three gentlemen left their horses at the livery stable, and while Bingley attended to his business at the solicitor's office, Darcy and Fitzwilliam strolled through several nearby shops.

During their stroll, Darcy caught sight of the young lady he had encountered while touring Netherfield the previous week, Miss Elizabeth Bennet. This time she was not alone. Beside her stood a fair-haired lady whom Darcy took to be her elder sister, owing to a resemblance of the young lady to his recollection of Mrs. Bennet.

They were accompanied by two younger girls with hair of varying shades of brown and an older woman who appeared to be their companion. A sixth lady—appearing slightly older than the woman he presumed to be the eldest Miss Bennet and more plainly dressed than those young ladies—approached and greeted the ladies.

With a quiet word to his cousin to identify the women, Darcy moved to join the party. Elizabeth turned at his approach, and her face broke into a delighted smile upon seeing them.

"Mr. Darcy," she said. "I had thought we would not see you again until after Michaelmas, but Papa informed me yesterday that you would visit the area again today." She laughed and shook her head in affectionate frustration. "He waited until this morning to inform Mama of the invitation he issued not only for a meal, but for you and your party to stay at Longbourn for a night or two while you completed your business in the area. My sisters and I were sent into the village to see what we could find to add to the evening meal."

She paused momentarily, not wanting to reveal too much, but feeling a greater sense of familiarity with the gentleman because of their previous meeting and the letters she had written on her father's behalf for so long. For a moment, she paused to determine if her words troubled him but supposed from his smile she was not overstepping.

"Mama always sets a generous table, but the addition of three gentlemen to our party nearly sent her into hysterics. I warned Papa that this would be the result and that he ought to have said something yesterday, but he says he still needs to find amusement where he can," Elizabeth admitted ruefully.

Darcy frowned. "We can return to London if our remaining here is too much for your mother. I would not want our hostess to be discomposed by our coming unannounced, even if we are not at fault," he said, not wishing to miss out on this time with the young lady but also not wanting to create trouble for her family.

Elizabeth reached out and lightly touched Darcy's arm. She withdrew her hand just as quickly, suddenly aware of the impropriety of such a gesture, and caught the reproving glance Mrs. Graham cast in her direction. A flush of embarrassment rose in her cheeks, and her voice was quieter when she spoke again.

"It is no trouble, sir, I assure you. Even without any additions, the meal would have been sufficient for our family and guests. Mama merely wished to present our family in the best possible light. She still recalls that dinner from so many years ago. While I was not at home at the time, I can well imagine what it must have been like. As you know, our family has changed a great deal since then. I only wish I might have met your father and thanked him for the difference his words made. When Mr. Livesay visited us a few years ago, the first time after that fateful meeting, and I was fortunate to have the opportunity to express my gratitude to him."

"Before he died, my father was gratified to learn he had an impact on his old friend," Darcy said seriously.

Darcy again responded to Miss Elizabeth's touch—even though it had been fleeting and barely felt through the material of his clothing—and yet the sensation lingered longer than it had any right to. Foolish, really, how the memory of so small a gesture could occupy his mind so completely. He did not have the courage to return it. A part of him —some insistent, unfamiliar part—longed to and wished that it would not breach propriety were he to do so.

It had been the same the last time: the faintest touch had sparked something in him, something warm and strange, like a flame coaxed to life beneath damp wood. It unsettled him. He was not accustomed to being so affected by mere contact. But neither could he deny it. The feeling was real—unwelcome, perhaps, but real—and it was growing harder to dismiss that his feelings for this woman were beyond the ordinary.

Clearing his throat, he straightened and said, "Might I introduce my cousin to you and your sisters? That is—if you would be so kind as to introduce your sisters to me first?"

She flushed, clearly abashed at the oversight. Colour rose swiftly to her cheeks, and he was struck—again—by how becoming her blushes were. The soft pink of her embarrassment lent her an unstudied grace, and to his own astonishment, he found himself smiling at her.

Strange, how easily his reserve slipped in her presence. He had not meant to smile—not in such a way—but the gesture had formed before he could suppress it.

Still flushed, she turned towards her sisters and began the introductions. "Mr. Darcy," she said, "allow me to present my sisters: Miss Jane Bennet, Miss Mary Bennet, and Miss Catherine Bennet. This is our companion, Mrs. Graham, and our friend, Miss Charlotte Lucas. Mr. Darcy is Father's friend—or rather, Mr. Darcy's father was Papa's friend from Cambridge."

He inclined his head to each in turn, offering the appropriate courtesies, his gaze lingering on Miss Elizabeth longer than was strictly proper. There was something in the way she spoke—light, quick, slightly ironic even in formalities—that caught and held his attention. The warmth of her earlier blush had not quite faded, and he remained delighted at seeing it, for it made her all the more lovely.

Pulling himself back to the present, he introduced his cousin, Colonel Fitzwilliam, whose affable manner seemed to ease the stiffness of the gathering. Darcy was grateful for it; charm had never come easily to him, and Elizabeth's presence—though undeniably pleasant—unsettled his usual composure.

"We would appreciate it if you would recommend a place," he asked once the introductions had concluded, "for us to wait for our friend without being entirely in the way?"

"Mrs. Graham and my younger sisters are going to the butcher's," Elizabeth replied. "Jane and I were on our way to the bookseller to collect an order for my father. Charlotte, would you care to join us—or had you another errand that you needed to complete?"

"I am free to accompany you, Eliza," Miss Lucas said with a smile.

That said, the party broke into two, with the gentlemen accompanying the older three ladies to the bookstore. Darcy was surprised to find the shop far better stocked than he had expected for a small village. "This is quite a collection," he remarked, glancing over the well-kept shelves. "I must admit, I did not anticipate such variety. If my friend's company proves lacking, I will be able to find books to amuse myself with here."

"We do our best to keep the bookseller in business," Elizabeth said, a mischievous gleam in her eye. "Between Papa's pamphlets and Jane's novels, I daresay we account for a significant portion of Mr. Thompson's trade."

Her wit struck him again—light, precise, effortlessly deployed. It disarmed him more than he liked to admit.

She laughed at his expression. "My father, though he reads less than he once did, still comes here weekly—either to seek out some obscure volume or to declare that my sisters and I are in need of further intellectual improvement."

"What are you picking up today?" Darcy asked.

"Some books of poetry he wished us to read together and the second volume of a novel by a lady," Elizabeth replied, watching Darcy for his reaction.

"I enjoy reading novels with my sister," Darcy replied, keeping his voice even. "While I do not always find the content particularly interesting, my sister reads with me, and we discuss the works with her. Do you read as a family in the evening, or do each of you read on your own?"

"We often read together in the evening after dinner," Elizabeth replied, feeling some relief that he did not criticise her family for the habit. "Not always novels, but we have enjoyed several this way, along with the works of Shakespeare and many other texts. We just finished *The Rime of the Ancient Mariner* recently, and my sisters still talk about the story."

"Then I look forward to participating this evening," Darcy replied, before his attention was captured by his cousin.

"I have just heard that the militia are expected in the area not long after our party arrives, Darcy," Fitzwilliam said as he approached the pair with Miss Bennet and Miss Lucas nearby. He indicated Miss Lucas as he spoke, implying that she was the one who had informed him of it.

Darcy frowned at this news, uncertain of why his cousin was telling him. "Does this trouble you in some way, Richard?"

"Not at all," Fitzwilliam replied, hurrying to reassure his cousin. "No, indeed, I am thinking it may be an opportunity for me to extend my visit beyond the fortnight I had requested. "I can suggest to my general that I extend my stay in the area and use my expertise to bolster whatever poor sot is assigned to duty here. My general often complains that the militia do not train very hard, and I can see about remedying that for at least this one company."

Merely nodding in reply, Darcy turned back to Elizabeth when she spoke. "I did not realise the colonel was joining your party," she said. The colonel had turned back to the other ladies, and the three were in a conversation about the coming arrivals.

"Yes, Bingley invited not only him, but also my sister and aunt, the colonel's mother, to join the party here. I will come with Bingley at Michaelmas, but my sister and aunt will travel from Derbyshire and will join us at Netherfield a week or two later," Darcy explained.

"Oh, I am delighted that Miss Darcy will accompany you to the neighbourhood," Elizabeth cried. "I have longed to meet her for years."

"I am looking forward to introducing you to her as well," Darcy replied. "The two of you will get along quite well, I am certain. Your two younger sisters might also be good friends to her since they seem to be close to her in age. She has often been alone—she has only one female relation in her generation, and our cousin Anne is nearer to my age. My aunt, the one she is presently staying with, tries to help her, but it is not the same as having friends and confidants nearer to her age. Unfortunately, she has had trouble making friends for her own sake."

Elizabeth looked at him for a long moment, remaining still as she considered his words. "They seek to befriend her for…other reasons?" she asked.

Darcy flushed slightly. "Yes, they did. Some because they had brothers whom they wished to connect to an heiress, and they believed my sister would be easily led, and others because they hoped to be introduced to me. That, and another incident, caused her to question herself and believe she had little to offer other than her wealth and connections. She had always been shy, but these events made matters worse."

This time, Elizabeth did not stop her hands from reaching out and pressing lightly on his arm. "I am sorry for her," she began. "And I do trust that, when she comes, my sisters and I will treat her as a sister instead of a means to an end. If she needs relief from her cousin and brother, or perhaps the aunt who will accompany her, then she will be welcome at Longbourn. We will treat her to the full sister experience if she desires it," she said with a laugh.

Fitzwilliam, who had been listening to Darcy's conversation with Elizabeth while he attended to his own, chuckled to himself at this jest, but her words caught Darcy in a different way altogether.

Suddenly, he imagined Elizabeth as his wife and Georgiana as her sister in truth. *What would she think about Pemberley,* he wondered idly and was startled from this momentary loss of focus when his cousin elbowed him in the ribs before returning to his conversation with Miss Bennet and Miss Lucas.

"Forgive me," he said, "I was not attending." He looked at Elizabeth and caught a troubled expression on her face. "What is the matter?" he asked her quietly.

"I apologise if my teasing offended you," she replied, her tone subdued and her eyes firmly on the floor.

"Oh," Darcy murmured, replaying her words and finally settling on what troubled her. "No, I assure you, you did not offend me. I…I found myself…that is, my mind wandered for a moment. Georgiana would be delighted to be welcomed to Longbourn as a sister and will likely find her time there a welcome relief from what she will find at Netherfield with my friend's sisters. Forgive me, I do not wish to speak ill of another, but you will meet them soon enough and form your own opinions of those ladies."

He watched as Elizabeth eyed him suspiciously. "I am all anticipation, Mr. Darcy," she replied after a moment of hesitation. "You have made me very curious about our new neighbours, and I look forward to seeing them soon." She paused again. "You said you will arrive shortly before Michaelmas?"

Darcy nodded his reply, wondering at the reason for her question.

"I am certain someone will mention it to your friend when he officially arrives, but our community's quarterly assembly will take place at the first full moon after Michaelmas," Elizabeth said, her voice once again subdued; this time, it was obvious to him she did not want to say too much and risk him thinking she was being forward.

"My friend will be delighted at the opportunity to meet all his neighbours at once," Darcy replied, attempting to put her at ease. "While I am not typically disposed towards attending assemblies and the like—truly, towards most social events—I will be pleased to attend this one where I can be certain of the company of a few good friends. Will your father attend?"

Elizabeth chuckled. "Not if he can help it," she replied, but then her face fell a little. "That is, perhaps, not completely fair. He does attend more often than not, and with you and your party in the area, he might find it more tolerable than usual. Papa has never been particularly sociable, and I know that attending these events is taxing for him. Although he has done better at chaperoning my sisters and me, it is still a trial to get him to attend, and he does so grudgingly."

Darcy chucked. "I can commiserate with him, Miss Elizabeth," he replied. "Might I take this opportunity to solicit your hand for a dance? I would find the whole thing far more tolerable if I knew I had at least one set I could look forward to."

Elizabeth flushed again at this. "Yes, sir, you may have any set you wish, other than the fourth. Although your party will add to our numbers, there are never enough men for all the ladies, and Jane, Charlotte, and I always sit out at least one set to ensure every young lady has the opportunity to dance."

"I would ask to claim the first, but I suspect that our party will arrive late," Darcy replied. "Is there a supper set or a break during the evening where I would have the opportunity to spend some time conversing with you?"

Elizabeth nodded. "There is usually a short break after the fifth set when refreshments are served. It is not as formal as a supper set at a private ball but is simply a short intermission."

"Then I would claim that set, Miss Elizabeth," he replied, bowing slightly over her hand, causing her cheeks to heat once again. "And perhaps another should it prove available?"

Just then, Fitzwilliam turned towards the pair, and while Elizabeth did not reply, Darcy delighted at seeing her blush. "We ought to return to Bingley, Darcy," he said. "He should be finished by now, and these young ladies need to return home to prepare for our visit."

Fitzwilliam turned to the rest of the ladies, "Miss Bennet, Miss Elizabeth, we will see you shortly. Miss Lucas, I look forward to seeing you again in October. Darcy?"

As they stepped outside, Darcy paused to bid the ladies farewell, requesting a set from both Miss Bennet and Miss Lucas for the upcoming assembly. The two young women, who had accompanied the gentlemen to the door, offered polite farewells in return. With parting words exchanged, Darcy and Colonel Fitzwilliam took their leave.

Elizabeth turned back towards the counter to collect the books her father had ordered. With the bundle in hand, she exited the shop, where Jane and Charlotte waited with the rest of her sisters and Mrs. Graham.

CHAPTER 8

Reintroductions

Around three in the afternoon, Mrs. Hill announced the arrival of the gentlemen callers and showed them into Bennet's study. Rising to greet his guests, he was surprised to see his second daughter lingering in the hallway—and even more so when she winked at him. Uncertain of her meaning, he gave a slight nod in return before shifting his attention to the gentlemen.

"I am pleased to see you again so soon, Mr. Darcy—and you as well, Mr. Bingley," he said, then turned to the third man. "You must be Darcy's cousin, Colonel Fitzwilliam, if I am not mistaken? Shall you introduce us now, Darcy?" Bennet smirked at the men.

His lips tilting up in a small smile, Darcy stepped forward to make the proper introduction, after which the four men took their seats and began to converse as Bennet handed them each a glass of brandy.

"By chance," Bennet began, his thoughts still occupied with Elizabeth's curious gesture, "did you happen to encounter my daughters while in Meryton earlier today?"

To his surprise, both Darcy and the colonel smiled. "Indeed, we did," Darcy replied, the faintest trace of amusement in his expression. "My cousin and I accompanied Miss Bennet and Miss Elizabeth to the bookshop, while the younger ladies and their companion visited other establishments. Bingley was at the solicitor's office, finalising the lease, and he did not have the same opportunity."

Bingley, for his part, had been rather disappointed to have missed them—especially after once again hearing from Mr. Phillips, whom he now knew to be the young ladies' uncle, about the beauty of the eldest Miss Bennet. During their luncheon at the village inn, the colonel had made several complimentary remarks regarding the charm of all the Bennet sisters. While he had offered no hint of particular interest in any one of them, his comments had only served to deepen Bingley's own curiosity. However, none of this showed on his face during this conversation.

Leaning back in his chair, Bennet steepled his fingers as he regarded his guests with mild curiosity. "Indeed? And was it a pleasant encounter? I trust my daughters conducted themselves with some degree of decorum?"

Colonel Fitzwilliam let out a quiet chuckle. "They were all quite charming, sir—particularly Miss Elizabeth. She kept my cousin and me well engaged with her observations, and her wit was not lost on either of us. Darcy's sister will be joining our party at Netherfield, and I am certain she will enjoy the company of all your daughters."

Bennet harrumphed at that. "Then I am glad that Lydia is still at school, for you would not wish to have your sister exposed to her influence. Your sister is near my Catherine in age, is she not?"

Darcy nodded, acknowledging that this was true. Idly, Darcy recalled that Elizabeth had shared only a little about herself, and what he knew of her came from letters written directly by her father.

"Yes, my sister is fifteen," Darcy replied. "As you know, my cousin shares guardianship with me, and we have decided that she would do well in coming to know your daughters. She has much in common with all of them, I believe, and she will enjoy spending some time with them."

"Aye," Bingley interjected with a slight chuckle, "particularly since my sisters are older than she is and far more interested in tittle-tattle and shopping than anything else. I fear they will not find much to please them in Meryton, though they are quite delighted to host Mr. Darcy and his family."

Bennet shot the younger man a sharp look, recalling what he knew of him. From Darcy, he understood that Bingley's family had made its fortune in trade. Although Bingley was no longer directly involved in the business, his wealth still stemmed from it. Without an estate of his own, he was not technically a gentleman although he was clearly striving to become one. Leasing Netherfield was his first step towards establishing himself, and Bennet wondered whether the attempt would succeed.

Interesting, Bennet mused, watching as the young man squirmed slightly under his scrutiny.

After a pause, Bennet turned back to Darcy. "Will other members of your family be joining you as well?" he asked, still uncertain what to make of Bingley. The man appeared young—not only in years but also in maturity.

"My cousin, along with his mother and my sister, will join us midway through October. Richard is obligated to remain in town for an additional fortnight after we depart, and his mother chose to wait until he could accompany them to join us," Darcy replied.

"And you will arrive just after Michaelmas?" Bennet asked. "Or was it before?"

"Technically, my lease begins at Michaelmas," Bingley answered. "However, Mr. Philips has given me leave to arrive a few days before. I met with him earlier today, and we discussed hiring a staff as needed for the estate and ensuring that all is in readiness for me to arrive on the Wednesday before Michaelmas. Once I am assured that all is in order, I will return to London on Friday or Saturday, and then my sisters will accompany me on that Monday. Darcy will arrive on Tuesday, is that not what you said?"

Darcy chose not to reply and merely nodded at his friend.

"That is good timing, sir," Bennet said, "although perhaps not for you, Colonel. The full moon will be on the second of October, the day after you arrive, Darcy, and Meryton's quarterly assembly will be held that evening. Our festivities will begin earlier than you are used to in London, I suppose, since dancing will begin promptly at half past six."

Bingley laughed. "That is extremely early," he replied. "My sisters will no doubt scoff at such a notion."

The colonel snorted, earning him a scowl from his cousin. However, Darcy felt it necessary to educate his friend about the differences between life in the country and that in town, something he would need to learn during his stay here.

"The distances one has to travel within the city limits of London are significantly less than in a country village such as this one," Darcy replied. "Not to mention, the streets in London are considerably better lit. In the country, one must rely more heavily on lanterns and the moonlight for travelling to and from such events. I daresay the early hour is meant to make the most of the lingering sunlight before it sets fully, and the event is scheduled on the night of the full moon to make travelling home easier for the families who live further afield. We do the same in Lambton and around Pemberley—remind your sisters of this fact, for I believe they had the same complaint during their one visit to my estate."

"Indeed," Bennet replied. "You and your sisters will have to become accustomed to the idea of country hours while you are in residence here. We tend to rise much earlier than our counterparts who live in town and return home much sooner. Yes, there is the odd occasion that lasts until dawn, but those are few and far between."

"I will do as you suggest, Darcy, and inform my sisters of how things are done differently in the country," Bingley replied with a laugh. "But you know as well as I do that it will make little difference."

"Indeed," Darcy replied coldly, realising that both Bingley and his sisters would find living in the country difficult. He wondered, not for the first time, if his friend was really suited for living the life of a landed gentleman.

"I am sorry I will miss the assembly, mainly because I would enjoy seeing how my cousin acts at one," Fitzwilliam interjected with a tease. Then he turned the conversation to a subject that was of interest to him. "Do you know anything about this militia regiment that is slated to arrive in Hertfordshire this autumn?"

"Yes, both my brother Philips, the solicitor, and Sir William Lucas have mentioned their coming to me," Bennet said, a frown forming on his face. "At least my daughters are used to being accompanied whenever they leave the house, even my Lizzy, much as she still dislikes it. With so many strangers around, I worry for my daughters' safety even more."

"It is good of you to protect your daughters in this way," Fitzwilliam replied. "Many a girl has fallen victim to an unscrupulous man in regimentals. A wise man would be on guard, much as I hate to admit it."

Bennet looked thoughtful for a moment and merely nodded at the colonel's words. After a time, he seemed to shake off whatever thought had overtaken him, and he turned the conversation yet again. "Come, enough of this. My wife and daughters are no doubt anticipating your arrival. Darcy, you have stolen my thunder by introducing the colonel to them, but I will still have the pleasure of introducing young Bingley here to my family. My wife is most pleased that you have come and that she will have met you before nearly all of our neighbours."

All three gentlemen chuckled at this, and they rose and followed their host from the room.

They found Mrs. Bennet and her daughters seated in a parlour that overlooked the front entrance. At the gentlemen's arrival, the ladies rose, and Bennet stepped forward to perform the necessary introductions.

"My dear, surely you recall Mr. Darcy though it has been many years since his last visit," he said, pausing as his wife offered a murmured greeting.

Turning to the others, he continued, "Gentlemen, allow me to present my wife, Mrs. Bennet, and our daughters—Miss Jane Bennet, Miss Elizabeth Bennet, Miss Mary Bennet, and Miss Catherine Bennet." Each young lady curtsied politely as her name was spoken.

He then addressed his wife. "Mrs. Bennet, daughters, this is Colonel Richard Fitzwilliam, Mr. Darcy's cousin, and beside him is Mr. Charles Bingley, our new neighbour. They are to remain with us for the evening before returning to London on the morrow. Mr. Bingley will take possession of Netherfield at Michaelmas."

With the introductions complete, everyone was encouraged to take their seats. Mr. Darcy gravitated towards Elizabeth, who was seated alone on a small settee. Meanwhile, both Mr. Bingley and Colonel Fitzwilliam made their way to the eldest Miss Bennet. The colonel, having been a step ahead and already acquainted with her, reached her first and claimed the spot beside her on her settee. Mr. Bingley, undeterred, settled into an armchair nearby.

Bennet rubbed his chin, only half-listening now to Jane's gentle tones as she addressed Mr. Bingley and Colonel Fitzwilliam. The colonel, ever gallant and good-humoured, appeared to be enjoying himself thoroughly; yet it was Bingley who leant forward with the greater interest, hanging on Jane's every word. The sight pleased Bennet. If Bingley had even half a brain, Jane might soon have an excellent prospect—and she deserved no less.

As for the colonel, Bennet was less certain of his interest. Although his wife remained unaware, Bennet knew Fitzwilliam to be the younger son of an earl, and he doubted such a match would suit his eldest daughter. While his daughters' dowries were improved from what they had been five years ago, they did not approach the level of what a man like Colonel Fitzwilliam might seek in a wife.

Chuckling softly to himself at the absurdity of such a notion at their first meeting, he turned his attention to Elizabeth and Mr. Darcy.

Mary and Catherine shared a settee with Mrs. Graham seated close at hand. Mrs. Bennet surveyed the arrangement with considerable satisfaction though she was taken aback to see Mr. Darcy so readily position himself beside her second daughter. No longer plagued by fears of being cast into the hedgerows upon her husband's death—and having come, somewhat grudgingly, to recognise Elizabeth's many merits—she was nonetheless astonished that such a handsome and wealthy gentleman as Mr. Darcy would choose to sit with her bookish daughter over the universally admired Jane. Still, her spirits rose again as she observed that the other two gentlemen appeared to favour her eldest.

At first, the conversation was general, but soon, small groups began to emerge. Bennet was seated near enough to Darcy and Elizabeth to engage in their discussion, which shifted easily between literature and the practicalities of land management. He was, at first, mildly amused by the pairing, having not expected a man of Darcy's wealth and status to pay attention to his second daughter despite their common interests. Yet the more Bennet listened, the more he realised how naturally conversation flowed between the two and wondered if, perhaps, the idea George Darcy had written to him about shortly after his visit to Longbourn was not as outrageous as he might have first surmised.

Darcy spoke of some of the more recent innovations he had implemented at Pemberley, and Elizabeth responded with thoughtful, and at times teasing, observations. When the conversation turned to the expense of maintaining tenant farms during poor harvests and difficult seasons, she asked sharp questions that Bennet could see gave Darcy pause—and pleasure.

That Darcy admired her wit was apparent; that Elizabeth was not entirely immune to his attention was equally so, though she masked it with her usual playfulness.

"I must say, Miss Elizabeth," Darcy remarked, following a particularly pointed comment she had made on a landlord's duty to his tenants, "you are more conversant in estate matters than many gentlemen I encounter in town."

Elizabeth tilted her head with mock-seriousness. "Indeed, sir? Then I fear for their tenants if that is truly the case."

Darcy laughed—quietly, but genuinely—and Bennet's brows rose ever so slightly. It was not a loud laugh, nor a lengthy one, but it bore no trace of artifice. Given all he had heard of his guest, Mr. Darcy was not a man easily amused, especially in the company of ladies.

Despite his history with the Darcy family, Bennet had written recently to his brother in London to enquire what was known of the two gentlemen soon to be residing in Hertfordshire. The report had arrived only that very morning and informed Bennet that Bingley had a habit of flitting from one pretty face to another, while Darcy tended to avoid any and all romantic entanglements—or even the suggestion of one. This knowledge made Bennet determined to keep an eye on both men and to see how any courtships might progress, or whether they would progress at all.

"I am beginning to suspect," Darcy said, sobering only slightly, "that if you managed an estate, Miss Elizabeth, half the county would prosper —or at least be required to read Cowper."

"And the other half would learn to spell," she replied with a smile.

That earned a second, quieter chuckle. Bennet leant back in his chair, mildly astonished. He had known Elizabeth was clever and quick—

but he had not expected Darcy to be so willingly drawn out of his shell by his second daughter.

"Darcy," he said, interjecting at last with a knowing glance, "you may find, if you continue this path, that my daughter will have you drawing up detailed plans to improve your estate before you leave the county."

"I should not object," Darcy said, looking straight at Elizabeth. "Provided she would consent to inspect the estate first."

Elizabeth flushed slightly, and Bennet, though outwardly calm, gave a silent huff of surprise. The man might not be making declarations—but his intent was clear enough to a father who had not ceased observing him since the drawing room doors opened.

Across the room, Mrs. Bennet sat in her usual place in the room's most comfortable chair, her hands tightly folded in her lap in an effort to appear composed. As she was unaware of Darcy and Elizabeth's previous meetings or the letters exchanged between them in her role as her father's sometime secretary, it was the scene unfolding around her eldest daughter that she watched closely.

Colonel Fitzwilliam, for all his ease and cheerful manner, seemed to Mrs. Bennet more the sort who would charm a room for the pleasure of it, whereas Mr. Bingley, the dear man, looked entirely besotted with Jane already. This delighted her; despite the changes in her conduct, Mrs. Bennet still saw a good marriage as the ultimate goal for her daughters.

"Oh, you must tell us more about Bath," Jane was saying, her eyes bright as she addressed the colonel. "I have never been, but I have heard so much about the Pump Room and the Assembly Rooms. Our neighbours, the Gouldings, went a few years ago and enjoyed it ever so much."

"It is delightful, to be sure," Fitzwilliam replied. "I found it a touch overrun with matchmaking mamas and ambitious aunts, and my cousin Darcy would not set foot in the place if he could help it. However, I escaped with my dignity intact—perhaps only because I returned to my regiment with haste."

Everyone laughed, though Bingley's smile faltered for half a second before he rallied. "I have not had the opportunity to visit Bath either," he said to Jane, a note of regret in his tone. "But I have heard it does not hold a candle to the tranquility of the countryside. I confess, I am very much looking forward to my stay at Netherfield with such neighbours as yourselves to befriend us. My sisters will be delighted to make your acquaintance when they come." Fitzwilliam struggled to contain his smirk at such a comment, knowing that at least one sister would be rather displeased by the connection.

Jane coloured prettily, and Mrs. Bennet could hardly contain the delighted gasp that tried to escape her throat at such blatant flattery. Oh, there could be no doubt now—he was as good as hers, if only Jane played her cards correctly!

"Mr. Bingley is quite right," Mrs. Bennet said suddenly, unable to help herself. "Nothing is so fine as the country. And when one has as agreeable a prospect as Netherfield—why, it is the very finest situation imaginable for a young man of good fortune. I hope your stay there will be of some duration."

Jane looked mortified, but Bingley only chuckled and nodded. "I could not agree more, madam. My friends and I are most anxious to make this county our home for the autumn."

Colonel Fitzwilliam, ever observant, hid a smile behind his teacup. It appeared Bingley had found his "angel" for the duration of his stay in Meryton, and Fitzwilliam briefly wondered how his cousin would respond to his friend's evident admiration of Miss Bennet. There was no question that Darcy held a vested interest in the Bennet family, and he would not look kindly upon Bingley trifling with the sister of the first woman who had ever truly captured his notice. For a moment, Fitzwilliam studied his cousin, who was deep in conversation with

SPORT FOR OUR NEIGHBOURS

Miss Elizabeth, and then glanced towards their host—who, he observed, was watching all three gentlemen with a discerning eye. Fitzwilliam offered Bennet a knowing smile and was gratified to receive a brief, acknowledging nod in return.

Meanwhile, Mrs. Bennet's eyes flicked again towards Mr. Darcy and Elizabeth. She had not missed the quiet way they leant into one another, nor the small smile that seemed to linger on Mr. Darcy's face. Good heavens, could it be? Mr. Darcy, of Pemberley, favouring Lizzy? Elizabeth, who preferred walking and books to ribbons and dancing?

After the Darcys departed all those years ago, her husband had made clear just how little regard the Darcys and Mr. Livesay had for her behaviour and that of their youngest daughters. Bennet had impressed upon her the immense wealth of both gentlemen and the likelihood that their opinions would be echoed by others encountering the family for the first time. That conversation had been the catalyst for her willingness to reform though the change had taken considerable time—and even now, she required frequent reminders of what was expected. The girls, with the exception of Lydia, had adapted well. Lydia, already spoiled at nine years old, had not taken kindly to the new order of things and had since been sent away to school where she remained.

Now, watching her second daughter converse with the young Mr. Darcy—whom she distinctly remembered looking at her with thinly veiled disdain all those years ago—Mrs. Bennet was astonished to see that such a man might take an interest in Elizabeth. Of course, it might all come to nothing, for this was only their first proper meeting. Still, even if Mr. Darcy proved not to be the one, this encounter compelled her to re-evaluate what she had previously believed about Elizabeth's marriage prospects.

With Jane so clearly admired by Mr. Bingley and Elizabeth in close conversation with Mr. Darcy, Mrs. Bennet could barely keep her mind from running ahead. Two daughters married! Two grand houses —Netherfield and Pemberley! No more talk of hedgerows and

71

economies. She would be the envy of Meryton and she could not wait to brag about her daughters' conquests to all and sundry.

Her gaze settled momentarily on Mary and Catherine, who sat dutifully near Mrs. Graham and worked on their sewing. Mrs. Bennet sighed. "Well," she whispered to herself, "two out of five is nothing to sneer at. Of course, these daughters are scarcely considered out, despite Mary's being eighteen, but Mr. Bennet insists they wait another year or two." She grimaced at this thought, and then she recalled that gossiping of her daughters' prospects was now forbidden. That had been one of the first lessons her husband, in combination with Mrs. Graham, had forced her to learn. A mother pushing a daughter towards a gentleman might have the opposite effect of the one intended, and she would not risk that.

She heard the group around Elizabeth chuckle once more, unsurprised to see that it was Elizabeth who had made some witticism that had her father and Mr. Darcy laughing. Even the colonel was smiling at whatever had been said. Whatever it was had flown over her own head, so Mrs. Bennet consoled herself by watching Jane and Mr. Bingley smile shyly at each other.

CHAPTER 9

Confessions

Dinner that evening was a pleasant affair. The groupings that had formed earlier in the day naturally carried over to the dining table with Elizabeth and Mr. Darcy flanking Bennet at the head. The three engaged in lively conversation, touching on topics as varied as estate management and the latest publications from London. Colonel Fitzwilliam, seated beside Elizabeth, occasionally joined in—particularly when the discussion turned to the ongoing war on the Continent—but for the most part, he entertained his end of the table with engaging anecdotes from his time in service.

Jane, seated next to her mother, was primarily occupied with Mr. Bingley who had taken the place beside her. Their quiet conversation, punctuated by soft laughter and gentle smiles, did not go unnoticed. Mary and Catherine, seated further down the table, listened with rapt attention to the colonel's tales, occasionally mustering the courage to ask a shy question or two.

Surprisingly, Mrs. Bennet contributed little to the conversation. Instead, she spent much of the meal observing the interactions at her table. While every maternal instinct urged her to nudge Jane more firmly in Mr. Bingley's direction, she seemed to have grasped—at least for the moment—that in such matters, restraint might serve her purposes better than interference.

After the meal, the party reconvened in the parlour, where the Bennets' usual custom prevailed. Bennet, ever fond of good literature, selected a volume and began to read aloud. The gentlemen joined in the activity with marked enthusiasm—Darcy especially, who surprised more than one member of the household with the warmth of his participation and the insight of his commentary. At one point, he even volunteered to read a passage himself, his deep voice lending gravity to the words and drawing the room's full attention.

Colonel Fitzwilliam maintained a dialogue with Jane and Mr. Bingley, occasionally drawing a smile from Elizabeth with a clever quip or teasing remark. Mary sat with a serious expression and nodded along with the readings though she rarely spoke. Catherine, quieter than usual, watched the room with wide eyes, clearly absorbing every detail. Mrs. Bennet kept to her corner, silently evaluating each gentleman's behaviour towards her daughters and trying—not always successfully—to temper her hopeful imaginings with reason.

The evening was marked by entertaining conversation, some rather obvious staring and shy smiles, and shared laughter that rose and fell with a natural rhythm. It ended far too soon for several parties, and the following morning, the gentlemen returned to London after an early breakfast that mirrored the evening before in its warmth and ease.

As they rode back towards London, Darcy and Fitzwilliam talked quietly about what they had observed, Bingley following a little behind with a besotted expression on his face. When he did speak, it was usually along the lines of "Miss Bennet is an angel" or a similar expression.

"Bingley," Darcy said, pulling on the reins to slow his horse and moving next to his friend. "You must take care not to show more interest than you intend. Young ladies in the country are not as accustomed to the types of idle flirtations you have typically engaged in in town. If you wish to seriously pursue Miss Bennet, then please continue as you did yesterday and this morning. However, if you are not yet ready to settle down, you will need to be more circumspect."

"Whatever do you mean, Darcy?" Bingley asked, his answer causing Fitzwilliam to snort.

"It is clear you are thoroughly besotted with the eldest Miss Bennet," Fitzwilliam interjected, "but what Darcy is trying to say is this—if you do not truly intend to settle down and marry the lady, then you must stop behaving like a mooncalf when you are with her. It is likely that Mrs. Bennet already assumes you mean to offer for her eldest daughter, and if you are not careful, you will not only raise expectations but also engage the young lady's affections. If you follow your usual pattern, within a fortnight your interest may wane, and you will move on to another so-called 'angel.'"

He also slowed his horse to come alongside Bingley and turned to him with a serious expression.

"Being in the country, where there is less variety, your attention may endure a little longer. But if you leave without making your intentions clear—without a proposal—you may damage her reputation and break her heart. Worse still, if others in the community have witnessed your attentions and perceive your actions as courtship, they will assume *she* has somehow failed or been cast aside. That sort of gossip lingers for a woman and could affect her reputation."

Bingley looked genuinely affronted. "When have I ever behaved so scandalously?"

"You may not have left a trail of ruined reputations behind you," Darcy said evenly, "but there have been more than a few young ladies who believed you meant to offer for them. I recall two in particular who had every reason to expect a declaration."

He paused as though he was attempting to recall both situations. "Admittedly, you had known each scarcely a fortnight—but your attentions towards each young lady were blatant: seeking them out at every gathering, dancing multiple sets at each event, singling them out in conversation. Their families believed you had serious intentions. So did they.

"When your interest shifted and you withdrew, they were left disappointed, deeply so. Fortunately, their relations chose not to confront you—but that does not mean your behaviour left no wound."

Bingley turned to his friend in surprise, pulling on the reins, causing the horse to stop in the middle of the road. "Surely not," he said. "You cannot be serious."

"I am, Bingley," Darcy said evenly. "And in both instances, I recall, it was a brother or a father who approached me, asking for an explanation. If you remember, I spoke to you about it each time it occurred."

He paused to think. "With Miss Matilda Smith, it was your sister who took issue—because the young lady's fortune came from trade. It was she who persuaded you to end the connection in that case, arguing that a connection with her family would hurt her own chances to marry well."

Bingley gave a small, uneasy nod, remembering the events referenced, but he did not speak to defend himself.

Darcy continued, his voice sharpening. "You must be more circumspect in Meryton—especially with the Bennet family. Mr. Bennet is a friend of mine, and I will not see his daughters trifled with."

There was a pause, heavy with meaning.

"You allow your sister too much influence," Darcy added, quieter now. "She may believe herself your guide, but she does not always act in your best interest, only hers. We have spoken of this before as well."

The final words landed with more weight than Bingley had expected. The note of steel in Darcy's voice was unmistakable—controlled, but not without edge. He had heard that tone before but never directed at him.

"I will take care, Darcy," came the reply, and all three gentlemen nudged their horses forward once more.

Darcy and Fitzwilliam resumed their conversation, while Bingley rode in silence—no longer lost in thoughts of Miss Bennet, but turning over the weight of his own decisions, especially in regard to his sister.

Up ahead, Fitzwilliam cast a glance over his shoulder, a familiar spark of mischief in his eye. "You would scold your young friend for his behaviour," he said, "when yours was hardly more commendable?"

Darcy turned towards him, affront clear on his face. "What in blazes do you mean by that, Richard? When have I ever led a young lady on?"

"You acted rather besotted with Miss Elizabeth," Fitzwilliam replied blandly, his tone all the more irritating for its calmness. "You cannot imagine she might have formed an idea or two from your attentions during this visit?"

Darcy stiffened in the saddle. "Attentions? I have done nothing improper. Polite conversation, perhaps. Civility. That is hardly—" He stopped, hearing the hollowness in his own defence.

Fitzwilliam gave a shrug. "Perhaps. But even an intelligent young lady may be swayed by some determined attention towards her. While we were in Meryton, you spoke often to her. Sought her company. Talked to her. Smiled, even."

Darcy grimaced. "It is not a crime to smile at a young lady."

"From you, it is practically a declaration," Fitzwilliam said, grinning.

Suddenly becoming more serious, he continued. "While Bennet may know you from letters, he does not know of your famous 'Darcy Reserve' that has you lurking along the walls of ballrooms."

There was a pause as they rode on, hooves thudding softly against the earth. Darcy said nothing. He was not in the habit of misrepresenting himself, and yet—he could not quite deny the pleasure he had taken in Elizabeth's company, nor the warmth her presence had begun to stir in him.

"She is clever," Fitzwilliam said more gently. "And she sees more than most."

"Yes," Darcy said at last, his voice low. "She does."

After a pause, he spoke again, so softly that his cousin barely could make out his words. "I like her, Richard. I know what my father said about marriage, but she is so different from the lady I believed I would end up marrying…" he paused and let the words linger. "What I feel for her…it is unexpected."

"You do not need to decide now, but you will need to be circumspect when you return to Netherfield until you come to a decision," Fitzwilliam replied seriously. "It will be several weeks before you see her again, and in that time, you will need to decide whether you intend to pursue her or not. If you decide against her, you will need to be even more cautious."

Darcy nodded and, like his young friend, rode the remainder of the way in thoughtful silence.

Upon reaching town, the three men parted ways. They would meet again at White's the following week, but for now, each had matters to attend to—and no small amount to consider—as they prepared for the journey into Hertfordshire.

SPORT FOR OUR NEIGHBOURS

That same day, once Darcy had attended to some of the business that had been awaiting him upon his return, he took out a clean sheet of paper. Instead of dipping his pen into the ink, he considered what he ought to write. He hoped to make his sister comfortable with the idea of joining him at Netherfield. To do this, he wanted to introduce his sister to the Misses Bennet before her arrival—by telling her about them ahead of time, he hoped he could alleviate any of the worry she might feel about meeting strangers. If he could tell her a little about each of the sisters ahead of time, it would be less like meeting a stranger and more like meeting a new friend.

He shrugged to himself at the thought; he was uncertain that it would work in truth but believed that it could not hurt to try. However, he struggled to compose the letter introducing the women, especially as he debated within himself what to do or think about one of the ladies in particular.

Darcy already knew from his cousin that it would be mid-October before his family would join him at Netherfield. He had debated waiting to go until they would arrive, but when Miss Elizabeth mentioned the assembly, he had wished to dance with her. Not knowing when they might have another opportunity, he had decided at that moment that he would come with Bingley or at least within a few days of his friend's arrival. While it would force him into Miss Bingley's company without others from his family, he would not disappoint Miss Elizabeth now.

Shaking his head to clear it slightly, Darcy dipped his pen into the bottle of ink and began writing:

Dearest Georgiana,

My dear sister, by now you have heard from our aunt about the invitation to Netherfield. I know I originally told you that I would not want you subjected to Miss Bingley, but I believe that between our aunt and Mrs. Annesley, you will be well protected from your hostess. At least you have the excuse of your studies that will allow you to hide yourself in your room if the company becomes tedious, and our aunt is quite adept at rebuking social climbers.

 I believe these challenges will be outweighed by the benefits of meeting the family of Father's old friend, Mr. Thomas Bennet. Since Father's death, I have kept up a correspondence with his friend, and it just so happens that Bingley's leased estate is nearby. While Mr. Bennet may not be of much interest to you—although he does have a few stories about Father that you may find enjoyable—I hope you will come because of the possibility of meeting his daughters. There are five ranging in age from two and twenty to nearly fifteen. I believe that the four sisters I met—the youngest is away at school—will be good companions for you.

 The eldest is Miss Jane Bennet, and Bingley is already enamoured of her. She is blonde and very pretty, and she seems to be kind, but since my friend monopolised her attention while I was at Longbourn, her family's estate, I cannot tell you much more about her. Her next sister, Elizabeth, is twenty, and is witty and intelligent. Miss Elizabeth has dark hair and green eyes, and she and her elder sister are a startling contrast in appearances. One would hardly recognise them as sisters if not for the fact that they have a very similar smile.

 I actually met Elizabeth as she was visiting the tenants on both her family's estate and at Netherfield when Bingley and I visited the area. Elizabeth assists her father in managing many aspects of the estate and has acted as his secretary on occasion. She joined her father and me in our

SPORT FOR OUR NEIGHBOURS

conversations about the estate while I was there. Moreover she has read many of the same works that you and I have, so you will have much to discuss with her about literature and poetry. Unfortunately, she shares some of the same ideas as you do regarding novels, but I suppose that must be overlooked.

After her come Miss Mary and Miss Catherine. I cannot say I learnt much about them, for they are not yet out, and while they were with the family, they remained mostly with their companion and did not put themselves forward. As I understand from Miss Elizabeth, Miss Mary is eighteen and Miss Catherine turned sixteen this summer, just a year older than you. Miss Mary is studious and enjoys reading and playing the pianoforte. She is talented though perhaps not as much as you. I believe you will enjoy playing together. Miss Catherine is quite the artist, or so I am told. There were portraits of several family members displayed in Mr. Bennet's study, and I was informed that Miss Catherine had drawn them. She is quite good for one so young, and she <u>might</u> be able to assist you with your art. I say might because I am not certain anything can improve your talent in this area, but perhaps Miss Catherine could.

I know, it is rare for me to tease you, but I hope that my small jest has made you smile. Richard expects that his mother will accept the invitation to Netherfield, so I look forward to seeing you there.

Something else to make you smile: Miss Elizabeth informed me of an assembly not long after Bingley takes up residence at Netherfield. Since I will be with him, I will doubtlessly have to attend. Fortunately, since I have already *met the Misses Bennet and at least two of them will be in attendance as well, I will be able to dance with them instead of just the Bingley sisters. I have already requested a set from both Miss Jane Bennet and Elizabeth, along with their friend Miss Charlotte Lucas. Can you imagine the look on Miss Bingley's face when she learns this?*

I miss you, dear sister, and hope to hear from you soon.

Yours, etc.,
Fitzwilliam Darcy

That done, Darcy took a moment to re-read what he had written. All seemed in order, and Darcy smiled again as he considered his sister's face as she read it. He would have to learn more of the younger two Bennet daughters when he was in the area, so he could tell his sister about them.

CHAPTER 10

A Threat

23 SEPTEMBER 1811

Fitzwilliam joined Darcy for a meal a few days later at Darcy House. They had met regularly since their trip into Hertfordshire and, each time, Fitzwilliam had taken the opportunity to tease his cousin about his flirtation with the second Miss Bennet.

"You have already asked her for a dance, which is quite unlike you," he jibed. "It is unfortunate that my general is requiring me to remain nearby for several more weeks. I would give anything to see you dancing."

Darcy grunted, not responding any farther to his cousin's statement. He had already told him about his delay and the reason for it, but he knew that the only purpose in bringing it up had been to tease him, yet again, about requesting the dance from Miss Elizabeth. That he had also asked for a set from Miss Bennet and Miss Lucas was beside the point since his cousin knew he had done that only as an attempt to save face.

"Perhaps the general will allow me to take a day or two to travel to Hertfordshire with you, at least for the assembly," Fitzwilliam continued. "Do you think you will recall the steps? I daresay you cannot even recall the last time you danced, and at a country assembly. So different from the balls you are forced to attend in London which you barely tolerate."

"I have danced often enough," Darcy replied tersely, knowing he had to say something and hoping that would be enough to stop the teasing.

He was wrong.

However, before Fitzwilliam could say much more, they were interrupted by a knock. Shooting his cousin a look, Darcy called for the person to enter.

"Mr. Darcy, your uncle is here. He says he was not expected, but he knows you will welcome him gladly," the butler said upon entering.

Rising, the two men exchanged a look, but said nothing, and Darcy indicated that the earl should be shown in.

"Uncle," Darcy said in greeting as the men all took their seats, "to what do I owe this pleasure?"

"My wife said that you had invited her to join you at Netherfield," the earl began, not bothering with pleasantries. "As I understand it, you are to join that tradesman you call a friend; Bungley, is it not?"

"It is Bingley, and he is not a tradesman," Darcy corrected, his back stiff as he spoke to his uncle. "While his father and grandfather may have made their fortunes in trade, Bingley attended Cambridge and has attended a levee. His leasing Netherfield is his first step towards becoming a landed gentleman, and he has asked for my assistance in learning to manage it."

"That is all well and good, I suppose," the earl said, waving his hand in the air, "but why should my wife and your sister be forced into their company?"

"Father's friend from university, Mr. Thomas Bennet, lives in the area," Darcy replied. "Georgiana would enjoy hearing Mr. Bennet's stories about Father, and he has several daughters near to her in age. I think Georgiana might benefit from their friendship."

"Bennet?" the earl repeated. "I do not recall any Bennets. Are they titled? Do they have any great wealth? What manner of estate does he own?"

Once again, Darcy exchanged a look with Fitzwilliam. He was well used to his uncle's snobbishness, and even though the earl and Bennet had been at Cambridge at the same time, the earl had allowed his title of viscount to prevent him making many connections with those he felt were beneath him.

"Bennet has a modest estate in Hertfordshire, and I believe it does well enough," Darcy replied, ignoring most of the earl's questions. Regardless, the earl noticed the lack of answers and deduced that the man had no great wealth nor connections of any value.

"You would do better to allow my wife to introduce your sister to some of the more notable families within the *ton*," the earl stated disdainfully. "There is little point to her meeting the daughters of some mere country squire even if their father did go to Cambridge with yours.

"How I wish your father had listened to me during his lifetime and taken an interest in politics. He was wealthy enough and, with my backing, could have petitioned for a title to be awarded. Since he would not, that task falls to you. If you were to marry Anne, you would have Rosings as well as Pemberley, and that would likely be enough for a title, but of course, that is not necessary. With your wealth and my support, you could marry the daughter of a peer. There are a few young ladies who will be coming out soon enough, and Viscount Halston has always had a soft spot for you."

"Viscount Halston's daughter is reported to be barely thirteen although he has kept her from view of society," Fitzwilliam interjected. "Surely she is too young to be betrothed at this time."

"The viscount needs Darcy's wealth," the earl retorted. "He would not need to marry the girl immediately; he can merely enter into a marriage contract with the viscount before the girl can be presented at court. Until then, he can do as he likes."

"I will not marry the viscount's daughter," Darcy stated. "As I have said several times before, Uncle, I do not need your help in arranging a marriage. When the time is right, I will marry a lady of my choosing, who suits both my desires and meets what my father wanted for me."

"How certain are you of that, Darcy?" the earl replied, his voice dripping with mocking scepticism. "You are nearing thirty and have thus far shown no inclination towards any of the women I have…encouraged you towards. I begin to fear that no lady will satisfy your obviously long list of requirements. Despite what you claim your father wanted for you, surely you have realised by now that alliances are made with sense, not sentiment."

His jaw tightening, Darcy gritted through his teeth. "I know that I would prefer to remain a bachelor than to barter my future for the marriage you wish for me. As I have told you before, I do not wish for a title, and I will not marry one of the brainless debutantes you have pushed at me. Nor will I bind myself to a mere child, simply because you believe it might be advantageous to you."

The earl sneered. "You speak as a boy, not a man who bears the weight of an ancient name. Your father understood duty. He would never have risked the family's standing for some childish fancy. I cannot imagine the man I knew having the conversation you claim the two of you shared. He knew as well as I did that his marriage to my sister was to benefit him and, had your mother not died when she did, he would have accepted the title when it was offered to him."

At this, Darcy's eyes flashed with restrained anger. "My father told me to seek a wife I could love. He trusted me to act in a manner that would constitute my best interest as well as the best interest of Pemberley. Towards the end of his life, we had many conversations on this matter. Unlike you seem to do, he trusted me to uphold the family's honour in my own way. I will not sully his memory by choosing my wife in this mercenary fashion."

Fitzwilliam shifted in his seat, eyeing his cousin with wary sympathy. "It would do you no good, Father, to force Darcy's hand. He will not be coerced in this matter. If you were successful in forcing him to wed, I dare say you would have little chance to get him to dance to your tune."

The earl leant back in his chair, steepling his fingers as he considered both his nephew and his son. His eyes gleamed with cold calculation. "Then be prepared to watch the family fortunes crumble. The world is changing, and sentimentality will not shield you from ruin. Mark my words, Darcy—marry wisely, or you will regret it when it is too late."

"I would sooner endure ruin than bind myself to a child or to a woman I cannot respect," Darcy said, his voice steady and cold. "You may plot and scheme all you like, my lord, but I will live—and marry—according to my own conscience and not to fulfil any plan of yours."

A sly, cunning expression appeared on the earl's face as he smiled knowingly at his nephew. "Conscience, is it? A fragile shield, that. Particularly when others are not so fastidious. After all, not every young lady escapes *unscathed* when careless guardians leave them vulnerable."

He tapped one long finger against the arm of his chair, almost idly. "A shame, truly, how easily a misstep can occur…and how quickly whispers might spread once they do."

Darcy stiffened, his hands curling into fists at his sides. Fitzwilliam shifted uncomfortably, his eyes darting to his father. They had told the countess about Georgiana's troubles from that summer but had deliberately kept the matter a secret from the earl, knowing he would easily use it against them.

The earl's smile widened, though it remained cold. "One would hate to see a young lady's prospects ruined by…lingering questions or rumours. Especially when a family has so much at stake."

A heavy silence fell over the room, broken only by the crackling of the fire. Finally, Fitzwilliam rose, casting a warning glance at his cousin before addressing his father.

"What are you implying, sir?" Fitzwilliam asked his father, raising his brow in question.

The look the earl fixed on both men was cold, menacing. He steepled his fingers together and regarded his son and nephew with the air of a man used to getting his own way.

"I imply nothing, Richard," he began. "I simply pointed out how fragile a young girl's reputation—and by extension her family—can be, even when she is so carefully looked after by her guardians. It only takes the slightest word to cast aspersions on her character, to make a minor, youthful indiscretion appear far more serious. Once the whispers begin…" he trailed off, leaving much unsaid.

Darcy stood slowly from his chair, every motion deliberate. When he spoke, his voice was cold. "If you mean to cast aspersions upon my sister, Uncle, your own niece, I suggest you tread with caution. You, with your great reluctance to have your family cast in a bad light, surely would not do anything that might harm your family."

"That depends, Darcy," the earl said, sitting up with a casualness that belied his words. "If that person seeks to throw away the…opportunities that are in front of him, for nothing more than some flight of fancy, then it may be worth my while to distance myself from that person, would it not? A poor marriage could be explained away if a man's sister were suddenly found to be less than…shall we say *pure?*" As he spoke, the earl's smile did not falter. If anything, it grew more patronising.

"Come, Darcy. You know as well as I that a young lady's prospects depend not only on her conduct, but on the *ton's* perception of her conduct and that of the rest of her family. It is fortunate, indeed, that your sister's…recent actions did not result in public scandal. London society is not so forgiving."

Darcy's hands curled into fists at his sides. Across from him, Fitzwilliam's jaw tightened. "What do you know of her actions?" Fitzwilliam said, rising himself. "It almost sounds, Father, as though you had hoped for a different outcome."

The earl turned his gaze upon his son, slow and disdainful. "Mind yourself, Richard. Georgiana may be your ward, but she is Darcy's sister. He will do everything he can to protect her, will he not? As for you, it does not become a son to question his father's loyalty to the family's interests."

"Interests, Father?" Fitzwilliam echoed bitterly. "Or ambitions? What does Mother know of your actions?"

The earl merely shrugged, as if the distinction were irrelevant. "Call it what you will. The truth remains—Darcy must marry advantageously. The sooner the better, for it appears that his position in society may depend upon it."

Darcy's voice was low and dangerous. "I will not be threatened into a marriage I do not desire, Uncle."

"You mistake my meaning," the earl said smoothly. "I offer counsel, nothing more. It would be a pity if the past—*anyone's* past—were to be dragged into the light, should the wrong alliances be formed."

There was a beat of silence after the earl's comment. It had not been an idle statement, but a threat—and not one that could be challenged openly without revealing more than was intended.

"Georgiana has done nothing wrong," Darcy bit out. "You imply she has been ruined, but you have obviously been misinformed."

"You forget that I have eyes everywhere, my boy," the earl said condescendingly. "You have until Christmas to think over my suggestion to you. You will announce your betrothal to the viscount's daughter early in the new year. She is young yet, so you may wait to wed, but mark my words, you will marry her."

"I will not," Darcy stated, having to hold back from shouting the words.

Moving to stand in front of his cousin, Fitzwilliam said in a clipped tone. "We have heard enough, Father. Darcy and I will speak of the matter and will let you know his decision."

The earl inclined his head as though granting a favour. "As you wish. But hear me, Darcy, if you persist in this foolishness, I will do whatever it takes to gain my point. Do not think that I will not do as I have said."

Without waiting for anything, the earl retrieved his gloves from the side table, pulling them on with slow, deliberate movements. He crossed the room with the easy arrogance of a man who believed he could not be touched, even here. At the doorway, he paused, glancing back over his shoulder.

"London thrives on scandal, Darcy. Pray you do not give it fresh cause to feast." He turned as if to go, and then threw over his shoulder. "By the by, George Wickham sends his regards."

And with that parting shot, the Earl of Matlock took his leave.

Darcy remained rigidly still until he heard the faint closing of the front door. Only then did he release a slow, shuddering breath.

Fitzwilliam cursed. "Damn it all. What was that reference to Wickham about? He must know something about what happened at Ramsgate. Perhaps not the whole of it, but enough to be dangerous. I cannot imagine Mother telling him, so we must find out what he knows about Georgiana."

Darcy turned, his eyes turning to flint. "Then we must be cautious. If he wishes for war, he shall find I am not so easily cornered. I will not be cowed by his demands."

Across the room, the fire crackled and hissed—the only sound in the heavy, charged air.

CHAPTER 11

Arrival at Netherfield

1 OCTOBER 1811

Darcy travelled to Hertfordshire the day after Bingley himself. Bingley had travelled back and forth to Hertfordshire twice more, and his sisters had joined him the previous day to take up residence. The lease was for a year, and Bingley intended to spend the whole of the autumn and winter there.

Early that the afternoon, Darcy's carriage arrived in front of Netherfield. He was greeted by his friend, and with a groan, he saw Miss Bingley standing just behind him.

"Welcome, Darcy," Bingley said, raising his hand in greeting as Darcy stepped from the carriage.

"Yes, Mr. Darcy," Miss Bingley said in what she clearly intended as an alluring tone. To Darcy, however, it grated unpleasantly—almost as much as the cloying perfume she wore, which reached him even from several feet away.

"We are *delighted* you have joined us," she continued, her voice smoothing into affected warmth. "And we are so looking forward to your family's arrival later this month. It is unfortunate they could not accompany you sooner, but I must say, I was quite pleased to learn that the countess accepted my brother's invitation. I understand it is quite a mark of her favour."

Darcy inclined his head politely, giving no indication of agreement or encouragement, but that did not deter Miss Bingley from continuing.

"I have always admired the countess from afar, and I look forward to making her acquaintance at last," she went on. "And dear Georgiana! I do hope she remembers me. She and I got on so well when she was in town two Seasons ago."

Darcy inwardly groaned, having not considered how Miss Bingley would view the countess's acceptance of the invitation. His aunt was coming to dissuade Miss Bingley from pursuing him, and to give him another level of protection from the social climber, but naturally, Miss Bingley viewed it as another matter altogether.

"*Miss Darcy* does remember you," he said, emphasising his sister's proper name, "and she is looking forward to visiting Meryton. In fact, I heard from her just yesterday. I do not know if you are aware of this, but my father's old friend lives nearby, and she is most anxious to meet him and his family." He kept his voice even and did what he could to tamp down Miss Bingley's expectations.

However, that did not deter her, and she responded in a cloying tone. "I am certain we shall be fast friends. I have already made a few plans for her stay. Outings, a card party or two, and perhaps a small *musicale*. That is, if we can find anyone worth knowing in this little village."

"Miss Darcy is not yet out, and is not overly fond of large gatherings," Darcy said, his voice cool but not unkind. "She prefers quiet company and walks and rides in the countryside. Additionallly, she will also be quite busy with her studies."

Miss Bingley's smile faltered for the briefest moment before she recovered with practiced ease. "Naturally," she said. "Perhaps she would enjoy a few rides or a drive through the park. It is sadly lacking compared to what she is accustomed to at Pemberley, but I would be delighted to keep her company. It must be so difficult for her—growing up without a mother to guide her." She tilted her head, adopting a sympathetic tone.

"I would be more than happy to offer what guidance I can—just as a sister might." She cast Darcy a coy look, her lashes fluttering in what she clearly believed to be a most becoming manner, once again attempting to imply a deeper connection between them.

Darcy's expression barely changed though inwardly he sighed. He could not fault Miss Bingley for seeking to ingratiate herself with his family—many ladies in society had done the same—but her persistence was wearying. Were it not for his friendship with Bingley, he would avoid her altogether.

Unfortunately, maintaining that friendship required a degree of tolerance. It would only be worse in such close proximity here at Netherfield, but he would bear it without too much complaining since it enabled him to be near the Bennets. However, he would remind his valet, again, that the doors to his rooms needed to stay locked at all times.

Before he could answer, Bingley interrupted her with a sharp tone. "Caroline, I have already told you there is little point in making so many plans when you do not even know the area yourself. Tomorrow evening, we will attend the local assembly, and you will meet the Bennet ladies. Perhaps Miss Bennet will be able to answer any questions you have about entertainments that are already planned or to share ideas about places to visit that will be of interest to us all. There will be other entertainments scheduled as well which our callers mentioned when they came today. Besides, Miss Darcy has Lady Matlock to guide her."

Bingley turned back to Darcy and said cheerfully, "Darcy! I am pleased you arrived before dinner." He drew them both inside as he passed by his sister. "We have enough time for a drink and a few hands of cards before we need to dress for dinner. Although, I suppose you will want me to show you to your quarters and to refresh yourself after your travels?"

Darcy nodded at this and watched as Miss Bingley's disappointment was poorly concealed. With a scowl, she stepped aside as her brother led his guest inside where they were greeted by Mr. and Mrs. Hurst who had just exited the drawing room to greet the new arrival. After a short conversation, Darcy allowed his friend to guide him towards his room.

"As you heard, your sister believes my aunt's visit means far more than it does," Darcy said quietly as they walked. "Bingley, I hope you will not object, but sometime in the very near future, I am going to have to speak very frankly to your sister. I do not wish to offend *you*, but I am afraid I will have to be unpleasant to make my point."

"She will grow worse when she sees how you are with the Bennets," Bingley said with a knowing grin. "Mr. Bennet called this morning, and my sister heard him mention you. At first, she was astounded that you would have made the acquaintance of the man, and she attempted, indirectly, to call him a liar, but when I confirmed that we had visited the estate together—I did not mention that we stayed there overnight—she was flummoxed. Another caller mentioned that the Bennets had five daughters, and I could see the wheels turning in her mind. She is determined to show them up at the assembly tomorrow night. I will be amazed if we leave Netherfield on time, if at all."

"Then perhaps I should order my own carriage readied and make sure Miss Bingley is aware of that fact," Darcy said. "I have already requested sets from Miss Bennet and Miss Elizabeth, along with Miss Lucas. I would not wish to disappoint any of them by not appearing as we arranged."

"If you indicate that you are anticipating the event, then perhaps she will be more inclined to attend, herself," Bingley replied as they

SPORT FOR OUR NEIGHBOURS

arrived at the room where Darcy would be staying during his visit. "I give you leave to say whatever you must to my sister for I know she can be a trial to you. Perhaps she will finally hear *you;* she has certainly never listened to *my* words on the subject."

"One can hope, Bingley," Darcy replied as he opened the door. "One can hope."

A SHORT TIME LATER, DARCY JOINED HIS HOST IN THE STUDY. AS THEY sat, each with a drink, Bingley recounted to Darcy about the visits from several men in the neighbourhood, including Sir William Lucas, the self appointed host of the area.

Bingley recalled the conversation with Sir William, who mentioned the quarterly assembly that would take place the following evening.

Having heard about the assembly while Longbourn, Bingley accepted the invitation without noticing the sneer on his sister's face at the gentleman's mention of the gathering.

From her seat, Miss Bingley stiffened, not attempting to hide her distaste at the idea of spending time with these country rustics. "How... quaint," she murmured, her lips tightening despite the smile she forced onto her face when her brother turned in her direction.

However, barely waiting until their guest departed, she turned on her brother as soon as the door closed behind him.

"Charles, how could you accept such an invitation without even consulting me?" she demanded, rising from her chair in a swish of silk. The movement stirred her perfume into the air, and her brother coughed softly, clearing his throat.

"Mr. Darcy arrives tomorrow, and you have already committed him to attend—without the slightest regard for his preferences. You know how particular he is about social engagements. He will not wish to suffer through some rustic gathering filled with strangers and their dreadful country manners."

Her voice dripped with disdain, and she made no effort to mask her irritation with her brother.

Bingley chuckled, undisturbed by her complaints. "On the contrary, I believe Darcy is rather looking forward to it. He knows about the assembly, as did you, since I informed you of it before we arrived."

Miss Bingley's brows rose in alarm, ignoring everything her brother said except the idea that Darcy was looking forward to the event. "How does he know of it?"

"I told you, Darcy and I met several of our neighbours on our earlier visit, and Darcy's friend resides nearby. He has said several times that he is glad to have this chance to visit Mr. Bennet," Bingley explained.

She narrowed her eyes. "You might have spared a thought for how such an event will reflect on the rest of us, Charles. What if I did not wish to attend so soon after arriving in the area?"

"You may stay at home then," he said, smiling to himself. "But I intend to enjoy the company of our neighbours thoroughly, and Darcy has no objection to attending. Had he not wished to attend, he could have merely delayed his journey."

As was typical for Caroline Bingley, she ignored whatever facts she chose, and took Mr. Darcy's agreement to attend the assembly as a compliment towards herself. She decided then that she would wear her best dress—a new gown of her own design—to the assembly the following night and let the country mushrooms look on her with envy.

Bingley reported this conversation to his friend when Darcy joined him in his study later.

"I have little doubt Caroline would offer to remain behind with you if you wish it, Darcy," Bingley told him as he finished the tale.

"She mentioned the idea to me again when I returned downstairs after showing you to your room. I am worried about her and fear I have judged poorly when I asked her to be my hostess. If I thought Louisa willing and able to stand up to her, I would ask her to be my hostess instead, but she will still let Caroline do whatever she wishes. Your aunt could serve when she arrives, but I am hesitant to ask such a favour from a countess. Instead, I will write to my Aunt Horatia and ask her to come. If Caroline objects to being replaced, she and the Hursts can return to London."

"Very good, Bingley," Darcy said approvingly. "I doubt my aunt would appreciate being called upon in that way when she intended only to visit. Have I met this aunt?"

Bingley frowned as he considered this. "I do not believe so," he replied. "She has always lived in Scarborough, and I cannot recall her ever travelling so far south. She has never married, and has no other family, so she may be willing to leave her home to come join us."

"Does she have a carriage to make the journey?" Darcy asked. "I do not mean to overstep, but, depending on her circumstances, you may want to eliminate any obstacles to her getting here—such as ensuring she has sufficient funds and a way to travel here easily. Sending a carriage that far would be difficult, but you could send a private messenger with the funds to hire one."

Bingley considered this for a moment before agreeing. That done, Bingley began a conversation about some matters that had already arisen since his arrival. Two of the issues had to do with staff—particularly related to what sort of authority his sister had over permanent staff at a leased estate. Apparently, Mrs. Nicholls, the housekeeper, had been unwilling to make a few of the changes that Miss Bingley ordered. According to the terms of the lease, the family could make changes to the decor, but not make any substantive changes to the structure of the house. Miss Bingley wished to enlarge her dressing room, which could not be accomplished without knocking down a wall.

Darcy could only shake his head when this was explained. "Bingley, I think that writing to your aunt is your best recourse at this point. Inform your sister what will be allowed and what will not be, and stand your ground."

As he had once before, Bingley agreed, but Darcy wondered if his friend would actually take the steps required. He would need to remember this and ask his friend about it before his aunt and sister arrived in a fortnight. A short time later, the two men departed to go to their rooms to dress for dinner.

CHAPTER 12
Early Morning Encounter
2 OCTOBER 1811

Rising early the next morning, Darcy set out on a solitary ride. The evening before had been interminable, and he could not help but compare it to the evening a few weeks ago that he had spent at Longbourn. That evening had been lively, and the conversation had been engaging and interesting.

Last night, Miss Bingley dominated the conversation, allowing little opportunity for anyone else to contribute. Much of the meal was spent with her complaining—about the house, the supposedly backward neighbours (most of whom she had yet to meet), and anything else she deemed beneath her. She repeatedly compared everything to Pemberley—or rather, to the grandiose version of it she had conjured in her imagination.

Darcy did, indeed, love his home, but anyone listening solely to Miss Bingley might mistake it for a palace on par with the Palace of Versailles, so lavish and majestic were her descriptions. He could barely reconcile her descriptions of it with the manor he had grown up in, and he wondered exactly where she obtained many of her ideas.

"Oh, Charles, I truly do not understand how you can be content in such an out-of-the-way place," Miss Bingley had said, her nose wrinkling as she glanced around the dining room. "The furnishings are… quaint, I suppose, and the company is charming in its rustic way, but it is nothing to Pemberley. The drawing room there is nearly twice the size of this entire floor, and Mrs. Reynolds is such a treasure—so efficient, so refined. I cannot imagine her refusing to do as the mistress orders and keeping her position. Why did you not take a house nearer to Pemberley, Charles? Netherfield is so lacking in comparison."

She turned to Darcy with a simpering smile. "Do you not agree, Mr. Darcy? There is truly no comparison between the society here and that of Derbyshire. One must make so many allowances for country manners in a place such as this."

"Pemberley is in the country and much farther from London," Darcy replied, his tone blank, as was his expression. "In fact, when your brother was considering leasing this estate, its proximity to town was one of the advantages. I believe that was at your request. London is merely half a day's journey."

"Regardless," Miss Bingley continued, once again glossing over information that did not agree with her opinion, "Netherfield is nothing to Pemberley."

"So you have said," came Darcy's dry reply.

Miss Bingley carried on in this manner for the entirety of the meal and into the evening. Hurst, as usual, contributed little to the conversation beyond the occasional grunt of agreement, and Mrs. Hurst's rare remarks served only to echo her sister's opinions. Neither Darcy nor Bingley managed to say much; whenever Bingley attempted to speak, Miss Bingley would talk over him, and whenever she directed a question to Darcy, he offered only brief, noncommittal replies, carefully avoiding any statement that might suggest agreement.

Darcy had excused himself as early as he could manage, claiming that he was tired from his journey that day. Miss Bingley pouted when he left the drawing room but could say little to dissuade him from his objective.

As he rode through the countryside, Darcy could not help but think about Elizabeth Bennet. Her image had remained vivid in his thoughts ever since he had made her acquaintance that day in the fields. He knew he ought not dwell on thoughts of her, and yet, he did not truly wish to forget her. He tried telling himself he was only curious, intrigued by such a unique lady.

However, he kept replaying his father's words from all those years ago, and his mind refused to let the memory of her go. He knew that he needed to marry soon—he had heard it from his relatives with growing frequency—but he had thought to wait until he was at least thirty before he truly considered it.

Nonetheless, Elizabeth was unlike any woman he had ever known. The ladies in town—particularly those pushed towards him by his uncle—were often beautiful, well-mannered, and completely uninspiring. Their conversation was composed of flattery, fashion, and carefully curated opinions that matched whatever man they were attempting to ensnare. In contrast, Elizabeth spoke her mind with intelligence and wit. She challenged him, surprised him. She made him think. She unsettled him, not in a way he wished to avoid, but in a way that left him wanting more.

Although his father had told him that a bride need not bring great wealth or grand connections to be worthy of marriage, making such a choice would still be far from simple. If he were to choose to marry a woman like Elizabeth Bennet, it would not be the memory of his parents that haunted him. No, it would be the very present voices of his Fitzwilliam relatives that would make themselves heard, loudly and frequently.

Lady Catherine would be the most vocal. She had long determined that he would marry her daughter and spoke of it as though it were already arranged. Despite him knowing otherwise, Lady Catherine attempted to claim his own mother had desired the match, but his father had assured him this was not so. That did not prevent his aunt from vociferously expressing her opinion on the matter; he had been equally frank in his refusal. That battle had been tiresome enough.

However, the greater resistance would come from his uncle, the Earl of Matlock.

The more he thought about it, the more his uncle's threats troubled him. In particular, the contrast between the evening in company with Miss Bingley and the dinner at Longbourn haunted him. The marriage his uncle expected him to make would mean many evenings like the previous one. Perhaps it would not have been so terrible if he had not also had the memory of the time spent with Elizabeth Bennet.

The more he thought about it, the more what his uncle threatened troubled him. The earl had hinted, not very subtly, that he knew about what had happened to Georgiana this summer. He could think of only two ways the earl could have had this information. Either his aunt, Lady Matlock, told him, or he was somehow involved in Wickham's pursuit of Georgiana. He knew he could trust his aunt; he would not have sought out her help with Georgiana otherwise.

Urging his horse into a brisk canter, Darcy attempted to shake the weight of conflicting thoughts from his mind. Although Elizabeth did have a modest dowry, her lack of a substantial fortune and her connections to trade would be the real obstacles in persuading society to accept her, at least according to his uncle. Regardless, these concerns did not dissuade him. He could not deny the admiration he felt for her, nor the way she lingered in his thoughts like no other woman ever had.

While he had not yet admitted—at least, not aloud—that his feelings for her went beyond mere regard, he could no longer pretend she meant nothing. With time, perhaps he would discover some flaw that would make him forget her, but somehow, he doubted it.

Unaware that he did so, he was riding towards Longbourn and soon encountered the object of his ruminations. He was gratified to see a groom following her at a discreet distance, recalling that conversation more than five years ago where he, barely out of school, had taken his father's friend to task for allowing his daughters out without any concern for their safety. He chuckled when this thought occurred to him, just as Elizabeth slowed her horse as she neared him.

"What is so amusing so early in the morning?" she called to him.

"Forgive me, but I was simply recalling my conversation with your father several years ago," Darcy replied. "I had only recently graduated from Cambridge, and, as you know, I visited Longbourn with my father as we travelled north. When your father mentioned your love of walking out unaccompanied, I was shocked that any father would allow a daughter to walk for miles without any form of protection, and I told him so."

Elizabeth scowled at him. "So I have you to blame for curtailing my walks," she said after a moment. "Had I known it at the time, I would have been most angry at you. However, I have learnt better now, and I know that my father was…unwise in allowing my sisters and me so much freedom. Although it was frustrating then, and still is occasionally now, I do recognise why such restrictions are necessary."

"Yes," Darcy agreed. "If my father had restricted me in the same way, I would have been upset as well. It is just that women face so many greater dangers than does a man on his own, and while it may not be quite…fair…I suppose it is for the best."

Although she frowned, Elizabeth knew she could not argue with his logic. He dismounted and then moved to assist her to do the same, while the groom approached and remained nearby.

"I am pleased to see you again," she said after he had helped her down from the horse. Once again, his touch had caused her cheeks to pinken beautifully, and Darcy cherished seeing her affected by him. He stepped back to allow her space, and for himself to regain his composure. "Will you return to London soon, or will you be here now for some time?"

"I intend to remain for some weeks, at least until the first of December," Darcy replied. "My aunt and sister are set to arrive within a fortnight. My sister is…shy, so I have been trying to introduce you and your sisters to her through my letters. However, I have been unable to tell her much about your younger sisters since they spoke only a little when I was at Longbourn."

"What if I were to write to her?" Elizabeth asked, sounding sincerely interested. "I can introduce not only myself, but the rest of my sisters as well. You said she likes to play the piano and that she enjoys reading, did you not?"

Darcy nodded in agreement, and Elizabeth continued. "Would you like to include it in your next post? I could write it this afternoon and give it to you this evening."

She considered it for a moment, and then cried, "Oh, that is a terrible idea, is it not? Perhaps I should have Papa give you the note, for it would be quite the scandal if I were caught handing you a missive, regardless of how innocent it might be."

Darcy chuckled. "I had not considered it, but, yes, you probably should not hand me a letter in the open this evening. It would do neither of us any favours to be caught exchanging a note."

"No," Elizabeth laughed. "Mama might be delighted, but Papa would not. He would be rather angry with me, I am afraid."

Despite his earlier thoughts about his relations, Darcy thought he would not mind at all if he were to become honour bound to this woman. Like his other thoughts this morning, he pushed it from his mind and attempted to give his attention to the woman before him.

"I intend to call at Longbourn tomorrow afternoon, and you could give me your letter then," Darcy replied. "Is that sufficient time for you to write it? My sister is still too young to need to prepare for most social events, but even attending the theatre seems to require hours of preparation. Surely it is more difficult in a household with four daughters."

Elizabeth laughed at this, her laugh a bright, tinkling sound that made Darcy wish to hear it again and again. Smiling down at her, he was surprised at her response. "Oh, it is best I stay well away from Mama on days like today, as long as I can. While Mama is much improved from when you first met her, she still views me as her most troublesome daughter. If she had her way, I would spend the entire day in my room receiving beauty treatments meant to enhance my 'meagre charms.'"

Darcy opened his mouth as if to object, but Elizabeth spoke before he could.

"She does not mean what she says," she began, her voice softening. "Or at least, I prefer to believe she does not—and Papa encourages me in that belief." She lifted her chin slightly and continued in a brighter tone. "In any case, if I stay out for a few hours, I will avoid the worst of the arguments. Mama will be resting, and Jane and I will have time to prepare in peace. Mary and Catherine are attending tonight as well although they will not be dancing. Papa has allowed them to join us at most entertainments lately, and while Mary could dance, she prefers to keep Catherine company."

"I recall something being said about that at Longbourn," Darcy said, reluctantly honouring Elizabeth's unspoken request not to comment on her mother's opinion. "I am looking forward to my dances with you and your sister, and with Miss Lucas. However, I have kept you here long enough, and I daresay we should both return to our breakfasts. The Bingleys are unused to keeping country hours, but my man intended to ensure I had something waiting for me upon my return."

Elizabeth laughed again at this. "Yes, you have said before that you are a 'mere country farmer' and prefer the country to London. I am looking forward to this evening and to meeting the rest of your party. Good morning," she replied cheerily, looking around for a rock or something she could use to mount her horse.

Seeing this, Darcy stepped forward once again. "Allow me," he murmured, and at her acceptance, he placed his hands around her waist to assist her back onto the horse. As had happened each time, he felt a jolt of something that seemed to go straight to his heart when he touched her.

"Good morning," he said, his voice rough, as he stepped away. "Until this evening." He remained where he was until she vanished from sight. Twice, she looked back over her shoulder, and each time, he raised his hand in a quiet farewell, a faint smile playing at the corners of his mouth.

The groom, to his credit, said nothing though Darcy caught the glint of knowing in the man's eye. He would not be surprised if the entire scene was relayed to Bennet with great detail before the servant sought out his breakfast.

CHAPTER 13
The Set Down

The remainder of the morning and afternoon at Netherfield dragged on with almost painful slowness. For his part, Darcy took great pains to avoid his hostess, employing every manner of subtle evasion short of fleeing the house entirely. He had no desire to be deliberately unkind to Miss Bingley, but his patience with her was already wearing thin.

Throughout the day, he dropped several carefully worded hints designed to discourage her attentions, but Miss Bingley remained undeterred. Her determination was, he admitted privately, both impressive and exhausting.

At one point, she intercepted him in the hallway outside the drawing room just as he was going into the library to search for a book.

"Mr. Darcy," she said sweetly, slipping her hand around his arm without invitation, leading him back into the room he had just departed, "how very good of you to keep me company. Shall we take a turn about the room?"

He gently but firmly disengaged her hand. "Miss Bingley, I must beg you to excuse me. I was going to the library to find a book to read until it was time to dress for dinner."

Tilting her head coyly, she reached out to wrap her hand around his arm again, seemingly unaware of the stiff manner in which he was holding himself or the motion he was making with his other hand to ensure the footman in the hallway stepped closer. Darcy had brought several footmen with him, and all were tasked with ensuring he was never alone with Miss Bingley.

"Surely you read enough at Pemberley, do you not?" she purred. "There must be some entertainment here more worthy of your attention than the stuffy old library. Come, I would love to hear your opinion of Netherfield. My brother does not have very many books, and the library here cannot compare to your own."

Darcy opened his mouth to speak but then closed it just as quickly. He drew in a deep breath, releasing it slowly, before he finally said, "We have all heard your opinion of Netherfield, and I cannot imagine you would truly wish to hear mine. Regardless, I have yet to see what is in the library here and wished to peruse its shelves. Likewise, I do not appreciate women who latch onto me without invitation or who attempt to coerce me into doing what I do not wish to do."

Her smile faltered at his harsh words, but she recovered quickly, laughing as though he had made a jest. "Oh, Mr. Darcy, you are always so amusing," she tried again, pulling at his arm.

He rather forcefully removed her hand from his arm again and clasped both arms behind his back to make another attempt impossible. "I was not attempting to be," he stated firmly. "Rather, I was attempting to convey how little I like your unladylike behaviour. Please desist from taking my arm in the future."

With that, he bowed politely and retreated to the library. He did not look back, but he rather imagined she was still watching him, waiting for an opportunity to try again. However, his footman followed him and stood just outside the door. Had Miss Bingley entered, he would have followed, but as it was, she did not.

That evening, as expected, Miss Bingley made a point of arriving downstairs well past the agreed-upon time for their party to depart. Her tardiness, paired with a lofty silence, made her lingering displeasure from the afternoon unmistakable. It was plain she was still smarting from her encounter with Darcy, though neither he nor Bingley appeared to notice—or, if they did, they gave no sign of caring beyond mild irritation.

Mr. Hurst, having been informed of the incident, found the matter more amusing than anything else. He had chuckled over his sister's efforts, murmuring something about her persistence, but even he seemed to grasp that Darcy's patience had its limits—and Miss Bingley was fast approaching them. Unwilling to be forced to return to London with his wife and her sister, he would do what he could to discourage her.

The ride was quiet, which Darcy found far more tolerable than usual, but still the smell of her perfume was strong in the enclosed space.

When they arrived, Darcy stepped down from the carriage first, as he was closest to the door. Needing a moment to clear his head of the overwhelming smell that had invaded his senses, he took a step away and allowed Bingley and Hurst to assist the ladies.

Despite the fact that it was her brother who handed her down from the carriage, Miss Bingley immediately stepped forward and grasped Darcy's arm. He attempted not to let his displeasure show and instead turned to look at his friend.

"Bingley," he said sharply, his tone aggrieved.

Bingley turned in his direction and saw what his sister had done.

"Caroline," he scolded.

"What, Charles?" she asked, feigning innocence as she tightened her grip on the gentleman's arm, ignoring his subtle attempts to remove it from her grasp.

"You know precisely what," Bingley said. "We have spoken about this."

"I do not understand," she replied, still affecting ignorance.

After exchanging a glance with his friend, Darcy spoke, addressing them both. "Miss Bingley, I know your brother has spoken to you about how you frequently take my arm when it has not been offered. *I spoke to you about it this very afternoon.* Beyond that, you know very well that entering on my arm at this assembly would imply a deeper connection than actually exists. The only association we share is my friendship with your brother. That is the only relationship there has ever been, or ever will be, between us. Please refrain from taking my arm when it has not been offered."

He paused at her gasp of surprise, then added, "If you must enter this evening on anyone's arm, it should be your brother's."

Miss Bingley stared at him in shock. "I do not understand you, sir. We are friends, are we not?"

Darcy sighed heavily before speaking. "As much as I was raised not to contradict a lady, in this case, you leave me with little choice. No, Miss Bingley, we have never been friends. I am friends with your brother. You, however, are obviously in pursuit of me. If we were truly friends, you would know that everything you love about town and society, I abhor. The two of us would never suit, and the sooner you realise this, the better off you will be. Please cease chasing me."

Miss Bingley gasped, scandalised by his directness. "Mr. Darcy! I cannot believe you would say such a thing."

Darcy's expression remained impassive. "Miss Bingley, I would not have had to say it if you had not forced me to. Your brother has attempted to make you understand this on many occasions, yet you have refused to listen to him. This afternoon, I asked you to stop grasping at me. And, before we left this evening, your brother spoke to you. You were explicitly told that you would not enter the assembly tonight on my arm. And yet, here you are, attempting to do just that."

He glanced down at her hand, still clutching tightly at his arm. "Despite having been asked three or four times to release me, you are still holding on, looking shocked at my words. You claim to be proficient in several languages—tell me, is English not among them?"

At this, Miss Bingley looked affronted, but she finally let go of his arm, albeit reluctantly. Lifting her chin, she sniffed and moved to take her brother's offered arm instead.

"I cannot understand what you mean, sir. I have never done anything improper and have always assumed we were friends. Otherwise, why would you have invited me to your home so many times?"

Darcy struggled to contain his frustration at her obtuseness. "Miss Bingley, I have *never* invited *you* to my home. You are an unmarried lady, and I could not invite you without breaching propriety even if I wished to. However, I have invited *your brother* to my homes on many occasions. That you have accompanied him has been entirely your own choice. Have you not noticed how often an extra plate had to be set for you because you were not expected? Or how a room at Pemberley had to be prepared for you when you insisted that your brother's invitation extended to you as well?"

He arched his brow. "You will recall that that particular visit was cut short when I discovered 'pressing business' that required my immediate attention. Did you never wonder about that?"

Miss Bingley's expression wavered.

Darcy continued, "Furthermore, you may have failed to notice that, beginning this past spring, Bingley has been invited to my house less often than usual. That is because we meet at the club instead—precisely to avoid giving you the impression that your presence is expected when I invite my friend to join me at my home for a meal or to talk over matters."

"But your aunt and sister…" Miss Bingley sputtered.

"Are coming at my request," Darcy interjected. "I had not intended to ask my sister to join me until my aunt agreed to accompany her. Georgiana is coming because I wish to introduce the Misses Bennet to her, having decided they would be good friends for her. As you know, she is very shy and speaks little when in your company, but I feel that the Bennet ladies will draw her out."

"But they are…" Miss Bingley tried again.

"Gentlewomen," Bingley replied. "And as such, they are above you in society. Their father is a landed gentleman, where I am only leasing an estate. Our money comes from trade. While I have a tentative claim to being a gentleman because I attended Cambridge, I do not own land. The Bennet ladies are above us both in status, and are on par with Miss Darcy. Perhaps not as high as she, given her fortune and her connection to the nobility, but still gentlewomen. You, dear sister, are not."

Still stunned, Miss Bingley allowed her brother to lead her and the rest of their party into the assembly. Darcy followed behind them at a deliberate distance. The evening would no doubt prove interesting, for Miss Bingley had never been particularly skilled at concealing her pique.

CHAPTER 14
The Assembly

As the Netherfield party approached the assembly room, the strains of music reached their ears, a clear sign that the dancing had already begun. But the moment their party stepped through the doors, the melody faltered and then ceased altogether. Every head in the room turned towards them in collective curiosity.

Darcy, much to his dismay, found himself at the centre of attention—a position he disliked intensely. Although tall and undeniably noticeable, he made a half-hearted attempt to retreat behind the others in their party, silently hoping the room's interest would settle on Bingley instead. After all, it was Bingley who had taken Netherfield, and he was far better suited to smiling graciously under a hundred watchful eyes.

A jovial looking man approached the party. He seemed to be of an age with Bennet, but where that man was rather dry in his wit, this man was more like Bingley in that he could not hide what he was thinking. It was obvious he was delighted with the newcomers and was intent on doing his duty in introducing the party to the entire room.

To Darcy's relief, Bennet came up almost immediately after the man. Bingley obviously already knew this gentleman, as did Miss Bingley, judging from the sneer she did not conceal. Bingley introduced Sir William Lucas to the rest of his guests, and then Bennet stepped up.

"Sir William, Mr. Darcy here is the son of my old friend," Bennet said. "I have matters to discuss with the gentleman, and I will take him with me, but I will leave you to introduce Mr. Bingley and the rest of his party to everyone else. Mr. Darcy has previously met my two eldest daughters along with your Charlotte, and has already requested sets with each of them. I will allow you to take Bingley around to find him partners."

"Capital," came the reply from Sir William, who looked happy enough to have four of the five visitors to take around the room. He headed straight to his family where Miss Lucas stood next to her sisters, Maria and Eleanor, who were near in age to Mary and Catherine.

"What business do you have to discuss with me, Mr. Bennet?" Darcy asked worriedly. "Is all well at Longbourn?"

"Oh, very well," Bennet replied with a small smile. "However, I am very familiar with my neighbours and believed you would fare better if you were left to me to introduce you to a few like-minded men rather than the entire room. I have warned my wife against spreading gossip about you and Mr. Bingley, but even if she is silent, that will not stop word of your income from making its rounds. I expect your friend's sister may have had her own part in spreading it, at least, that is the impression I have formed of her from what her brother said about her at dinner."

Darcy sighed in relief as he turned to examine the room. Bennet had led him to a secluded corner, and he noticed that Miss Mary and Miss Catherine were sitting quietly nearby, but he could not spot Bennet's other daughters.

"What set is this?" Darcy asked after several moments had gone by and he had still not spotted either Miss Bennet or Miss Elizabeth.

"Alas, it is only the first," Bennet replied with a touch of humour in his voice. "My daughters are dancing already; do you see them next to each other in the line just now? Ahh, look at my wife. She is delighted that we have already met your party, and that she is not dependent on Sir William for the introductions. That was her complaint when Jane first entered society, that I refused to attend most events with her. Still, while I might prefer to be at home with a good book, it is better that I accompany my wife and daughters. At last, I have learnt to be cautious."

"Did something happen to prompt this realisation?" Darcy enquired with a raised brow, intrigued by the way Bennet said this last.

Bennet visibly drooped. "Unfortunately, my youngest daughter, Lydia, was unwilling to adjust her behaviour with the rest of us. She refused to follow my wishes regarding not venturing out on her own and escaped from the schoolroom a few too many times for my liking. On the last occasion, she had a run in with a man from town. While he did not harm her, he easily could have. We sent her to school as a last resort, and she remains there for now. This summer, we attempted bringing her home for a time, but she was still unwilling to abide by our rules, and we sent her to a different school. However, this will be her last opportunity, for if she continues as she has done, we will have to see what other alternatives might be available."

"My Aunt Matlock may be able to make some suggestions when she comes," Darcy replied. "She does not have any daughters herself, but somehow, she has become an expert in these matters. On several occasions, she has helped a family find a more appropriate place for a daughter who refused to follow the dictates of society."

"I will speak to her when she comes," Bennet agreed. "Now, tell me what is troubling you."

Darcy laughed, having rarely met someone who could so easily deduce what he was thinking. "Father was very good at that same trick, sir, and always seemed to know what I was thinking before I did," Darcy replied, delaying any possibility of confession.

"Yes, your father and I grew close at school and exchanged letters for many years," Bennet said. "You are very like your father and have the same look that he did when something was weighing on him. However," he paused, taking the opportunity to examine his young companion closely.

"Whatever is troubling you is likely not fit to discuss in so public a manner. Come visit me tomorrow at Longbourn; call as early as you like. Lizzy is the only early riser in the household, and tonight's assembly will likely last until at least midnight. Even she might sleep later on the morrow, but regardless, I will rise before the sun. If you come to the kitchen door, the housekeeper will not only show you in but will likely give you a hot bun to enjoy while we speak."

Darcy smiled at being encouraged to such informality. He had long made it a habit to rise with the sun, if not earlier. For many years, he had slipped into the kitchen at dawn to watch the cook prepare the day's meals, often pilfering a pastry fresh from the oven. It was a tradition he had learnt from his father, and one they had shared frequently during the last months of his father's life.

"I will do so," Darcy agreed with a smile, but then, as he once again considered the matters that were troubling him, his face fell. "There are several matters troubling me, and while I am uncertain how much I ought to confess, I know I can trust you, and may find relief in speaking of at least part of it to you."

Both gentlemen fell silent for a moment before a thought occurred to Darcy. "Did you know my uncle, the Earl of Matlock, when you were at Cambridge with my father? I believe my father once said they were there at the same time, as it was my uncle who introduced him to his sister. He was only the viscount then, but I seem to recall them speaking of making the acquaintance while at university."

"The earl is a few years older than your father and me," Bennet said, his voice deliberately even. "He was finishing his studies just as I was beginning mine. Your uncle did not think much of me—nor, truthfully, of your father—at least not until he learnt how wealthy the Darcy family was. As the Bennets were never so well endowed, he continued to dismiss me though he made a show of befriending your father. I doubt your father had any real wish to encourage the acquaintance, not until your mother arrived for a visit with the old earl. Once he saw Lady Anne, his heart was fixed. She was very young then, only sixteen, I believe, but your father declared almost at once that she would be his wife."

Darcy looked at the older gentleman for several moments. "Yes, Father once told me that their marriage was a love match, but my uncle claims it was agreed to for other reasons."

"That is partially true, I daresay," Bennet replied with a nod. "Your maternal grandfather was not pleased when a mere country gentleman asked for his daughter's hand in marriage, and he attempted to withhold his permission. However, your paternal grandfather made some sort of deal with the earl, and permission was granted for the two to wed. Your father never said much about it, only expressed his delight in finally being permitted to marry his Anne, but I know that the Fitzwilliam and Darcy families never did get along particularly well."

"Yes, I recall some of that," Darcy agreed. "Mother always encouraged us to spend time with her brother's family though I believe it was as much for her friendship with my aunt and their children as for any duty to her brother. As for my grandparents—I remember very little about them, on either side."

"Your father and mother were very much in love, but I do not believe either family was particularly pleased to be tied together," Bennet said, a faint smile playing about his mouth. "I recall your father writing to me about the difficulties between them, both before and after the wedding.

"Lady Catherine, as the elder sister, had already endured two seasons without a single offer. When she learnt her younger sister—who was not even out—had already attracted a suitor, it drove her to distraction. Your father was considered quite handsome, and Lady Catherine claimed that Anne marrying a mere gentleman would harm her own chances. Naturally, she argued fiercely against the match. At the same time, she tried to persuade her father to allow her to marry George herself. A contradiction, of course—but once she learnt how wealthy the Darcy family was, her objections softened considerably. I suspect she even admired your father though she would never have admitted to it openly."

Bennet chuckled softly before continuing. "Your uncle objected as well, claiming that the Darcy family, lacking a title, was not worthy of a Fitzwilliam. He overlooked the fact that the Darcys owned far more land and were significantly wealthier than many a noble house, including his own. Had they desired it, they could have purchased a title—likely one loftier than an earldom—but they had no interest in such trappings.

"In the end, George would have no one but Lady Anne. They married a few years later, after she had been presented at court, but several years before your grandfather Darcy passed away."

"That lack of a title in my family still plagues the earl," Darcy said bitterly. For a moment, he said no more, then turned to the older man. "Bennet, I will take you up on your offer. My uncle is causing trouble—perhaps you will have some suggestions for dealing with him."

"Aye," Bennet said, his eyes gleaming with thinly veiled amusement. "I would not mind crossing swords with Matlock again. It has been far too long since I had the pleasure of frustrating his schemes."

He shifted his weight slightly, the corner of his mouth quirking in a grin. "I will also write to Livesay, if you do not object, once we have discussed the particulars. Like me, he was never held in high esteem by your uncle—lacking sufficient wealth, and of course, the all-important title."

Bennet's mouth twisted into a grin. "He has since remedied the matter of fortune—though some of it came through trade, and we both know how Matlock scorns anything that smacks of honest work." He gave a brief, satisfied chuckle. "Regardless, Livesay will almost certainly relish the chance to assist you in defeating whatever your uncle has in mind. I imagine we will both enjoy it more than we ought."

"Thank you, Bennet," Darcy said quietly. "I do not believe I have ever properly expressed my appreciation for your continued friendship after my father's death. It meant…more than I can easily say."

He paused, his gaze dropping briefly before he forced himself to continue. "In truth, while I know that meeting was significant for you and your family, it had a greater impact on my father and me than I understood at the time. Before we left Longbourn, he and I had a serious conversation—something we had managed all too rarely. It opened the way for further discussions, and in those final months…"

He trailed off for a moment, gathering himself before finishing quietly, "we were able to speak with a frankness and understanding that had long been missing." He hesitated again, his voice tightening.

Drawing a steadying breath before finishing, Darcy continued: "Since his death, your letters have filled a place he could no longer occupy. Not as a replacement, but as a…source of counsel and steadiness when it was most needed."

Bennet met his gaze, his voice gruff but kind. "I am glad I could be of some service, lad. Your father was a good man, and I have missed his friendship since he died. I speak for both Elizabeth and myself when I say that the feeling has been mutual." Clearing his throat of the unusual emotion, Bennet said more gruffly. "Come, that is enough of this. Did you not ask my daughters to dance some time this evening?"

With that, Bennet led the younger man towards a group of other landholders in the area and introduced him. The men spoke on mutually agreeable topics until the current dance ended, and it was time for Darcy to dance.

CHAPTER 15

First Dances

Finally, the fifth set arrived, and Darcy was at last able to claim Elizabeth Bennet as his dance partner. They had exchanged only a few brief words earlier in the evening, both having been otherwise occupied. Elizabeth had sat out one set while Darcy had been obliged to dance that one with Charlotte Lucas. He had also danced with Jane Bennet but had thus far avoided Miss Bingley.

As he led her to the line, Elizabeth glanced up at him with a warm, familiar smile and asked, "Are you enjoying the evening, Mr. Darcy?"

"Surprisingly, I find that I am," he replied, a slight, almost sheepish smile lifting the corners of his mouth.

Elizabeth's brow arched. "And what, pray, is so surprising about it?" she asked, her voice light, though there was a warning glint in her eye at the implied insult.

Darcy hesitated a fraction too long before answering, causing her ire to grow. "I do not often find much pleasure in crowded rooms," he admitted slowly when he finally found the words to say. "Tonight has been…an unexpected exception to that."

He caught the faint flicker of doubt that crossed her features and hurried to continue. "I mean only that—here, I am new, and while there has been some curiosity, it is nothing compared to what follows me in town. There, whispers of my fortune and connections accompany me and attract far more attention than my company ever could. Those who have spoken to me this evening have done so—" he paused, searching for the right word "—kindly. Authentically. It is refreshing and unusual for me."

Elizabeth's expression softened, the anger fading into something more reflective. "I see," she said. "Forgive me—I thought, for a moment, you meant something else entirely, that you found the company here lacking. My father has often accused me of rushing to judgement and has warned me repeatedly against the habit. I mistook your meaning and immediately assumed you meant the worst."

He shook his head slightly, a touch of colour rising to his cheeks. "You are not mistaken to be wary," he said quietly. "Particularly since some of my party—" His eyes flicked discreetly towards Miss Bingley, and Elizabeth followed his glance without comment. "—have not acquitted themselves well this evening."

Shifting uncomfortably, he lowered his voice further. "I was forced to speak to Miss Bingley sharply on two separate occasions today. More directly than I ought to have done, but it was necessary. She presumed too much—and, due to my friendship with her brother, I have remained silent for too long. I asked her brother to address her, and he did, but to no avail. She would not listen…"

There was an awkward moment, and Darcy looked away briefly, as though gathering himself. "I fear I have spent too much of the evening speaking with your father," he said, half-apologetically. "His manner invites a degree of frankness…and I find myself less guarded than I ought to be. I should not have said that about my hostess."

He hesitated, then added in a lower voice, almost conspiratorial, "I am afraid that I am not showing myself at my best this evening, first angering you, and, then proving myself to be nearly as bad as the gossiping matrons I try to avoid."

"I will not hold it against you, sir," Elizabeth teased. "I too, have spent too much time in the company of my father and often find myself with a similar frankness. The fault is as much mine as it yours, for it was my hasty rush to judgement that forced you to say what you did."

Elizabeth laughed quietly, not unkindly, and Darcy, still slightly flustered but heartened by her amusement, allowed himself a small, genuine smile.

Their set began, and for a little while, the noise and press of the assembly faded, leaving only the two of them moving together in an easy, familiar rhythm.

Several moments later, Elizabeth glanced up at him, her eyes bright with mischief. "It seems your dancing, Mr. Darcy, is as surprising as your conversation," she said, her voice low enough that only he could hear. "For someone whose cousin expressed surprise at your knowing how, I find you quite adept at the art."

Darcy felt a rush of heat climb the back of his neck, but he managed to answer, his tone wry, "I did not wish to disappoint you, Miss Elizabeth. And I believe my cousin was more surprised at my willingness to dance, not my skill. I have often partnered with my sister during her lessons, and I enjoy the activity. It is the...other parts of navigating society that trouble me."

Throughout the dance, Darcy found his gaze drawn to Elizabeth. They spoke, though he could not have said about what, lost as he was in the quickness of her smile, the grace of her movements, and the intelligence shining in her eyes.

When they passed in the pattern of the dance, Elizabeth tilted her head slightly—an almost imperceptible gesture, as if to reassure him. Each time, Darcy's chest tightened with an emotion he dared not name. Their gloved hands brushed in a touch no more intimate than the dance required, yet each touch burned against his skin. He wondered if she felt it too and noticed that a faint, secret flush coloured her cheeks.

When Darcy first met Miss Elizabeth, he knew at once that he *wished* to pursue her—but he had hesitated, uncertain whether he *should*. Now, his concerns had shifted to his uncle's likely reaction. What did his uncle know? What might he suspect? And what would he say—or do—if Darcy were to openly court Elizabeth?

Given his attraction to her, which only grew each time he was in her company, it was more imperative that he speak to Bennet as soon as possible. He needed to see what could be done to circumvent his uncle from carrying out his threat—implied or otherwise.

The final measures played, and Darcy offered his hand once more. Elizabeth placed hers lightly in his, and when he bowed over it, he allowed himself the smallest indulgence—holding her gaze a heartbeat longer than propriety allowed.

She did not look away.

Neither did Caroline Bingley.

Her brother had told her often enough that Darcy would never offer for her, but she had ignored him. Watching him that evening had been painful since it was obvious that he was actually enjoying himself for once.

Unlike all the events she had attended with him in town—not truly with him, since he was right, he had never invited her, but she had always convinced herself that he had not done so due to the impropriety of it, not because she was unwelcome—he appeared to be at ease in the company that night.

For some time after they entered, she watched him as he first spoke to an older gentleman, likely the friend of his father's, before that man began to introduce him to others in the room. Most of these first introductions were to other men, and though he had been stiff at first with each of them, Miss Bingley noticed that it did not take long for him to appear at ease.

When he began to be introduced to some of the matrons and young ladies in attendance, she noticed that, while many appeared interested in him, most approached him demurely. Although she was at a distance from most of these, she saw enough to know that these women did not appear interested in him solely for avaricious reasons.

Yes, he was handsome, and she noticed the admiration in many of their glances, but not the same sort of flirtations that she so often witnessed in town. Nor the same sort of flirtations or improper behaviours that she had so frequently demonstrated towards him.

It was a startling realisation, made all the worse when she heard her own name and the account of Darcy's comments to her outside the assembly hall whispered about by a few young ladies in attendance.

"What has you thinking so seriously, Caroline?" Mrs. Hurst said quietly as she approached her sister, observing her rather fierce scowl. "It is not quite the same as in town, but I have met several interesting ladies here. Our brother seems to be enjoying himself, but I worry about his typical behaviours. I hope that Mr. Darcy has warned him to be careful about his usual exuberance. Such behaviour would not be welcome in a small country society like this one. I would speak to him, or have my husband do so, but I am certain that if Mr. Darcy were to say something, he would take the matter much more seriously."

Miss Bingley grimaced. "I think you must be correct. We have warned him away from women so often for various reasons, but most of them were because we did not approve of the lady," she said with a sigh.

She continued, shocking her sister greatly. "Have I been inappropriate in my actions towards Mr. Darcy?"

For a moment, Mrs. Hurst could not speak. "What…what do you mean?" she stammered.

"Have my actions towards Mr. Darcy been inappropriate? Have I been…pushy, grasping, clingy? Am I too forward with him or with other gentlemen?" Miss Bingley asked in a brisk manner, not noticing her sister's face as the colour seemed to drain from it. She stopped and looked at her sister as she finished.

Mrs. Hurst had become very pale, and her mouth was opening and closing without any sound coming out of it.

"Never mind," Miss Bingley retorted icily. "I suppose your reaction is answer enough. My actions have been unbecoming, and Mr. Darcy was likely correct to speak to me the way he did. It seems," she continued, her tone becoming bitter, "that I could not have attracted him regardless since his taste appears to run towards the society here. He has been more personable this evening with strangers than he ever was in my company or at society events. I suppose that, should I have managed to force his hand somehow, we would have been miserable together."

Mrs. Hurst nodded. "You enjoy society far more than Mr. Darcy has ever seemed to do," she agreed. "I think that you would have found very quickly that you would not have enjoyed a marriage to him, and it would not have been the marriage you desired. Once he is married, Mr. Darcy will spend very little time in London."

Miss Bingley scowled at this. "I thought I would have been able to change his mind on that count. As his wife, he would have given in to my insistence that we spend the majority of the Season in town and to host house parties in the summer. Still, watch him now," she ordered, and both women turned to look at where Darcy stood talking to Miss Elizabeth. There were others around them, including their brother, who already seemed to be smitten with the eldest Miss Bennet, but

SPORT FOR OUR NEIGHBOURS

Darcy seemed entranced by his companion, and the two were lost in conversation.

"What do you know about her?" Miss Bingley asked after a moment.

"She is Miss Elizabeth Bennet, second of five daughters in the Bennet family," Mrs. Hurst began. "The family owns a modest estate that is apparently adjacent to Netherfield, but I do not know much about it. I did meet her mother who had much praise for the elder daughter, Miss Jane Bennet, but complained that Miss Elizabeth was too much of a bluestocking to attract a husband. The lady seemed to recognise our brother's interest in Miss Bennet and seeks to encourage the match. However, she implied that Mr. Darcy was well known to the Bennet family and informed me that our brother, Mr. Darcy, and Mr. Darcy's cousin had all dined at their estate, Longbourn, during one of their visits to the area."

Miss Bingley scowled again. "Five daughters," she huffed. "Do they have dowries?"

"That did not come up," Mrs. Hurst replied. "Mr. Bennet approached when Mrs. Bennet was denigrating her second daughter and pulled her aside, presumably to speak to her. When she returned, she was much subdued."

"I could understand it if Mr. Darcy married the daughter of a peer or a woman with a larger dowry than my own," Miss Bingley huffed. "For him to appear interested in a mere country miss, even if she is the daughter of a gentleman, is more than I can stand. I have told my friends that I would return from Netherfield engaged to Mr. Darcy. If he is not to marry me, the least I can do is ensure he chooses a bride who is better placed. I would not be able to hold my head up in London otherwise."

Mrs. Hurst was already shaking her head before her sister finished talking. "I do not think that is wise, Caroline," she said. "While I cannot disagree with you giving up your pursuit of Mr. Darcy, I do not think you ought to interfere. I imagine he will make a decision that best suits him and will not take into consideration your desire to save face with people you hardly even like. If he decides Miss Elizabeth is the one he wishes to marry, then you should not do anything to meddle with them."

Huffing, Miss Bingley turned to her sister. "It is not meddling. His family could barely condone such a match. Just wait until Lady Matlock arrives, and we will see what she has to say about the matter."

CHAPTER 16

Revelations

The day after the assembly, Darcy rose early and rode to Longbourn to meet with Bennet. He did not waste time in recounting both the incident involving Georgiana that summer and his meeting with his uncle only a few weeks earlier.

"My cousin and I thought that Georgiana would benefit from a few months at the seaside this summer after a difficult spring in London," Darcy began. "Both Richard and I interviewed the companion, who had been recommended to us by his father, Lord Matlock, who he said had been recommended to him by a friend. I should have suspected him then, but there was so much else going on, and while I have had my problems with my uncle, I believed he would have had my sister's best interests at heart. Now, however, it would appear that I may have been wrong."

Darcy paused for a moment and thought about what he now knew and what he and his cousin had discussed after speaking with the earl.

"Mrs. Younge was not who we thought she was. Instead of protecting my sister as she ought to have done, she encouraged my sister to meet with a much older man, a former friend of mine, named George

Wickham. Georgiana did not know he was no longer my friend and had not been for some time due to his depraved behaviour. Regardless, Wickham persuaded my sister that they were in love, and he attempted to convince her to elope with him. Fortunately, I arrived in time to put an end to the scheme before any real damage could be done, but my sister was heartbroken."

Again, Darcy paused, running his fingers through his hair as he considered his next words. "I have since learnt that Mrs. Younge and Wickham were lovers. Initially, I believed their plan had been to abscond with Georgiana for her thirty thousand pounds, but after our last meeting, Richard and I believe the earl was behind the plot. We think he intended to use this to blackmail me into marrying as he wishes, using my sister's reputation as leverage over me."

"What will you do?" Bennet asked, his hands steepled in front of him as he considered the younger man. He had seen how Darcy reacted to his second daughter and wondered if that was not behind some of his troubles.

"I do not know," Darcy admitted after a moment. "My…my father and I spoke after we visited here; did he ever speak to you about it?"

Watching Bennet shake his head, Darcy sighed and continued. "We spoke of marriage and the kind of woman I should one day take as my bride. I had been out in society a little at that point but had not been impressed by any of the young ladies I had met. Little has changed since then, as most young ladies I meet appear vapid and entirely unappealing."

Pausing again, Darcy shook his head to clear his thoughts. "Your description of your daughter on that visit intrigued me. I liked the idea of a well-read, intelligent wife who could be a partner to me, and I said as much to my father. His reply surprised me, for I expected him to encourage me to wed someone who brought wealth and connections to the match. Instead, he told me to seek a lady whom I could fall in love with, as he had done."

Huffing out a reluctant laugh, Darcy shook his head slightly. "In truth, he told me that, given what we knew of her, Miss Elizabeth would make an ideal bride for me one day. However, we were both too young at the time to even consider such a thing—and, at that point, I had not even met the young lady."

His smile faded. Straightening in his chair, Darcy met Bennet's gaze directly, his tone becoming more serious.

"I will admit to you now that she intrigues me," he said quietly. "But I am uncertain what I ought to do, given my uncle's threats."

There was a pause. Bennet, steepling his fingers thoughtfully, considered his companion for a long moment.

"What if," Bennet said at last, his tone deliberate, "there were a contract—signed by your father and myself—formally binding you and Elizabeth in marriage? If such a document existed, it would take precedence over any arrangement your uncle might attempt to impose. He could do nothing to prevent the marriage in that case."

Darcy froze. For a heartbeat, he could only stare at Bennet, the suggestion landing in his mind with the force of a blow. His mind raced, struggling to absorb it all.

A contract. Signed by his father. A shield against his uncle's interference. Relief stirred in him—swift, almost dizzying. It was an elegant solution, far better than any he had dared imagine at this point. He could marry Elizabeth, a lady who, even if he had not quite fallen in love with yet, he certainly felt as though he could. At the very least, he respected her and enjoyed her company, which was more than he could say about the girl his uncle proposed he marry.

But, just as quickly, concern followed. His brows drew together, and he leant back slightly, as if to put space between himself and the enormity of what was proposed.

"And the earl?" he said finally, voice low and rough. "If he cannot prevent the match, he will almost certainly seek to destroy it—

through scandal if he must. He will threaten to reveal—or invent—disgraceful stories about Georgiana. He will demand that I find a way to void the contract, either by bribing you—or by ruining your family if you refuse."

Darcy's hands had curled into fists on his knees. He forced himself to unclench them, breathing out slowly through his nose. He looked back at Bennet, searching his face for any sign of hesitation.

"How are we to protect Miss Elizabeth—and your family—from the consequences of his anger?" he asked, his voice rough with suppressed emotion. "And how are we to shield Georgiana, if he chooses to speak of what may—or may not—have happened at Ramsgate?"

"Take a breath, Darcy, and calm yourself," Bennet said, leaning closer and placing a steadying hand on the young man's shoulder. His voice was low but firm. "Nothing must be decided this instant. But yes—your father secretly sent me a marriage contract before his death."

Darcy stiffened, but Bennet pressed on, his tone measured.

"It contains an addendum," he explained, "that would render it void should either you or Elizabeth object. Your father, even then, feared the earl might attempt to exert his influence and force you into a marriage against your wishes. He also made mention of Lady Catherine's ambitions towards her daughter, but he was more worried about what the earl might attempt."

Bennet leant back in his chair, studying Darcy carefully as he continued. "As you know, he wished for us to maintain our correspondence after his death. If I developed any concerns regarding your potential marriage, I was to inform you of the contract. Otherwise—" he allowed a faint, wry smile "—I was to keep it secret. He thought that having a formal contract in place had the potential to protect you if it became necessary."

Darcy let out a slow breath, his hands tightening briefly where they rested on his knees. For a moment, he stared at the floor as if hoping it might offer answers.

When he spoke, his voice was low, edged with something almost like hurt.

"Why would he not tell me of this himself? Before he died?" he asked quietly.

"He intended it to be revealed only if necessary," Bennet said. "Had you and Elizabeth met and decided for yourselves to marry, it would not have mattered. The same would have been true if you had met another lady and chosen to marry her instead. The decision of when —or if—to disclose the contract was left to my discretion.

"In this case," he continued, "I believed it might serve to your benefit. As I said, there is no obligation on your part to marry my daughter, and I cannot even guarantee that she would wish to marry you. But if your uncle proves difficult, the knowledge may make your path easier."

Attempting to lighten the moment, Bennet said with a wry smile, "Still, the two of you danced twice last evening and have already spent several hours together. I think she must like you at least a little."

He gave a short chuckle at his own jest, though it fell flat; his companion seemed not to hear it at all.

For a long moment, Darcy said nothing. He sat very still; his gaze fixed on the space between his tightly clasped hands.

The idea that such a contract had existed for years unsettled him more than he cared to admit. That his father had kept it a secret, hoping to shield him from a future threat he had scarcely imagined at the time, unsettled him even more.

He could not decide which troubled him more: the secrecy, or the sense that his father had predicted his attraction to Elizabeth.

However, he also felt relief. It was a strange, welcome feeling, born not of obligation, but of possibility. The knowledge that his father approved of the match was liberating. If what Bennet said was true, then the path ahead, difficult as it might be, was not entirely closed to him. There were still options he could pursue and, what was more, the most significant option was Elizabeth, the first woman he had ever encountered who had fascinated him.

He looked up. "Might I see the document?" he asked.

Bennet inclined his head in agreement. "Of course."

Before either man could say more, the door opened unexpectedly.

CHAPTER 17

A Private Meeting

Elizabeth stepped into the room; her cheeks flushed from the wind. She stopped short at the sight of the two men, the tension between them still hanging faintly in the air.

"I beg your pardon," she said, glancing between them. "I did not realise you were engaged, Papa. Mr. Darcy, I am surprised to see you here so early in the morning, especially after such a late evening at the assembly."

Both men rose at once—Bennet with a faintly amused expression while Darcy appeared more conflicted. Something unspoken lingered in his manner, and Elizabeth regarded him with quiet wariness.

When Bennet spoke, his tone was even, his expression unreadable. "There is no need to apologise, my dear. You are always welcome in my study."

Darcy gave a slight bow. "Miss Elizabeth."

She returned the gesture with a nod though her eyes lingered on him for a moment longer than was necessary. "I hope I have not interrupted anything of importance."

"On the contrary," said Bennet with a dry smile. "Your timing, as ever, is impeccable, Lizzy. I believe you may be able to add to our discussion."

She inclined her head, eyes flicking briefly to his, her expression neutral. From the corner of her eye, she noticed that Darcy had paled and wondered about the cause.

"I will not remain; I only came to return this," she said, holding up a small book. "I found it in the drawing room upon my return from my walk." She crossed to place it on the desk, her movements unhurried, though Bennet —keen observer that he was—noted the slight tension in her shoulders.

"Thank you," he replied, watching her closely. "You arrived at an opportune moment. Darcy and I had nearly concluded our discussion."

Elizabeth glanced again at Darcy. "Indeed?

"Not serious," said Bennet with a faint smile, "but not insignificant, either."

She gave him a questioning look, but before she could speak again, Bennet turned to Darcy. "If you are in no great hurry, sir, I wonder if you would remain a moment longer. I should be very glad of your opinion on a matter relating to the northern fields."

Darcy hesitated briefly at the change in topic of their conversation, then nodded his agreement. "Of course, sir."

"Excellent." Bennet gestured towards chairs in front of his desk. "Lizzy, I imagine you have nothing against remaining a few moments yourself?"

Elizabeth raised an eyebrow, amused but obliging. "If I must," she said with a teasing air.

They all took their seats. Bennet remained behind the desk while Elizabeth and Darcy sat in the chairs facing him. He studied them with the same unassuming sharpness he often reserved for more delicate passages in books and saw how they each turned, ever so slightly, towards the other.

There was a pause before he spoke again, this time with a careful casualness to his tone that caused both his companions to turn to look at him for a moment.

"I have been considering a few changes to the crop rotation in the north field," Bennet said, leaning back in his chair once again. "The soil has been growing tired, and I wonder whether it might be time to rest it—or perhaps introduce barley in place of wheat. Darcy, what is your opinion?"

Darcy turned to Bennet, thoughtful. "I have seen similar cases at Pemberley. We rotated in clover and vetch for two seasons, then barley in the third. The yield improved steadily when we did this. It was Father's idea, but we have done it for nearly a decade now, and it seems to have helped."

"Hmm," Bennet murmured. "We have not tried clover before. Although I have some doubt whether the tenants would favour the change. As you know, Lizzy, several of the older tenants are not fond of surprises, nor are they willing to make changes to the way they have always done things."

"They are not alone in that," Elizabeth said lightly, but her brow was drawn in thought as she wondered about the purpose of this conversation. It was one they had debated several times, and while Elizabeth had read about several different options, the one she had proposed was different. "But if the soil is exhausted, as Papa says, then barley would take less from it. And clover would need to be introduced gradually—perhaps only on the far end at first, near the tree line, where few notice what is grown anyway."

Both men turned towards her. Bennet's expression showed quiet approval, but it was Darcy who spoke.

"You are likely correct, Miss Elizabeth," Darcy began. "I do not know precisely what field you refer to, but if it is near a tree line, it is likely the edge of the field is underused and shaded. That would be enough to slow the growth of anything planted there. But with clover, that might actually be of benefit."

Elizabeth looked surprised but not displeased. "I read about it in a pamphlet Mr. Davies lent us. There was a diagram and several tables showing the benefits of such a scheme."

"Then you were more thorough than most," Darcy said. His tone was not patronising, only matter of fact, and Elizabeth noted, with a small flicker of something like satisfaction, that he addressed her not as someone less than himself, but as an equal.

Bennet, who had opened a ledger and was flipping through the most recent notes on crop yields, said without looking up, "It seems I shall soon be out of a position. Between the two of you, there may be no need for me at all."

Elizabeth smiled and laughed at the familiar tease. "I cannot say I mind if we manage the land a little better. As you well know, it has been Mr. Darcy's agreement with my plans for the estate that has persuaded you more than once, Papa, when we disagreed about what would work best."

Darcy inclined his head, the corners of his mouth lifting slightly. "Then it seems we make a good team, does it not? At least from afar. But I suppose we can only improve now that we are in the same county for a time."

"That seems likely," she replied, a touch of colour rising in her cheeks as she met his gaze.

There was a pause as they simply held each other's gaze. It was comfortable but charged. For a moment, neither spoke.

Finally, Darcy glanced towards the window, where the early morning light lay soft across the lawns. "Would you like to walk with me, Miss

Elizabeth? I should very much like to see the orchard path your father mentioned on a previous visit."

Elizabeth hesitated for only a breath. "Of course, sir. Let me collect my things and notify a footman to accompany us."

"It is not necessary, Lizzy," Bennet replied, feeling that it was best to allow the two to speak in privacy. They would be outside, and there were enough people about that they would not be unobserved. "You need a footman only if you go out alone, and I trust Mr. Darcy to be adequate protection for you. Take your maid Sally instead."

Elizabeth nodded at this, and the two stepped out into the corridor to claim their outerwear and hats. These in place, Elizabeth led Darcy through the kitchen and out a side door that led towards the garden. Before they exited, she claimed two of the rolls that were sitting on a sideboard, cooling in preparation for the family's breakfast.

The air remained cool beneath the pale sun of early autumn. For a time, they walked in companionable silence—her hand resting lightly on his arm, their boots quiet on the packed earth, the rustle of birds in the hedgerow their only company.

It was Darcy who spoke first.

"I had not expected, when I arrived this morning, that I would be drawn into estate matters quite so quickly," he said with a dry smile.

Elizabeth cast him a sidelong look. "You are not disappointed to find me out of the drawing room, then? And intruding on my father's matters of business? I know that you are aware of my involvement, but perhaps after meeting me, you have formed a different opinion."

"On the contrary," he said. "It is…refreshing to speak of these matters with you. I cannot say I often find conversation on estate management both intelligent and spirited. My steward mostly listens, and while he does suggest alternate ideas, he rarely does so in such a pert manner."

She smiled. "Careful, Mr. Darcy, or I shall begin to believe you are impressed by me."

He glanced at her, something warm flickering just behind his usual reserve. "I am."

The admission was quiet, but unmistakable. Elizabeth's brow arched, though her tone remained light. "Well. I shall do my best not to let it go to my head," she replied, her tone revealing nothing.

However, a moment later she ducked her gaze and slipped her hand from his arm, quickening her pace by a few steps. The movement was not dramatic, but it was enough to give Darcy pause.

"Have I offended you, Miss Elizabeth?" he asked, speaking quietly but loud enough to be heard from her position ahead of him.

"No," she replied, without turning.

He tried again. "Have I upset you?"

"No, sir."

Her tone was even, but too brief to be reassuring.

He reached forward, hesitating only a moment before his fingers touched her arm—gentle but firm enough to make her stop.

"Then what is the matter?" he asked, his voice low, earnest.

She turned to face him at last, chin lifted, though a faint crease had formed between her brows. Her hands, now clasped tightly before her, belied the calm set of her features. There was a slight flush at her neck, the kind that came not from embarrassment, but from the effort of keeping one's composure.

"You should not say things like that to me, Mr. Darcy," she said, her voice controlled, although her eyes did not quite meet his.

Darcy regarded her with quiet confusion, his brow furrowing as he searched her face. "Might I ask why?"

Elizabeth hesitated, her hands clasped before her as if bracing herself. "Because I do not know how you mean them. And I would rather not imagine meanings where none were intended."

There was a heavy silence between them as neither spoke for several long moments.

Darcy's reply came slowly, as though he were choosing each word with care. "Then allow me to be clear. I meant what I said."

She met his gaze, her own still cautious. "And what, precisely, did you mean?"

"That I admire you," he said simply. "Your intelligence, your willingness to speak your mind. Ever since I discovered it was you who wrote to me, not your father, I have been intrigued by you. Now that I have met you, it is bordering on fascination." Darcy repeated his initial comment. "As I said, I admire you, Miss Elizabeth."

Elizabeth did not answer at once. She looked away, towards the trees, where a breeze stirred the leaves, causing a few to fall. When she finally spoke, her voice was quiet.

"I am not in the habit of being admired for such things," she admitted.

"Then it seems many have not looked closely enough," Darcy said. His tone held no embellishment—only quiet sincerity, as though he stated a truth rather than offered praise.

Elizabeth glanced back at him, studying his face as if to discern whether he truly understood what he was saying—and whether she believed him.

Something in her expression softened.

"You are different than I expected," she said at last.

Darcy allowed a faint smile. "And how did you expect me to be?"

Elizabeth did not respond, and after a moment, Darcy offered her his arm. Elizabeth took it without hesitation.

They walked in silence for some time, meandering beneath the thinning canopy of trees, the crisp rustle of leaves beneath their boots the only sound that was heard. Eventually, the path brought them back towards Longbourn—in their distraction, they had not gone to the orchard as intended, but had merely walked in a wide circle.

"I believe my friend intends to call at Longbourn tomorrow," Darcy said quietly. "I mean to accompany him—both to conclude my conversation with your father, and because I hope to speak with you again. Tell me, Miss Elizabeth; will I be welcome?"

She looked up at him, searching his face, trying once more to judge his sincerity. Whatever she saw there seemed to settle something within her. She nodded.

"I would enjoy that," she said.

At her reply, he smiled—more fully than before—and she caught, for the first time, the dimples that softened his usually solemn expression. Gently, he took the hand resting on his arm and raised it to his lips, pressing a brief, chaste kiss to her gloved fingers.

Aware that should he remain much longer in her presence he would say more than he was ready to confess, with a brief wave goodbye, he turned and made his way towards the stables.

Elizabeth remained at the edge of the drive, watching as he mounted his waiting horse and rode down the lane, the figure of him growing smaller with each stride.

CHAPTER 18

Letters

Once Elizabeth and Darcy left his study, Bennet pulled out several pieces of paper. He examined his quill to ensure it was ready to write and began composing the first of several letters he would need to write that morning.

The first was to his brother Gardiner. As a merchant, Gardiner heard things that others may not. He also had a number of connections, and he could use those connections to find out what he could about both the Earl of Matlock and the viscount who wished Darcy to marry his daughter. It seemed odd to Bennet that the man was using an intermediary to manipulate—or was it an attempt to compel? —Darcy into a marriage with his daughter, particularly since the daughter was reported to be young, of a similar age to his daughter Lydia, or perhaps even younger. Darcy had known little about the girl his uncle wished him to wed, but Gardiner would, hopefully, be able to discover more.

The second was to his old friend James Livesay. Since that fateful visit five years ago, the two had kept up a steady correspondence, with Bennet far more regular in his writing than he had been before. Although Bennet had kept up his relationship with the son of his late friend George Darcy, writing to the son had not been the same as writing to his father. However, his relationship with Livesay had not changed.

Instead, Livesay had become, for a time, more of a mentor while Bennet had attempted to make changes. After George Darcy had become ill, Livesay had been the one to sometimes cajole, sometimes threaten Bennet to "remove his head from his arse" as Livesay had once put it during a visit to Longbourn a few months after the first one.

In fact, Livesay had visited at least annually since then, although he had come more than that during the first year. It had been Livesay who had sent one of his own under stewards to assist at Longbourn. At first, the steward had written to Livesay frequently, updating him on what was going on at Longbourn, and when Bennet had begun, once again, to rely too heavily on his second daughter to manage things, Livesay had written a scathing letter to his friend.

That had been a needed catalyst to force Bennet to again take hold of the reigns of the estate. While Elizabeth had been fairly competent, she was young and did not have the same knowledge and experience as the trained steward or of Bennet himself.

Now, Bennet contemplated what to write to Livesay.

Since the two men enjoyed a close friendship, he did not hesitate to tell Livesay all he could safely write in a letter. Some was in a sort of code that only the two men would understand, but, ultimately, the letter was a plea asking Livesay to come as soon as he was able. The harvest should be done on his estate, and he had two sons to oversee any necessary business.

Both Livesay and Darcy had married several years before Bennet himself had done so, and so their sons were older than Bennet's children. Livesay's elder son was likely near of an age to Fitzwilliam Darcy, and he had one other who was probably a few years younger. For a moment, Bennet attempted to remember the ages of the daughters, and he added a note to the letter encouraging Livesay to bring his family with him.

Once these letters were finished, Bennet picked up the letter he had received a few days before from his cousin Collins. While he had considered not responding to it at all, especially given how the man had seemingly invited himself to Longbourn, Bennet decided that it was best he write to delay the man's visit. Since he was inviting so many others to his house, there would not be room at Longbourn for Mr. Collins.

Reluctantly, he wrote a third letter, denying the man's request to visit, indicating that the house would be full at that time. Instead, he suggested that Collins visit the following spring. Bennet hoped that perhaps two of his daughters might be engaged or wed by then. Mary might like to marry a clergyman although Bennet had not been impressed by the man's letter and thought it unlikely. Since he had taken an interest in the management of his estate, he had ensured his wife and children would be well cared for upon his death, even if none of his daughters were wed when that occurred. Of course, if the two married as he was inclined to hope, the steps he had taken mattered far less than they had a few months before.

Once the letters were sitting on the silver salver waiting to be posted, Bennet stood and went in search of his wife. While he had not intended to speak of his cousin's visit, Livesay's visit was another matter entirely. Although nothing was yet decided, he still felt it was for the best that he inform his wife he had invited Livesay and his family to visit so she could prepare.

THE FOLLOWING AFTERNOON, DARCY AND BINGLEY CALLED AT Longbourn. They were joined by Miss Bingley and Mrs. Hurst, the former of whom arrived with an air of reluctant duty rather than genuine courtesy. Mrs. Hurst appeared more interested and attempted to be pleasant, but the presence of Miss Bingley made any private conversation between Elizabeth and Darcy difficult.

The following day, the Bennet ladies returned the call at Netherfield. It was painfully obvious, upon the announcement of their visit, that the hostess was displeased by their company. Miss Bingley received them in the drawing room with forced politeness and offered no refreshments beyond a single tepid pot of tea, placed on a table and subsequently ignored. She sat upright, her spine straight and her smile tight with disdain as she began to ask a series of thinly veiled, rude questions that were clearly intended to highlight the social divide.

Mrs. Bennet, unusually restrained, appeared to recognise the impropriety. After years of Mrs. Graham's patient instruction, she now understood that certain topics were best avoided with new acquaintances. Her answers, therefore, were notably brief.

"Have you and your daughters never been to London for the Season?" Miss Bingley asked, her tone edged with affected surprise. "I am astonished we have not made your acquaintance there before—especially given your family's *supposed* connection to the Darcys." Her voice dripped with disdain, and the very notion of a link between this family and the Darcys made her grit her teeth.

Elizabeth, seated beside Jane, exchanged a glance with her sister. She could feel Jane tense ever so slightly at this, for even Jane had recognised that Caroline Bingley was not quite as sincere as she might like.

Mrs. Bennet lifted her chin. "No, we have not gone to town for the Season," she said evenly. "My brother resides there, but we prefer to remain in the country."

"How…charming," Miss Bingley replied, a thin smile on her lips. She turned her attention to Elizabeth, eyes narrowing just slightly. "And you, Miss Elizabeth? Have you never wished for the advantages of a London education? Or exposure to a more refined society?"

"I cannot say that I have," Elizabeth replied, folding her hands in her lap, gripping them tightly as she attempted to hold her tongue. "The society I find in the country suits me quite well without needing to immerse myself in the falseness of those who believe themselves superior to others. My education has been sufficient and quite the equal of any other gentlewoman."

Mrs. Hurst gave a soft snort of laughter, quickly disguised as a cough. She knew her sister did not like the Bennet family, yet she could not help but be impressed by the family's willingness to allow her sister to insult them without comment. Miss Elizabeth's barbs were sharp, yet subtle, and often flew straight over her sister's head.

Miss Bingley continued, undeterred by Elizabeth's wit, "Yet you seem to have made quite an impression on Mr. Darcy. I understand he has been a regular visitor at Longbourn along with my brother. He mentioned that they had dinner there one evening this summer."

Elizabeth tilted her head slightly. "My father enjoys Mr. Darcy's company. He was friends with Mr. Darcy's father at Cambridge. After the elder Mr. Darcy's death, his son maintained the correspondence."

"Indeed?" Miss Bingley's eyes gleamed. "Your father attended Cambridge?"

"Yes, Miss Bingley," Elizabeth retorted. "He was even presented at court as befits a gentleman upon completion of his university studies, not that he finds the society in town to his liking. However, he has kept up an acquaintance with a number of friends from university, and we have had the opportunity to meet several when they have visited."

Miss Bingley furrowed her brows, unaware of additional friendships. She wondered who else the Bennet family might know and began to wonder if their connections were better than reported.

However, she was not deterred and sought to find another mark against the Bennet family. "Did you not mention you have a brother who lives in London, Mrs. Bennet?" Miss Bingley asked again. "Where does he live?"

"On Gracechurch Street," Mrs. Bennet replied, keeping her answers short.

"I am unfamiliar with that street," Miss Bingley replied. "Is that near Mayfair?"

"It is not," Mrs. Bennet said.

"Where is it?" Miss Bingley snapped, but her question was covered by her sister's.

"Mrs. Bennet, I understand from the housekeeper that your family looks after the tenants here at Netherfield," Mrs. Hurst interjected, attempting to shift the topic from the inquisition her sister intended. "My husband's family owns an estate that he will one day inherit. Would you answer a few questions I have about how you handle the needs of the tenants? In fact, I would like to accompany you on a visit or two, if I might."

Mrs. Bennet flushed a little at this question. "My daughters do most of the visiting these days," she admitted, unwilling to say that tenant visits were something she had never bothered to learn about. "Lizzy handles most of the visits here at Netherfield, and she is assisted by Jane and Mary. Catherine focuses more of her time on household matters since she is unable to do much that requires her to be out of doors; her health has never been good, and she cannot walk or ride so long as is required."

"Your daughters visit tenants?" Miss Bingley asked, her nose wrinkling in distaste. "How can your husband allow them to do such a distasteful task? Is that not the responsibility of the steward of an estate?"

"It is not," came a deep voice, and Miss Bingley coloured brightly at hearing Darcy speak. Both he and her brother entered the room then, bowing and greeting the three ladies.

"Welcome to Netherfield, Mrs. Bennet, Miss Bennet, Miss Elizabeth," Bingley said, nearly bouncing in his excitement. "A maid mentioned in passing that you arrived some time ago; we would have joined you sooner had we known."

Miss Bingley grimaced; she had explicitly informed the housekeeper that her brother was not to be informed of these callers. She would investigate that matter later.

"Did you not order tea, Caroline?" Bingley said next, calling more attention to her less than gracious behaviour.

"They brought us cold tea," she complained, turning to ring the bell. "I will ask them to bring fresh." However, even as she did this, she turned towards her guests. "Although I suppose you will be going soon," she said. "You have already been here for a quarter hour."

"Caroline," Bingley reprimanded, speaking at the same time as his sister.

"Caroline," Mrs. Hurst cried sharply.

"What?" Miss Bingley asked, turning to look at her brother and sister.

"I think you must be ill," Mrs. Hurst said, rising to her feet. "Come with me, and I will escort you to your room where you can rest for a time. Surely your behaviour just now is indicative of a headache or some other ailment."

She turned towards their guests. "Forgive me, Mrs. Bennet. I will be just a moment, and I will ask the housekeeper to be sure there is hot tea when I return. Brother, I think I will need to speak to you later."

Bingley nodded, surprised by this, but grateful, nonetheless. He turned to his guests. "Forgive my sister, Mrs. Bennet," he said. "She can be rather…unpleasant when she feels a megrim coming on. It is likely it will cause her to keep to her bed for several days."

"It is of no matter, Mr. Bingley," Mrs. Bennet said graciously.

Beside her, Jane and Elizabeth shared a look. While Jane no longer viewed the entire world as ideal, she had rarely encountered someone as unpleasant as Miss Bingley and struggled to understand what would have caused a virtual stranger to act in this manner.

"Mr. Bingley," she said, "please express our sympathies to your sister when she feels better. A megrim can be unpleasant to experience, and I do not envy her the pain she is suffering."

Darcy stifled a chuckle at this undeserved kindness. Elizabeth observed this and merely raised a brow at him. Although the two had not spoken of Miss Bingley beyond that first dance at the assembly, Elizabeth recognised the symptoms of jealousy that Miss Bingley exhibited. While she knew Mr. Darcy admired her, she still doubted it would matter very much, for surely, he would seek a wife with wealth and connections far beyond her own. She could admit that she returned the admiration, but she was doing what she could to keep it contained.

By the time Mrs. Hurst returned about ten minutes later, a fresh pot of tea had been delivered. Mrs. Bennet did attempt to withdraw, refusing the beverage given how long their visit had already lasted, but both Mr. Bingley and Mrs. Hurst encouraged them to remain a bit longer. With a minimal amount of persuading, she relented, and the six enjoyed a pleasant half an hour until Mrs. Bennet insisted that it was truly necessary they depart.

Elizabeth arranged with Mrs. Hurst to call the following day to take her around to a few tenants. It would remain Longbourn's responsibility, but Mrs. Hurst was grateful for the opportunity to learn from Elizabeth's example.

CHAPTER 19

Getting to Know You

The next fortnight followed a similar pattern. Elizabeth and Darcy saw each other daily—either by apparent chance during their morning rides across the fields or when Elizabeth found him already seated in her father's study, deep in quiet conversation, when she returned from her morning walk.

His early visits became so routine that even Mrs. Bennet ceased remarking on them—though not without a pointed glance or two in Elizabeth's direction, accompanied by the occasional knowing smile. She would have said more, as she did about Jane and Bingley, but her husband had warned her to keep silent, even within the family, about any potential connection between their second daughter and the son of his former friend.

"Lizzy, do not think your meetings in the fields with Mr. Darcy have gone unnoticed," Bennet said to his daughter one morning a few days after Darcy's first early morning visit to Longbourn. "I am pleased the groom is always with you, but I must warn you to be careful lest someone get the idea that these meetings are intentional. Mr. Darcy could walk away with little harm to his reputation, but it would be more difficult for you to avoid the speculation."

"Father," Elizabeth scolded, "how could anyone think that our meetings are anything but chance? I have ridden early in the mornings for years, and I recall very well the arguments we had about my not gadding about unaccompanied. When we have met on our rides, neither of us dismount, nor do we remain longer than a few minutes. You have taught me to consider my own reputation, and that of others, so you cannot suppose that either I or Mr. Darcy would do anything to jeopardise that."

Reluctantly, Bennet acknowledged the truth of her statements, having heard the same from the groom. However, he still worried about these meetings and how someone might misconstrue them. He wondered if he should make the marriage contract between Darcy and Elizabeth known to her, or if perhaps he should determine her feelings about the gentleman. Although he had observed the two of them, and they seemed to be inclined towards each other, that did not mean that either desired to marry the other.

First, Bennet would need to ascertain Darcy's interest—he had indicated some interest, but Bennet was uncertain if the man actually wished to marry his daughter—and willingness to pursue the match with Elizabeth before speaking of it with his daughter, for he would not wish her to be injured if the gentleman was not inclined towards marriage.

In the afternoons, visits were exchanged between Longbourn and Netherfield. Mr. Bingley called regularly, often accompanied by Darcy, while the Bennet ladies returned the calls to Netherfield.

Since Miss Bingley rarely left Netherfield after that first visit, afternoons at Longbourn were always more pleasant. When she did make an appearance during a visit from the Bennets, she sat stiffly and spoke little—her once-constant stream of barbed comments notably absent. This was appreciated, but still Elizabeth, in particular, was wary.

Whatever Mrs. Hurst said to her following that first disastrous visit had clearly left an impression. But no one at Longbourn could be certain of how long her newfound restraint would last.

For her part, Miss Bingley was determined to bide her time. She observed each interaction with sharp, narrowed eyes, listening intently and saying little. Bits of seemingly trivial conversation were stored away—hoarded and twisted in her mind into ammunition she intended to use later at just the right moment: the moment the countess arrived.

She would not allow Mr. Darcy's interest in Elizabeth Bennet—or this insufferably provincial family—to go unchecked. She had already composed in her head the conversation she hoped to have with the countess: gently expressed "concerns" about the Bennets' lack of connections and their vulgar relations. Through the servants, she had learnt that the Bennets had connections actively in trade—apparently the uncle in London was a merchant, and the uncle who lived in Meryton was a mere country attorney.

Of particular interest to Miss Bingley was the missing youngest sister. Miss Bingley's maid had learnt that the youngest daughter had been sent away to school and had hinted of some scandal causing her to be sent away. The age of the daughter was irrelevant, in the absence of real details, Miss Bingley delighted in inventing them.

As she considered this, she imagined the countess's disdain sharpening into outrage upon hearing of this "ruined" sister who had been sent away to school in disgrace. With luck, she would insist that both Mr. Darcy and Miss Darcy be removed from Hertfordshire at once.

If things unfolded as she hoped, the Bingleys and the Hursts would depart as well.

Finally, Miss Bingley could no longer delude herself—Darcy would never be hers. She had accepted that bitter truth the night of that ridiculous assembly. But Elizabeth Bennet? She most certainly did not deserve him either. Miss Bingley intended to ensure that *that* match would never come to pass.

She said little about her intentions, her sister no longer in her confidence, but one afternoon, as the Bennets prepared to leave Netherfield after a rather civil visit, she allowed herself one small dig.

"You must find it quite different, Miss Elizabeth, to entertain gentlemen callers so frequently" she said as the ladies stood to take their leave. "I imagine your mornings are quite altered of late since you are no longer spending time digging in the dirt with your tenants."

Elizabeth turned, her smile cool. "Not so very much, Miss Bingley. Although I confess it is a rare thing indeed to find a conversation partner in the countryside who speaks as thoughtfully as your brother and Mr. Darcy. They are very welcome company at Longbourn. I cannot imagine what else you might mean."

Miss Bingley's smile faltered though she recovered quickly. "Indeed," she murmured. "Mr. Darcy is always so generous with his attention—when it suits him."

Darcy, who had just entered the drawing room in time to hear the remark, glanced between the ladies with a frown.

"Miss Bingley," he said, his tone carefully neutral, "you must forgive me, but I do not think I understand what you mean by that statement. I am very generous with my attention with my friends although those who only pretend friendship find me less so. Mr. Bennet has long been my friend, and I have been delighted to spend time with his family while we are in the area."

Elizabeth suppressed a smile, and Jane quickly intervened with a comment about the weather, turning the conversation onto safer topics.

But Miss Bingley's eyes narrowed slightly as she dipped into a shallow curtsy and turned away, retreating to the window with all the appearance of a woman above it all—though her mind raced furiously again. That Mr. Darcy had heard her had been unfortunate, as Miss Bingley intended to hint at something far less savory than the calls exchanged between the two estates.

A few days later, the Bennets again called at Netherfield. On this particular visit, Mary and Catherine accompanied the older girls, and Mrs. Graham attended, for Mrs. Bennet had been occupied.

While Jane, Elizabeth, and Mary spoke with Mrs. Hurst, Miss Bingley managed to corner Catherine to speak to her. Catherine had been looking at a few pieces of art around the room, and had wandered away from the others. Miss Bingley approached her and struck up a conversation, first about the art, and gradually turning the conversation to the missing Bennet sister.

"Tell me, Miss Catherine, how do you like being the youngest in your family?" she began, hoping that her words would have the desired outcome.

"Oh, I am not the youngest," Catherine replied. "Lydia is younger than me by a year and a half, but she is away at school."

"I did not realise that," Miss Bingley replied. "I had thought I heard there were five daughters, but I supposed that I had heard wrong when we did not meet the fifth one."

"Lydia has been at school for several years now," Catherine said. "I think that is why few people speak of her."

"She does not return home?" Miss Bingley asked.

"She does, but she does not remain long," Catherine said, pursing her lips as she recalled the last visit.

"Whyever not?" Miss Bingley prodded. "Is she the only one of your sisters to go away to school? Have you not often wished to join her?"

"Not at all, Miss Bingley," Catherine said. "Lydia can be... rather stubborn, and I have always enjoyed staying at home. I would not wish to be at school with her."

"What manner of school is she in, if she rarely returns home?" Miss Bingley asked. "When I was at the ladies' seminary I attended, I returned home at the end of each term, and spent several months at home in the summer months. Did your sister not spend the summer term at home?"

"No, she did not," Catherine said, attempting to put an end to the conversation.

"That is a shame," Miss Bingley continued. "I cannot imagine a family not permitting a daughter to return home as often as possible. Your sister must be very stubborn indeed."

Suddenly feeling uncomfortable with this conversation, Catherine attempted to change the direction, making a comment about the piece of art she was viewing. "The subject of this painting is lovely, is it not?" she asked.

"It came with the house," Miss Bingley said, waving her hand as though it did not matter. "I have little interest in paintings such as this one and cannot imagine anyone being particularly drawn to it."

"Oh, but look at the brush strokes," Catherine began, but quickly stopped when she saw a look of distaste pass over Miss Bingley's face. Feeling increasingly discomfited, she moved back to where the others sat. As she listened to the conversation around her, she wondered why Miss Bingley had appeared so interested in Lydia. She would speak of it to Mary later or perhaps Mrs. Graham. Surely one of them would be able to explain the sudden interest in her sister.

CHAPTER 20

New Arrivals at Netherfield

15 OCTOBER 1811

Almost a fortnight after the assembly, the expected visitors finally began to arrive at Netherfield. Miss Bingley was delighted that the countess of Matlock would be joining them that afternoon. She had imagined this visit for days, planning precisely how she would present herself and carefully preparing remarks to steer the countess away from any warm opinion of the Bennet family.

She was significantly less pleased, however, when her brother informed her that not only would Mr. Darcy's family arrive today, but another visitor as well. For the first time during this visit, she was grateful that Darcy had absented himself from the morning meal even if it meant he was likely in company with those Bennets he seemed to admire so much.

"Aunt Horatia arrives this morning," he said casually, reaching for the marmalade. "Her carriage should be here within the hour."

Miss Bingley lowered her knife mid-slice, her surprise clearly on her face.

Horatia Bingley had always been a stern, unyielding woman with no patience for pretension or ambition. She disapproved of her niece's aspirations and was unmoved by either tears or charm. When Edwin Bingley sent his daughters to a fashionable seminary near Oxford, Horatia called it a mistake, insisting it only taught girls to think above their station. Her niece had never forgiven her. Even in London after their education, Horatia remained critical, claiming Louisa had improved while Caroline had become "insufferably pleased with herself." The connections she made with well-connected young ladies meant nothing to her aunt who dismissed her ambitions at every turn.

"Aunt Horatia? Whyever is she coming?" Miss Bingley asked when she recovered her voice.

Bingley did not look up, refusing to meet his sister's eyes as he stated calmly. "I asked her to. After seeing how little regard you seem to have for our neighbours, I thought it wise to have someone here who would welcome them properly when we have guests visiting. As you know, we have been invited to many places, but we have yet to invite anyone here."

"You thought it wise to replace me as your hostess?" she asked sharply, her voice dripping with disdain and undisguised anger.

"I did not say that," Bingley replied evenly. "But your feelings towards everyone in Meryton, particularly the Bennets, have been made quite plain—and I have no desire to offend Darcy or Lady Matlock. Aunt Horatia will bring the necessary…steadiness and welcome that has been missing. I would have asked Louisa, but I did not want to put her in that position."

Miss Bingley pressed her lips together, her brother's words landing like a slap. "How thoughtful of you," she said coldly, each syllable clipped with disdain.

She said nothing more for the remainder of the meal. Instead, she finished her breakfast in silence, her posture rigid, her appetite clearly diminished. The moment her plate was cleared, she rose without a word to anyone and left the dining room, her heels striking sharply against the floor as she went.

Once within the sanctuary of her bedchamber, Miss Bingley did not hesitate to give vent to her frustration. She seized a porcelain shepherdess from the mantel and hurled it against the far wall, where it shattered with a satisfying burst. Two more figurines followed before she called out, voice raised, "Jenny! Come and clean this mess—immediately!"

Her maid entered with a wide-eyed glance at her mistress, but said nothing, setting to work at once to clean up the mess.

Miss Bingley stood at the window, breathing hard after her exertion. The crash of porcelain had provided some release, but not nearly enough. Her mind churned. Her aunt's arrival at this time was not just a slight—it was a complication. A serious one. Her aunt's presence would make it far more difficult to carry out her intentions without scrutiny. Horatia missed nothing and trusted no one, least of all her.

She closed her eyes and exhaled slowly. If she was to salvage the countess's visit—and prevent the ruinous match she most dreaded—she would need to be cleverer than ever.

Horatia Bingley had long been a thorn in her side. Older, unmarried, and possessed of a fearsome command of silence, she had never approved of her younger niece's conduct or aspirations. That she had now been summoned to manage the household at such a critical moment rendered Miss Bingley's humiliation complete.

With Aunt Horatia under the same roof, it would be far more difficult to set her plans into motion.

Miss Bingley greeted her aunt alongside her brother and sister, doing little to conceal her displeasure at the new arrival.

Only a short time earlier, she had burst into her brother's study, intent on persuading him to reverse his decision to replace her as mistress. She stopped short, however, upon seeing Mr. Darcy present. Unable to express herself freely in front of the gentleman, she had been forced to hold her tongue while her brother calmly—and firmly—restated that their Aunt Horatia would indeed be taking charge of the household during Lady Matlock's visit.

It had taken every ounce of self-control to keep from erupting. Although she privately insisted she no longer harboured any real hope of securing Mr. Darcy's affections, she was unwilling to appear ill-bred or ungoverned in his eyes. That he had borne witness to the exchange was mortifying enough; she would not give him further reason to report to his aunt—or any of his illustrious relations—that she had behaved in a less than seemly manner.

Having read her nephew's letter, Horatia Bingley had formed her own opinions before she boarded the carriage south, and was hardly surprised at her niece's cold welcome.

"Caroline, I understand additional guests are expected today," she said, handing her wraps to the waiting maids. "As your brother has asked me to serve as hostess, should I consult with you or the house-keeper regarding the arrangements already in place?"

Her voice was calm, laced with effortless poise, but the underlying message was unmistakable: she knew exactly why she had been summoned—and she would brook no opposition.

Miss Bingley sniffed at the pointed reminder of her new position within the household.

As the women entered the drawing room, Aunt Horatia immediately took charge.

"What arrangements have already been made for our guests, Lousia, Caroline?" she asked.

Miss Bingley sputtered at the direct question. "Lady Matlock and Georgiana…"

"Miss Darcy," Aunt Horatia corrected. "As I understand it, Miss Darcy is rather young and not a contemporary of yours. Has she given you leave to address her by her Christian name, or did you merely begin to do so in order to curry favour with the girl and her brother?"

"I…" Miss Bingley stammered again, suddenly aware that she had, in fact, done precisely that. Mr. Darcy had corrected her more than once regarding the informality, and although his sister had never voiced an objection, Miss Bingley now realised—with a slow, sinking clarity—that Miss Darcy had always appeared uncomfortable when addressed so familiarly. She had never once returned the liberty.

The silence stretched between them. Mrs. Hurst merely looked on, waiting to see how her sister would react as she glanced between the two.

Aunt Horatia raised a brow. "I thought as much. It would be best, going forward, to observe the proprieties. Familiarity, when unearned, tends to reflect more poorly on the speaker than the subject."

Miss Bingley pressed her lips together, colour rising in her cheeks. She managed a faint nod but could summon no words.

"Although Miss Darcy is younger, she is more highly placed than you in society, seeing that she is a gentleman's daughter and connected to an earl. By rights, you should have allowed her to control the level of informality between you," Aunt Horatia said.

Outwardly composed, Miss Bingley was seething about being lectured by her aunt in this manner. She was very aware of both her place and Miss Darcy's in society, and that was exactly why she had so often pretended, if not outright forced, an intimacy between them. Did her aunt not recognise that their success depended upon the connections they made?

"Enough of that," her aunt concluded a few moments later, her tone sharp. "One would think you would have learnt these things at that expensive school your father insisted upon—but evidently, the lessons did not take."

Without waiting for a reply, Aunt Horatia launched into a flurry of pointed questions. Her enquiries came so swiftly that neither Miss Bingley nor Mrs. Hurst could keep pace, and both began to flounder under the weight of her scrutiny.

At last, with evident displeasure, she turned and rang the bell.

When Mrs. Nicholls, the housekeeper, entered a moment later, Aunt Horatia faced her directly.

"Mrs. Nicholls," she said sharply, "what precisely have my nieces done to prepare for the countess's visit? Or have the arrangements, as I suspect, fallen entirely upon your shoulders?"

Mrs. Nicholls, a capable woman with a calm manner and keen sense of hierarchy, gave a respectful curtsey before answering.

"The drawing room and parlour were seen to by the maids under my direction, ma'am," she said evenly. "Cook and I planned for refreshments to be served soon after the guests' arrival, but the dinner tonight will be rather extensive at Miss Bingley's orders. There are not enough footmen who have been trained properly to serve, but we will do the best we can with the meal. Miss Bingley requested several additional dishes just this morning, and we have done our best to accommodate her."

Aunt Horatia's eyes narrowed slightly at that. "Is bathwater being heated for the newcomers? What if the countess or Miss Darcy do not wish to dine with the family this evening, or if their carriage is delayed? What arrangements have been made?"

"None, madam," Mrs. Nicholls replied. "I did order bathwater to be warmed when your own arrival was imminent, and it is still sitting on the stove. More will be added when our other guests are expected."

"I see," Aunt Horatia said, pursing her lips in obvious displeasure. "Well, Mrs. Nicholls, what do you need from me to assist you as you prepare?"

"Mr. Darcy selected several rooms near his own for his sister, aunt, and cousin," Mrs. Nicholls explained. "Those have been cleaned and aired. Mr. Darcy also lent us the aid of some of his own staff since we have not yet been able to hire enough servants for a house this size. I believe he sent for a few maids from London to assist those already here, and his footmen have been helping out as necessary."

"Are there not enough servants in the area available?" Aunt Horatia asked.

"We had several more, but a few left, deciding they could earn more elsewhere," Mrs. Nicholls said evenly.

Although she had spoken plainly until now, she chose her words with greater care in Miss Bingley's presence. She did not add that those who had departed had done so for similar wages in nearby households, but also for kinder treatment and more reasonable expectations—matters better left unspoken before present company.

There was a brief pause—just long enough to be noticeable—and long enough for Mrs. Nicholls to know what she had left unsaid had been understood.

"I see," Aunt Horatia said, her voice cool. "You have done well, Mrs. Nicholls. You may return to your duties."

The housekeeper curtseyed again and withdrew, leaving an uneasy silence in her wake.

Aunt Horatia turned back to her nieces, her gaze steady and unrelenting.

"Louisa," she said, her voice cool, "I would have thought *you*, at least, would know better than to leave the oversight of everything to the servants. Mrs. Nicholls appears competent, to be sure, but you have been married several years now, and your husband will one day inherit an estate. At some point, you must cease following your sister's lead and take up the responsibilities you have married into. This would have been good practice for you—yet you chose to step aside and let Caroline seize the reins, rather than standing up to her."

Louisa's complexion visibly paled at the rebuke. She opened her mouth as if to respond, but no words came. Instead, she pressed her lips together and stared at the carpet, her hands knotting themselves into the folds of her gown.

Unmoved, Aunt Horatia turned her attention to her younger niece, scowling when she saw the disdainful look on her face.

"And you, Caroline," she said sharply, "I am well aware you attended that expensive seminary of yours, but it seems you learnt very little of proper behaviour. Your brother writes that you hold yourself higher than the local population—and that your conduct towards your neighbours has been more hostile than hospitable."

Miss Bingley merely sniffed in response, lifting her chin in silent defiance. She would not give her aunt the satisfaction of seeing how bitterly she resented being spoken to like an errant child.

Observing them for several moments, Aunt Horatia grimaced, then stood. "I will seek out the housekeeper and speak to her about a few more arrangements. Since you are no longer the hostess, Caroline, I will join your brother to welcome our guests when they arrive. However, I will speak to him first to see what he expects from me. You are, of course, welcome to wait for us in the drawing room—tell me, is this room best suited to welcome guests, or is there another that you prefer? Since the house is merely leased, I presume you have not made too many changes, and from what I have seen, it is tastefully decorated, if not a little overly embellished in places. That can easily be resolved. Louisa, I will find you later to speak to you further about our guests."

Having said all she intended, Aunt Horatia swept from the room, leaving an oppressive silence in her wake.

No sooner had she gone than Miss Bingley gave vent to her frustrations, failing even to ensure the door had properly closed following her aunt's departure.

"How could our brother have replaced me as his hostess?" she seethed, pacing furiously across the room. "And on the very day of the countess's arrival—and Georgiana Darcy's?"

"It is done, sister," Mrs. Hurst said cautiously, attempting to placate without fully agreeing. "And perhaps it would be best if you held your tongue. If you are not acting as hostess, you will have more time to spend with Miss Darcy, and you can further your friendship with her. You may not marry her brother, but her friendship would still benefit you."

"What good is that now?" Miss Bingley snapped, her voice rising. "There is no point in currying favour with that mealy-mouthed child! I only ever paid her attention to gain Mr. Darcy's notice—to make myself indispensable to him by flattering his *precious sister*. And what has it earned me? Nothing! Less than nothing! I spent months fawning over her and offering her compliments after nearly every word that came out of her mouth."

She began to pace the room, her skirts rustling sharply with each angry turn.

"I demeaned myself," she muttered furiously, more to herself than to her sister. "I endured endless, tedious conversations about pianoforte lessons and watercolours, pretending every word was brilliance—and for what? To be cast aside and humiliated in my own brother's house, while others—those Bennets, of all people—climb higher and higher in his estimation."

She stopped abruptly before the fireplace, her cheeks flushed with anger.

"All wasted," she said bitterly. "And now I am expected to stand meekly aside, while girls of no consequence—no fortune, no connections—are elevated before me! He invited his sister and aunt here to introduce them at Longbourn, and I have been displaced by my aunt. Why did I ever bother with Georgiana Darcy? I ought to have known she was just as useless as Charles."

A noise from the doorway made them both turn.

Darcy stood just beyond the threshold, his expression cold, his posture rigid.

"It is fortunate," he said, his voice clipped with barely restrained contempt as he glared at Miss Bingley, "that I never had any intention of offering for you. For anyone who could speak so of my sister is no friend of hers—or of mine."

Miss Bingley blanched, her mouth opening and closing without a sound.

"Forgive me," Darcy said, his voice unyielding, his brief apology directed at Mrs. Hurst. "I had no wish to overhear. Yet, with the door left so carelessly open, I could hardly help it."

Then he turned, fixing Miss Bingley with a look as cold as ice. "Rest assured, Miss Bingley, I shall see that Georgiana does not trouble you with her company. I expect she will find far more genuine friendship among the Misses Bennet."

With a curt bow, he turned and departed, leaving Miss Bingley frozen in place, humiliated, furious, and, for once, utterly speechless.

CHAPTER 21
The Countess Arrives

Later that afternoon, a lone horseman in a blue coat arrived at the front door of Netherfield. He knocked sharply, and was quickly ushered inside.

Darcy, passing through the foyer, caught sight of the visitor and paused.

"Richard—welcome," he said warmly. Then, glancing around and seeing only the butler standing nearby, he asked, "Where is the rest of your party? Georgiana and your mother? Should they not be with you?"

"They are just behind me and should arrive within the half-hour," Fitzwilliam replied, removing his gloves. "I rode ahead to speak with you privately for a few minutes."

Darcy's brows furrowed, his curiosity mingling with a trace of anxiety about what his cousin might have to say. "Yes? What is it?" he asked, his voice low, as he pulled Fitzwilliam closer to the door and further away from the retreating butler.

"Nothing to trouble you, Darce," Fitzwilliam said lightly. "I have had a letter from my father. He wanted me to remind you—rather pointedly—to consider the young lady he mentioned."

Darcy's expression darkened at once. "I am even less inclined to marry her now than when he first raised the subject," he said in a firm tone. "Bennet and I have already discussed my uncle's interference, and he has written to his old friend James Livesay. They were both at school with your father and mine—though neither, it seems, held much affection for your father."

As they stood speaking quietly in the hall, Darcy brought his cousin up to date on his recent conversations with Bennet. Fitzwilliam, listening closely, could not help but notice how often Miss Elizabeth's name crept into the discussion—spoken with a warmth and familiarity that left little doubt as to where Darcy's true interests lay.

Their conversation was soon interrupted by the arrival of Bingley and his aunt.

"Fitzwilliam! You are already here," Bingley exclaimed, surprise clear on his face. "The footman said you were expected shortly."

"My mother and cousin will be here momentarily," Fitzwilliam replied easily. "I needed some exercise and rode ahead to give the warning."

"Ah, good," Bingley said brightly. With a discreet nudge from his aunt, he remembered himself and turned to formalities.

"Oh—Fitzwilliam, allow me to present my aunt, Miss Horatia Bingley. Aunt, this is the Honourable Colonel Richard Fitzwilliam, cousin to Mr. Darcy and an officer in His Majesty's Army."

"Colonel Fitzwilliam, I am pleased to make your acquaintance," Aunt Horatia said, offering a small, dignified curtsy.

"My aunt will be acting as my hostess during your stay," Bingley added quickly, eager to smooth any potential awkwardness.

Fitzwilliam cast a sidelong glance at Darcy, one brow arching in silent amusement.

Darcy made no reply, but he knew well enough the matter would be raised again when they were alone.

Before anything more could be said, the sound of carriage wheels crunching on the gravel drive drew their attention. Instinctively, the entire group moved to greet the new arrivals.

Having not seen his sister in several weeks, Darcy found himself keenly anticipating their reunion. Although they had exchanged frequent letters—and though Georgiana's spirits seemed to have improved somewhat since he began writing to her of the Misses Bennet—this correspondence was no substitute for seeing and speaking with her in person.

He watched as the carriage rumbled to a halt in front of the house. There was a flurry of activity as grooms approached from the stables to hold the horses while the footmen stepped down from their posts on the back of the coach. One footman stepped forward to place the carriage step while the other stood ready to assist the ladies down from the coach.

Smiling broadly, Bingley moved towards the newcomers with his aunt just behind him. Darcy followed, allowing Bingley to greet his guests while Fitzwilliam lingered slightly to the side.

The first to emerge from the carriage was the countess. She descended with grace, accepting the footman's hand lightly. Although no longer young, she carried herself with the easy authority of a woman well accustomed to deference. Her dark travelling cloak and understated bonnet spoke of quiet taste rather than ostentation, but her sharp grey eyes missed nothing.

Right behind her was Georgiana Darcy. Although she stood tall, there was a tentative air about her, and she glanced anxiously towards the house until her gaze found her brother. At the sight of him, her face brightened, and some of her unease melted away.

"Mr. Bingley," Lady Matlock said as she approached, inclining her head with polite familiarity. "It is good to see you again. Thank you for allowing my niece and me to join your party."

Bingley bowed low. "Lady Matlock, we are honoured to have you at Netherfield. May I introduce my aunt to you?"

At her nod, Bingley performed the introductions, including Georgiana Darcy in the greeting even though she had yet to speak. She moved closer to her brother, and he wrapped his arm around her side and pulled her close.

"Are you well, Sprite?" he asked her quietly once the introductions had concluded. She had barely spoken in response, but at least she had spoken.

"I am, Brother," she replied. "Perhaps I should be accustomed to travelling, but this particular trip has been exhausting. Some of it was the anxiety of meeting so many new people, but earlier today I attempted to imagine what Miss Elizabeth might do in this situation. What you have written of her has given me confidence, and I am less anxious now than I was."

A wide grin broke out across Darcy's face. "Then I look forward to introducing you to Miss Elizabeth and to her sisters. I have little doubt that they will welcome you wholeheartedly."

Georgiana looked up at him to respond, but before she could do so, she heard the grating voice of Caroline Bingley.

"Dear Georgiana," she cooed as she descended the front stairs with her protesting sister in tow, "how delighted I am that you could join us here. The society in this miserable little town is positively dreadful, but now that you and your aunt have arrived, I am sure it will be infinitely more tolerable."

"Miss Bingley," she said quietly, acknowledging the greeting. She stiffened her spine and began the introductions with a steady voice: "Aunt, may I present Mrs. Louisa Hurst and Miss Caroline Bingley, our host's sisters."

Inclining her head towards both ladies in response, the countess turned her sharp gaze towards Miss Bingley, assessing her with a glance that was neither warm nor discourteous. She offered the barest inclination of her head, a gesture that acknowledged the introduction without inviting intimacy.

"How do you do, Mrs. Hurst, Miss Bingley," the countess said, her tone perfectly polite but notably lacking in warmth. Addressing Georgiana, she asked, "Does she have your permission to address you informally? You should be careful in allowing such liberties, dear niece, for you are not yet out and must be careful about the friendships you make at this time."

"Yes, Aunt; I mean, no, she does not have my permission, but yes, I understand that I need to take care," Georgiana said quietly, her head bowed.

Lady Matlock cast an assessing glance at the young woman before turning towards her nephew.

"Fitzwilliam," she said warmly, moving towards him in greeting. She extended her hand which he took, and then she leant forward, allowing him to kiss her cheek. "I trust all is well with you. It has been several months since I saw you last."

"Well enough, Aunt," Darcy replied, stepping forward to offer his arm which she accepted, allowing him to escort her into the manor.

"Come, Georgie," he said gently, extending his other arm. She came forward immediately, allowing him to lead her inside, Fitzwilliam following in behind them.

Caroline Bingley, standing just behind the others, fought to school her features into a pleasant expression at being roundly dismissed. Every instinct urged her to step forward, to insert herself, to attach her name firmly to these distinguished guests—but her Aunt Horatia's watchful eye remained upon her. She stood with her hands clenched tightly behind her skirts as she grudgingly followed the party inside.

She continued behind the party to the drawing room. Apparently the countess had decided to take refreshments before being shown to her room.

Entering after the others, Miss Bingley was displeased to see that the only seats still available were not next to either the countess or Miss Darcy. Despite her aunt's warnings, she had intended to begin her campaign to insinuate the less-than-honourable intentions towards the Darcys by those at Longbourn, but she could not do so unless she could speak privately to either of them. More troubling, she was unaware precisely which rooms the ladies would use and would have to enquire to find them.

Before long, the party broke up, and each sought out their rooms to dress for dinner. With a whispered word, the countess indicated her desire to speak privately with her nephew before the evening meal. Darcy presented himself at her sitting-room door a little more than half an hour before they were due downstairs.

"Thank you for accompanying Georgiana to Netherfield, Aunt," Darcy said, bowing and kissing her cheek in greeting, his lips tipped up in a slight smile and his eyes flashing with warmth.

"When my nephew, who consistently avoids the company of young women, asks me to travel hundreds of miles to introduce his sister to a house full of young ladies," the countess said sharply, "then naturally I will come to see what mischief he is about. I was even more intrigued when my husband wrote to inform me that this same nephew is soon to be wed to the daughter of an old crony of his. And to complete my confusion, my own son writes that the same nephew is enamoured of a country lass who has any number of very pretty sisters—all of whom come with no particular connections and indifferent fortunes.

"Since I know my nephew to be an honourable and upright young man," she added, her eyes glinting, "I nearly suffered whiplash from such prolific—and conflicting—reports."

To her great surprise, her normally stoic nephew flushed hotly at these words. Looking up, he allowed himself a brief, wry smile at her bluntness and bowed his head in acknowledgement of the varied reports.

"There is some truth in what you have heard, Aunt," he said hesitantly. "Yes, the earl is attempting to force me into a marriage to the daughter of the Viscount Halston. As far as anyone knows, she is young, younger even than Georgiana, but she has been kept from society, so I know little of her. I informed my uncle that I would not marry the child, but he implied that he knew enough to ruin Georgiana. I am uncertain whether he actually knows anything, or merely suspects something occurred, but as he departed, he mentioned George Wickham by name."

Lady Matlock gasped softly at his words. She and her husband had not shared a roof since the previous spring, and she had taken great care not to discuss personal matters regarding either her niece or nephew within the hearing of the servants she knew would report faithfully to Lord Matlock. Although some were completely loyal to her, she knew others were well paid by the earl to only appear so.

Darcy, seemingly undeterred, continued with his defense.

"Moreover, I suppose there is some truth in what you have heard from your son," he said. "Mr. Bennet is an old friend of my father's—and, to some extent, of mine. My father encouraged me to maintain the connection between our families, and since his death, Mr. Bennet has been a valuable correspondent and a steady source of advice."

He paused, gathering his thoughts before proceeding.

"He has five daughters," he said at last, "and I confess I am rather intrigued by his second eldest, Miss Elizabeth. She is... quite unlike the young ladies one typically encounters in town."

Another brief pause.

"She is lively, intelligent, and accomplished without being affected. I have found her company—refreshing. More than that, I believe she and her sisters are precisely the sort of companions Georgiana needs at present. They are lively without being exuberant, spirited without vulgarity, and—perhaps most importantly—they appear entirely genuine. None of them would prey upon Georgiana for her fortune or connections; they have not been taught to value such things as highly as many of their peers in society."

Lady Matlock said nothing for a long moment. Her fan tapped lightly against the arm of her chair, each deliberate beat a quiet measure of her thoughts.

Finally, she spoke.

"You have been often in their company, then?" she asked, her tone even. "Enough to judge that they will be proper companions for Georgiana? How can you be so certain they are not mercenary? Country manners differ vastly from those of the *ton*, and while that can be refreshing, it can also mean they may be more adept at hiding their true objectives by appearing different."

Darcy stiffened slightly but replied without hesitation.

"I have known Mr. Bennet for years, and my father always held him in the highest esteem. Since arriving in the area, I have spent considerable time in the Bennets' company, and everything I have observed thus far suggests they are genuine in their behaviour—unguarded, without calculation."

Lady Matlock's fan stilled at last, and she studied her nephew seriously.

"You speak warmly of them, and perhaps your judgement is sound in this matter," she said slowly. "Do you care for this Miss Elizabeth?"

Darcy closed his eyes and let out a slow breath. "I admire her, but I am unwilling to say more at this point. We have met several times since my coming into the area, but I cannot say yet what I feel towards her."

Again, Lady Matlock studied her nephew. "And what of this girl your uncle wants you to marry? Or his threat to ruin Georgiana?"

"I am uncertain," Darcy admitted. "I refuse to consider marrying a child, and I cannot imagine any circumstances that would induce me to enter into a marriage contract with the viscount. The earl said the viscount needs my wealth, but I still cannot understand his role in this. I did not even know the two were friends."

Lady Matlock pursed her lips. "Neither did I, or at least, that they continued to associate with each other," she said after a moment. "Richard shares the guardianship of Georgiana with you; what does he say about this?"

"He also does not feel I ought to give into the earl's demands," Darcy replied. "And you ought to know that my father was in favour of my marrying Miss Elizabeth."

At Lady Matlock's small gasp of surprise, Darcy went on. "When we visited all those years ago, Miss Elizabeth was from home. However, Father knew I was intrigued by hearing her father speak of her, and I admit to you that I have corresponded with her, after a fashion, over the years since my father's death. She sometimes has acted as her father's secretary and scribed letters to me from him, but added some of her own thoughts and opinions. It allowed me to know something about her before I arrived."

"And now that you have met her?" Lady Matlock asked, her voice deceptively mild, deliberately masking her concern, dismayed at such forward behaviour by this young lady.

Darcy hesitated, then said quietly, "I find myself drawn to her as I have never been to any other lady."

He paused, gathering his thoughts before continuing.

"We danced twice at the assembly that was held soon after my friend took the lease of this estate. Since then, we have been in company nearly every day. Conversation with her is easy—remarkably so, given my tendency towards being taciturn when in the presence of ladies."

He paused, as if weighing his next words with care. "She is lovely, both in appearance and in character. There is a brightness to her that draws others in—an intelligence and warmth that make her company both engaging and comfortable. I do not find myself grasping for words in her presence, nor do I feel the need to guard my every thought. I feel as though she is an equal and am certain that she does not pursue me for material gains, but out of genuine interest in me."

Hesitating briefly again, he spoke with candour when he finally found the words to speak, "I can easily imagine her by my side at Pemberley. She would suit the place—would bring it life and grace without artifice.

"I like her," he finished simply, though the weight behind the words made the admission anything but casual.

Lady Matlock sat back in her chair, momentarily speechless at what amounted to a near heartfelt declaration.

"Well," she said at last, a chuckle escaping her, "high praise indeed, coming from you."

Her amusement faded quickly, replaced by a more serious expression. "And what will happen if you pursue her? Can she withstand the scrutiny of the *ton*? What if my husband carries out his threat and spreads rumours regarding his own niece?"

She tapped her fan sharply against the arm of her chair.

"Although," she added, her voice cool and sharp, "I shall have something to say about that, should he dare attempt it."

Anger was written clearly on her face, and Darcy wondered what she could do to block him. Lady Matlock had many friends and commanded attention within the *ton*, but would that be sufficient to keep gossip from spreading regarding his sister?

"I have one final matter to disclose," Darcy said after several moments of silence. He cleared his throat before beginning. "Before he died, my father signed a marriage contract with Mr Bennet, binding me to marriage with Miss Elizabeth."

He hesitated a moment, choosing his words with care.

"I cannot explain every detail of how it came about, but I have seen the document myself. I met with Mr. Bennet, and there can be no doubt—the signature is my father's. I did not question him further, but should anyone, even the earl, seek to dispute it, I can state with certainty that it is genuine."

Lady Matlock stared at him, her shock plain.

"There is an addendum," Darcy continued, "stipulating that if either Miss Elizabeth or I wished not to marry, the contract would be rendered void. My father apparently arranged it as a safeguard—to protect me from undue influence."

His mouth tightened and his fists clenched ever so slightly as he continued.

"He knew of Lady Catherine's determination to see me wed to her daughter, and he feared that my uncle might one day attempt something similar. The contract was intended as a shield, should it ever be necessary to protect me."

"Seems convenient," she said tartly.

"Perhaps," Darcy admitted. "But right now, I consider it a salvation. I cannot enter into a marriage contract with another if I am already bound to Elizabeth Bennet. Should I proceed and make this public, then the earl can do little about it since it is obvious my father condoned the match. He will bluster about my refusal to comply with his orders, yes, but I am most worried about his knowing anything about what happened to Georgiana this summer. I find it difficult to believe he would actually act to harm a member of his own family, but still…." He trailed off, uncertain what else might be said.

"Yes," Lady Matlock agreed. "I will send a few letters to ask what the servants at Matlock House might have heard. There are a few who will report to me, even if it means defying the earl. Were it not for my father's funds, my husband would barely be able to afford his servants, and many of them are aware of that fact."

She eyed her nephew carefully. "You have not said anything to Miss Elizabeth about this marriage contract, have you? And neither has her father? I would like to meet the young lady before anything further is discussed about this possible marriage. In fact, I would like to be the one who tells her about it."

"Absolutely not," Darcy said firmly, his tone leaving no room for argument. "If I choose to honour the marriage contract, I will be the one to speak with Elizabeth to inform her of the arrangements our fathers have made, and the addendum."

He shook his head and exhaled slowly, pinching the bridge of his nose.

"Miss Elizabeth deserves a choice in whom she marries. She should not be told that she is promised to a man without any regard for her own wishes. Yes," he added, lifting a hand to forestall his aunt's protest, "I am aware that she is not yet of age and, by law, must obey her father's will. But truly, Aunt—what man of sense would want a wife who does not wish to be his?"

He looked directly at her now, his voice quieter but no less resolute.

"Should Elizabeth and I marry, it will be because we both choose to do so. I would not have that choice taken from me—nor will I take it from her. I would not allow it for Georgiana, and I cannot allow it for Miss Elizabeth."

There was a pause.

"I wonder," Lady Matlock said at last, her voice softer than he had ever heard it, "that you insist you have not yet decided, Fitzwilliam—when you have referred to her by her Christian name several times in this conversation."

Her eyes held his, calm and assessing. "Your mind may still wrestle with the decision, but I believe your heart has already made it."

Darcy blinked, caught off guard by the uncharacteristic gentleness in her tone.

But the moment passed. She straightened her shoulders and resumed her usual commanding bearing.

"Still," she continued crisply, "I would like to meet the young lady and speak with her myself. Perhaps, once you have proposed, I might discuss with her what will be expected of her as your wife. The mistress of Pemberley will have obligations—significant ones—and if she has not moved in society, she may have no notion of what lies ahead."

CHAPTER 22

Plotting

Miss Bingley seized her first opportunity to speak to Lady Matlock after dinner.

Earlier, she had attempted to seat herself beside the countess during the meal, but Aunt Horatia had firmly directed her to the chair at her own left, far from Lady Matlock who was placed in the seat of honour beside their host.

To Miss Bingley's left sat Mr. Hurst, who offered little conversation beyond asking for more wine, while to Aunt Horatia's right was Colonel Fitzwilliam, who had occupied much of the countess's attention throughout the meal.

Thus, despite her best efforts, Miss Bingley had found herself effectively cut off from both her intended targets.

However, when the housekeeper called Aunt Horatia away, Miss Bingley used the opportunity to speak to the countess and Miss Darcy.

"Lady Matlock, I am perfectly delighted to have this opportunity to grow better acquainted," Miss Bingley simpered. "We have never had the pleasure of meeting in town, but I was so pleased when my brother informed me that you and Miss Darcy would be joining us here. It is so dreadfully dull in the country—full of little nobodies who believe themselves far more important than they are. Worst of all is that Bennet family, with whom your nephew seems so enamoured."

She gave a light, affected laugh, oblivious to the darkening expression on Lady Matlock's face—or to the look of open shock on Georgiana's.

"I know Darcy claims a connection to the father through his own, but surely that Bennet fellow is making far more of it than truly existed. We shall be a much more agreeable party with you here, my lady. With your presence, my brother will have no reason to call at Longbourn so often, nor need we endure their frequent visits. I cannot imagine you would wish to be acquainted with such a family." Miss Bingley sniffed with disdain.

Lady Matlock straightened, her posture imposing, and regarded Miss Bingley with a look of icy derision. When she spoke, her voice was cold and cutting.

"First, when we arrived you addressed my niece by her Christian name without her permission. Now you attempt to imply a familiarity with my nephew by referring to him by his surname as though you were of his intimate acquaintance. It is said you attended a seminary for young ladies, Miss Bingley, yet it appears you mastered none of the lessons taught there."

The countess drew herself even more erect, her gaze firm and unwavering as she glared at the interloper.

"Were you not instructed that it is for the person of higher rank to initiate an informal address? Did they not teach you that it is for the superior to open a conversation with an inferior, not the other way around? You ought not to have approached me but waited for me to acknowledge you."

Her eyes narrowed slightly. "My nephew has already informed me that he was obliged to remind you of the proper decorum owed to a gentleman to whom you are not related. It grieves me to see that you have taken no greater care in amending your conduct."

She let the words hang in the air a moment before continuing, her tone as cool as glass. "If you are truly determined to raise yourself above your current station, Miss Bingley, I suggest you begin by acquiring the manners to match your ambition. At present, it seems a most unlikely prospect. It is fortunate your sister has already married; otherwise, your conduct might well have jeopardised her prospects. As for your brother—he would be wise to establish a respectable distance once he takes a wife, if he values peace in his household."

Miss Bingley's mouth opened, then closed again, no words finding their way past her mortification. A blotchy flush rose along her neck and cheeks as she struggled to summon a defence, any defence, in front of this woman whom she had hoped to impress.

Before she could stammer out a reply, Lady Matlock turned away with cool finality, addressing Georgiana in a tone of polite warmth. "My dear, would you care to demonstrate for me the music you have been practising? I am certain your brother will be most eager to hear your progress at the instrument."

Gratefully seizing on the opportunity to distance herself from Caroline Bingley, Georgiana rose at once, casting the lady a fleeting, pitying glance.

Still reeling from yet another set-down by a prominent member of society, Miss Bingley rose unsteadily and murmured an apology for retiring early, claiming she was suddenly unwell.

Not even her sister acknowledged her departure.

To her dismay, she found her aunt waiting in the hallway. One look at the expression on her aunt's face confirmed what she feared most: the conversation had been overheard.

"Caroline Bingley," her aunt hissed, taking her arm and nearly dragging her into an empty alcove behind the stairs. "When one does not know how to behave in company, the wisest course is silence. You would do well to remember that."

With that final pronouncement, Aunt Horatia turned and walked away, leaving her niece standing alone in the hallway.

Miss Bingley remained frozen in place for several moments, her pride stinging and her thoughts spinning. The muffled sound of the gentlemen rejoining the ladies in the drawing room reached her ears —a sharp reminder of this group of people she had so desired to be a part of continuing without her.

Mortified, she gathered her skirts and fled up the stairs, retreating to her room with as much dignity as she could muster. She seethed with anger at her treatment that evening, in truth the treatment she had been subjected to ever since she had come into this part of the country.

It is often said that angry people are not wise, and Caroline Bingley was no exception to that. Rather than reflect upon her own behaviour or make any attempt to amend it, she chose instead to direct her resentment towards the easiest target: Elizabeth Bennet. In Miss Bingley's eyes, it was Eliza Bennet who had ruined all her hopes of securing Mr. Darcy, and it was her influence that had altered his manner so completely.

Returning to her room in silence, her face burned with humiliation as she entered it. Her maid was waiting, but she quickly dismissed her, telling her to return when she rang. Once the door was shut behind her, the stillness of her thoughts shattered. She tore off her gloves and flung them onto a chair, annoyed further when they missed and landed on the floor beside it, and then she began to pace.

Her eyes flashed, and her expression was tight as she seethed.

How dare they say those things to me? What right does the countess have to scold me as if I were a mere child? She may be higher placed in society than I, but I have heard whispers about the earl's habits. Everyone in town knows of his mistress, but she thinks to tell me that I will never rise above my station.

If anyone had expected her to amend her behaviour and gracefully retreat—well, they were fools to think that. No, she would do what she had always done when denied what she wanted: find another way to have it. She no longer wanted Mr. Darcy; he had proven too intransigent. *He* was not worthy of *her*.

However, her thoughts turned, as they always did of late, to Elizabeth Bennet.

That chit—smug, sharp-eyed, too clever by half—she has ruined everything. How dare she engage Mr. Darcy, challenge Mr. Darcy, yet no matter what she said to him, he only seemed to fall further under her spell.

That grated on Miss Bingley. Mr Darcy's affections, his attention, his changed manner…all of it could be traced back to that Bennet chit. From the moment she appeared in their company, everything had shifted. Miss Bingley could see it plainly, even if the others refused to acknowledge it.

Well. If Elizabeth Bennet thinks she has won, she will soon learn otherwise. I will ensure that she will not obtain the prize she expects.

Her steps began to become more frantic as her mind lit with possibilities. If she could not ruin the Bennet family in truth, she would do so in the eyes of those gathered at Netherfield.

Let them see how vulgar she is. How low. How ill-suited she is to everything he represents. She cannot possibly be Mrs. Darcy; she is unworthy of the name. If I cannot have the title I covet, then neither will she.

Miss Bingley could whisper doubts, sow discomfort, raise the sorts of questions that would linger in an insignificant little village such as this one. She knew the power of gossip, and she would shine a light on every weakness the family displayed—lack of connections, rural ignorance, improper manners—anything that might turn admiration into disdain.

Let her stumble. I will be there when she does. With luck, I will set the rock in her path that causes her to fall.

Of course, Miss Bingley was no longer content to ruin just the Bennet family. If she could damage more than that *Eliza*—if perhaps there was something that could be done that would cause Georgiana's image to suffer, or if word of Lord Matlock's liaisons made their way more prominently into gossip and embarrassed the family—so much the better. However, those would be only additional highlights to her master plan: to separate Darcy and Elizabeth, causing each to despise the other, and if she could, to ruin Elizabeth entirely.

A slow smile curled at the corners of her mouth as a thought occurred to her. The missing sister. Her smile turned even more vengeful with this final thought: *I may have failed to win him, but I will not fail to destroy the one he has chosen over me.*

The following morning, Miss Bingley rose with renewed purpose—and a plan. She needed to learn more about the elusive Bennet sister and begin quietly raising doubts about her conduct. If she could find someone willing to assist her in discrediting Elizabeth Bennet, all the better.

Although she had not engaged with the local society at the events she had attended, she had listened closely. In villages like Meryton, gossip flowed freely, and Caroline had already noted a telling coolness between Lady Lucas—the only titled woman in the area—and Mrs. Bennet. *That*, she thought, *might prove useful.*

With this aim in mind, she informed her maid they would be going into the village that morning "to shop," offering no further explanation. She did not trouble herself to tell her brother or sister, merely summoned the carriage and ordered it to take her to Meryton.

Since she had never ventured into the village before, no one thought to question her instructions. None of her relations imagined she might act independently—and so no one forbade her from doing exactly as she pleased.

As she strolled through the streets, she recognised several faces from past encounters. A few greeted her with distant civility, but none went out of their way to engage her.

Still, she thought, *no matter. I do not need their friendship—only their tongues.*

While she was looking for her target, she noticed the prevalence of redcoats in the area. *Oh yes,* she thought, *the militia was to quarter in Meryton for the winter.*

She smiled to herself. *One of these men will do nicely. The only question is which of them might be persuaded to indulge in a little ruin—for the right price.*

The problem there would be getting her brother to give her the funds in ready cash. Still, she had some hidden away, preferring to save some of her allowance while allowing her brother to cover the overages. While she contemplated this, she looked about for Lady Lucas.

"Ah, there she is," she said aloud, surprising her maid. They turned in the direction of the haberdasher, where Lady Lucas and her younger daughter stood. Miss Bingley could not remember the girl's name.

When Lady Lucas turned around and saw Miss Bingley approaching her as if she wished to speak, her brows lifted in mild surprise. However, she inclined her head with polite reserve.

"Miss Bingley," she said. "I had not expected to see you in Meryton. I had heard you had guests arriving yesterday; your brother mentioned the newcomers to my husband a few evenings ago at Lucas Lodge."

Miss Bingley offered the lady her most practiced smile. "I confess it is my first time venturing into the village. I thought it might be refreshing to escape the house for a short while. One can only speak of weather and wallpaper so long before one longs for fresh air—and news. My sister and aunt were busy this morning, so I struck out on my own to see what I could find in Meryton. Surely you must know of all the best shops and where all the best wares are to be found?"

Lady Lucas chuckled faintly. "That I do, Miss Bingley, but I am afraid there is little to be found in Meryton that cannot be procured in London. I doubt someone of your..." here, she hesitated over the word, "*taste* would find much to her liking here."

Miss Bingley laughed at this jest, believing the lady to be complimenting her. She did not waste time, however, and quickly turned the conversation to the topic she wished to discuss. Tilting her head, she asked, "I understand, Lady Lucas, that your family is long acquainted with the Bennet family."

"Yes, indeed. We are neighbours, after all," came the tart reply.

"How fortunate for you all." Miss Bingley's tone was smooth. "They are such a lively family. Mr. Darcy seems most taken with the second daughter, Miss Elizabeth though I understand there are five daughters in all. I confess, I have only been introduced to four. I do hope nothing is amiss with the fifth?"

Lady Lucas blinked. "Oh—Lydia. She has been away at school these past few years. Poor girl had little inclination for learning from her governess, and eventually her parents thought it best she continue her education elsewhere. She returns now and again, and it is always… eventful when she is at Longbourn."

Miss Bingley nodded slowly, as if hearing a revelation rather than something the neighbourhood likely knew well. "How curious. So, she is rather—rebellious? Unrestrained?" Her tone carried the edge of barely contained satisfaction.

"Not exactly," Lady Lucas replied, her expression turning more guarded. She tilted her head, studying the other woman with mild caution. "The family simply concluded that it would be best for her to continue her instruction away from home."

"How old is the young lady?"

Lady Lucas glanced towards her daughter. "I believe she has recently turned fifteen—or will, quite soon." Maria gave a small, uncertain nod but did not speak, clearly unwilling to address Miss Bingley directly.

"Surely there's a story behind it," Miss Bingley pressed, her tone growing overly eager. "A family would not send a child away for a mere childish offense."

At that, Lady Lucas straightened. The friendliness slipped from her expression, replaced with polite formality.

"There is no story," she said evenly. "Now, if you'll excuse me—my daughter and I have errands to complete. It was lovely to see you, Miss Bingley."

Without another word, she turned and walked away, Maria trailing behind her.

Miss Bingley grimaced at her lack of success at this first overture. She would need to be more careful, moving forward.

Rather than return to Netherfield in defeat, Miss Bingley continued to stroll through the streets of Meryton, casting disinterested glances into the shop windows. She paused occasionally to examine the wares on display, though always with thinly veiled disdain. There may have been a few items of interest, but she had long since decided that nothing in Meryton could possibly be worthy of her attention.

Determined not to let the excursion be a complete waste, Miss Bingley was pleased to come upon two militia officers accompanied by a rather handsome gentleman in civilian dress. She recognised one of the officers—though his name entirely escaped her—and, undeterred by the lapse in memory, approached with a carefully composed smile. Her tone, lofty but attempting friendliness, did little to disguise the condescension beneath it.

"Captain," Miss Bingley said with an air of affected warmth, "how do you fare on this lovely day?"

"I am well, Miss Bingley," he replied, clearly taken aback by her sudden approach. When they had met before, she had barely acknowledged any of the officers, and it was obvious from his face that he had not expected her to remember him.

"Will you not introduce me to your companions?" she asked, her tone light but expectant, with the air of a grand lady commanding those beneath her.

The captain complied with a polite nod. "Miss Bingley, may I present Lieutenant Jonathan Sanderson and Mr. George Wickham, lately of London. Mr. Wickham will be joining the regiment shortly—he met with the colonel this morning and is to be fitted for his uniform at the tailor's now."

Miss Bingley inclined her head with the regal detachment of a queen acknowledging her inferiors. "Good morning, gentlemen," she said, the greeting gracious in form, if not in spirit.

The three men exchanged uncertain glances, silently debating whether they ought to remain or take their leave. Before any of them could speak, Miss Bingley forestalled the decision with another question.

"And how are you finding the neighbourhood, gentlemen?" she asked, her voice light while concealing her true intentions. "I myself am newly arrived though my family has been quite social of late—visiting the estate of Longbourn frequently."

Miss Bingley let the name hang in the air a moment longer than necessary, watching their expressions shift with quiet satisfaction.

SPORT FOR OUR NEIGHBOURS

"There are four young ladies in the household," she said smoothly, "all quite charming—and, if local gossip is to be trusted, each expected to bring a respectable dowry. I daresay a regiment stationed nearby might find their company…agreeable."

She smiled as though the suggestion were no more than a casual observation.

"The second daughter, Miss Elizabeth, is particularly notable. It's said she assists her father in managing the estate. I wouldn't be at all surprised if he named her his heir. She's often seen wandering the grounds, more like a steward than a young lady of her station, and quite alone, more often than not."

She paused delicately, letting the implication drift through the air like a trace of expensive perfume.

The two officers acknowledged her words slightly, departing quickly when they were hailed by another. The third gentleman, the one in civilian clothing, appeared particularly intrigued by this notion and leant in to whisper: "Intelligent, independent, and unaccompanied? A rare combination in a country miss. But I dare say, she is not one who would be easily tamed."

Feigning innocence, Miss Bingley tilted her head and offered a light, practiced laugh. "Oh, but I am sure you will find her…most engaging, Mr. Wickham. Her father's lack of foresight is to *your* advantage, I should think," she said smoothly, though the flicker in her eyes betrayed more of her motives than she realised.

Wickham's gaze sharpened, amusement gleaming as he caught the edge of jealousy woven into her words. "Then she and I shall get on famously. Perhaps you might arrange a meeting?"

"I would be delighted," she replied, her smile curling with satisfaction. "In fact, I may be able to ensure she is alone—and I could offer an incentive that would make it worth your while."

Wickham arched a brow at her boldness, intrigued by the offer.

Oblivious to the true nature of the man before her, Miss Bingley congratulated herself on a plan well set in motion. Let that lieutenant pursue Miss Eliza. Whatever came of it, the results were sure to be entertaining—at least for her.

CHAPTER 23
Visiting Longbourn

While Miss Bingley wandered about the shops of Meryton, the rest of the Netherfield party—except for Mr. Hurst—paid a call at Longbourn, entirely unaware that she had even left the manor. When a servant informed them that Miss Bingley would not be joining the visit, it was assumed she had simply chosen to remain in her room. No one questioned the message nor suspected that she had discreetly paid the maid to report her as indisposed, disguising her absence from the house.

Once the introductions were performed, the older ladies—Mrs. Bennet, Lady Matlock, Mrs. Hurst, and Miss Horatia Bingley—settled into one corner of the drawing room. Darcy and Bingley each made their way to the lady who increasingly occupied their thoughts. Georgiana quickly took a seat between Mary and Catherine, content to engage in their quiet conversation under the watchful eyes of Mrs. Graham and Mrs. Annesley.

Colonel Fitzwilliam positioned himself within earshot of his cousins, his demeanour casual though his eyes missed little. From his central vantage point, he could observe the entire room with ease.

He watched as Darcy leant a little closer to Miss Elizabeth, his eyes bright with interest and his expression unusually unguarded.

"I confess, I was surprised to find Maria Edgeworth so well represented at the village bookseller," Darcy was saying, recalling his recent visit. "One does not often encounter such a collection outside London. Once again, Meryton has exceeded my expectations."

There was a note of genuine admiration in his voice, and Elizabeth, catching the implication beneath his words, felt a warm flush rise to her cheeks.

Elizabeth smiled. "My father insisted Mr. Thompson stock her entire catalogue—he claims she is far more instructive than most sermonizers. And when he tires of her morals, he moves on to her footnotes."

"A thorough reader, then," Darcy teased, knowing how much Bennet still enjoyed his books, although perhaps not so much as he once did.

"Insufferably so," she replied, her eyes dancing with merriment. "He once read *Belinda* twice in a fortnight to determine whether the ending truly suited the rest of the novel. I am still not sure he is satisfied. He has also read the newer edition and was quite displeased with the changes."

Darcy laughed—quietly, but genuinely. It surprised even him.

"You find that amusing, Mr. Darcy?"

He glanced at her, the corners of his mouth still lifted. "I do. I did not expect to find such amusement in a discussion of *Belinda*."

"Then clearly, sir," she said, mockingly prim, "you underestimate both Edgeworth and the Bennets."

He looked at her for a moment longer than was strictly proper, and then said, more softly, "It would seem I have."

Darcy gave another soft laugh, and Fitzwilliam noted the rare sound with some amusement. Miss Elizabeth seemed pleased by it, as well; she tilted her head slightly, her eyes alight.

So, he thought wryly, *the great Fitzwilliam Darcy does know how to flirt with a young lady—though I doubt he realises he is doing it.*

He turned his attention towards his mother just in time to catch her watching the pair. Her fan moved in a slow, deliberate rhythm, her expression polite and unmoved—but her eyes were sharp and unblinking as she observed the ease between her nephew and the country gentleman's daughter.

"I daresay," she said with gracious detachment, turning back to Mrs. Bennet, "you must find it quite lively here with so many daughters at home."

"Oh, indeed, Lady Matlock," Mrs. Bennet said brightly. "There is never a dull moment—not with four girls under one roof! We quite miss our Lydia, but we hope to have her home before too much longer."

Lady Matlock offered a serene smile. "Yes. Quite so."

Fitzwilliam, watching her, knew better than to assume that calm reply indicated approval. His mother rarely voiced her opinion before it was fully formed—and when she did, her words carried weight. Iron beneath velvet, as always.

After a moment, Lady Matlock caught her son's gaze across the room. She held it briefly, then rose with an unhurried elegance and made her way towards Darcy and Elizabeth, joining them in an empty seat next to the settee the couple were settled on.

"Fitzwilliam," she said smoothly, "you are far too engrossed in this conversation to spare a word for your poor aunt."

Darcy turned towards her and smiled. "Forgive me for my inattention, Aunt. We were discussing Miss Edgeworth's novels—Miss Bennet's father is an enthusiastic reader. You know how easily I become lost in a conversation of books."

Lady Matlock's eyes flicked briefly to Elizabeth. "Indeed? How very modern of him." She turned to Elizabeth with a polite smile. "Do you share your father's literary inclinations, Miss Elizabeth, or merely endure them? Are you able to keep up with my nephew on this subject?"

Elizabeth met the older woman's gaze with composed assurance. "I do enjoy reading, although I take pleasure in many pursuits. My parents ensured I received the education expected of a young woman of my station. I am moderately accomplished in literature, languages, music, and the usual refinements. At the very least," she added with a light laugh, "I know enough to be a tolerable companion for anyone brave enough to speak of books in mixed company."

The remark drew a quiet laugh from Darcy which did not escape his aunt's notice.

Lady Matlock offered a cool, measured smile. "How fortunate for my nephew, then, that you are…accomplished in so many ways."

"I am always pleased to find someone who can engage in good conversation," Elizabeth replied lightly. "And gentlemen who are not intimidated by a heroine who thinks for herself."

Lady Matlock tilted her head ever so slightly, her brows lifting at the thinly veiled challenge. "A rare breed, indeed."

A pause followed—brief, but deliberate.

"I hope, Miss Elizabeth," she continued, her tone smooth, "that we might speak again while I am in the neighbourhood, perhaps more privately. I should like to hear more of these accomplishments you claim. One morning, you should call on me at Netherfield for tea; I think our hostess would not be offended if the two of us hid ourselves away for an hour."

Elizabeth smiled graciously. "Of course, Lady Matlock. I should be honoured. Simply name the time and day, and I will be certain to call."

"Excellent," the countess replied, her fan pausing mid-motion for the briefest instant. "I look forward to knowing you better, my dear." She patted Elizabeth's hand briefly before moving back to her seat with the other matrons.

"I think she was pleased with you," Darcy whispered into her ear.

Turning to her companion with a raised brow, Elizabeth took a moment to look at Darcy.

"She means well," Darcy said before Elizabeth could speak.

Elizabeth chuckled. "I feel as though I was just examined, but I am uncertain what mark I may have received."

"My aunt and my mother were close friends during my mother's lifetime," Darcy said quietly. "Since my mother's passing, my aunt has, at times, tried to fill that role for my sister and me. The letters I wrote to Georgiana introducing you and your sisters…they were quite unlike me. And—" He stopped, uncertain how much to admit.

He cleared his throat, his gaze dropping. For a moment, an unusual silence hovered between them. Then, as though unaware of the others nearby, Elizabeth gently laid her hand atop his where it rested between them on the cushion.

He looked up, startled at first, then softened. A faint smile touched his lips.

"I believe I ought to speak with your father," he said after a moment. "And, if he permits, request a private audience with you. There's something I must discuss—but I feel it is only right to confirm a few matters with him first."

Elizabeth's eyes widened, and her mouth fell open slightly. "What?"

Darcy blinked at her, then realised what she had assumed. Colour rose to his cheeks.

"No—no, forgive me," he said quickly, with a touch of remorse. "It is not…that, not yet. There are—some business matters I must speak with him about, and certain concerns you ought to be made aware of regarding my uncle."

Elizabeth's colour deepened, but she did not withdraw her hand from where it rested upon his, now hidden beneath the folds of her skirt. "I see," she said slowly, though her voice betrayed some confusion. "You startled me, Mr. Darcy. I assumed something quite different from your words. Forgive me—for presuming."

Her voice was quiet, uncertain, and Darcy found himself wishing he could remove the cloud of doubt from her eyes.

A flicker of frustration crossed his face. "Yes," he said softly. "I am discovering that I am not always as clear as I imagine myself to be. There are…certain matters that you have not yet been made aware. It is…they are important, and I need to ask your father for some guidance."

"Then I will follow your lead," she replied, her tone was light and still a little uncertain—or perhaps hurt, Darcy thought.

He looked down at where their joined hands still rested under her skirts, then back at her. "The truth is, there are matters concerning my family—particularly my sister—that I believe you should be aware of. Not because they are scandalous," he added quickly, "but because they may one day concern you. Or rather…they may come to matter."

Her brows rose, just slightly. "That is very nearly a proposal."

"Only nearly," he said with a quiet smile. "You must forgive me. I find I cannot speak to you without meaning more than I say."

Elizabeth's heart beat a touch faster, though she tried not to show it. "And yet, you would not mean too much too soon."

"No," he said, serious once more. "Not before I have spoken to your father."

She studied him for a long moment. "That sounds ominous."

"It is not," he said firmly. "Only necessary."

A silence fell between them, but it was not uncomfortable. Elizabeth gently withdrew her hand, but the warmth of the gesture lingered between them.

"I trust you will speak plainly when the time comes," she said at last.

He inclined his head. "That is my intention."

Just then, laughter rose from the corner of the room where Lady Matlock and Mrs. Bennet were engaged in conversation. Mrs. Hurst and her aunt were chuckling over something, while Mrs. Bennet leant in with an eager smile, and the countess observed it all with a faint, amused expression. When Darcy's eyes flicked briefly in their direction, he caught Lady Matlock turning her gaze towards him as well.

Elizabeth followed the direction of his gaze. "She is concerned?"

"She is," he replied, his eyes still fixed ahead. "And I have no doubt she will make her opinions known."

"I have never been particularly troubled by the opinions of others," Elizabeth said calmly.

Darcy turned to her then, a flicker of wonder in his expression. "No, you are not," he agreed, a hint of a smile tilting his lips upwards. "But I do wonder how you will respond to what I must say to you."

He hesitated, then gave a slight shake of his head. "Excuse me—I must speak with Mr. Bennet."

Rising, he offered a brief nod before leaving the room and making his way swiftly to Bennet's study.

CHAPTER 24

Confessions

D arcy knocked at the study door and entered at the sound of "Come."

"Bennet," he said without preamble, his voice low and taut, "We need to speak."

Bennet rose from his chair, blinking at the gravity in Darcy's tone.

"My aunt said something yesterday," Darcy went on, already pacing. "She claimed the earl received funds from her father—to maintain Matlock House." He paused, frowning. "At the time, I dismissed it. But now…" His voice trailed off as he turned sharply on his heel. "Have you heard from Gardiner? Has he discovered anything?"

He drew a hand through his hair, obviously distracted. "I was too preoccupied yesterday to give her words proper consideration, but now I'm wondering what she meant—what that might mean? Why would the earl need funds from his father-in-law?"

Darcy fell silent again, his steps marking slow, restless lines across the rug.

Bennet remained still, watching him with a thoughtful, unreadable expression, and said nothing.

"I wish to tell Elizabeth about the difficulties with the earl—especially as they concern Georgiana," Darcy said at last. "She may see something we have overlooked. She is insightful and may be able to approach the matter in a way that neither of us have considered."

He paused, exhaling slowly before continuing.

"There is something else," he said quietly. "I believe the time has come to tell her about the marriage contract. As I have said before, I would never hold her to it—not if she were unwilling. But the truth is…" His voice softened. "I am nearly certain that, given the choice, I would choose her. The fact that my father approved the match gives weight to my own desire to have her as my wife. Judging from our conversation just now, I feel that, perhaps, Elizabeth would choose the same, but I can no longer withhold this information from her."

"Do you still wish to be the one to speak to her about the contract?" Bennet asked.

Darcy nodded, not speaking for a moment as he considered the idea. "I do," he finally said.

Nodding, Bennet stood and sent a maid to request that both Elizabeth and the colonel join them in his study. Darcy looked up at him in surprise.

"As much as my wife has changed in recent years, if she believed I were calling Elizabeth to speak with you privately, she would immediately assume a marriage was imminent," Bennet said drily. "By requesting her presence along with your cousin's, it will appear to be about estate business. She disapproves of Elizabeth's involvement in such matters, but in this case, it provides convenient cover for what you actually wish to discuss."

He glanced towards the adjacent wall. "There is a small sitting room through that door. Colonel Fitzwilliam and I can speak here, and you may speak with Elizabeth in the other room. It offers some measure of privacy—enough for what is necessary."

He paused, fixing Darcy with a glare. "I am placing a great deal of trust in you by allowing this. Keep it brief—and join us as soon as you are able."

Darcy nodded his agreement and opened the door Bennet indicated and entered the small room, pacing as he waited.

A few moments later, Elizabeth entered the small sitting room and closed the door softly behind her, not quite latching it, but enough to give them privacy. Darcy was pacing near the hearth, his hands clasped behind his back, his expression taut with thought. At the sound of the door, he turned quickly.

"Miss Elizabeth," he said, then stopped. "Elizabeth."

She raised a brow slightly at the correction, but said nothing, waiting.

"I—thank you for coming." He took a step towards her, then stopped again. "There is…something I need to speak to you about. Something I wish we had both known about earlier, but until recently, I was unaware of it myself."

Elizabeth's posture stiffened slightly. "Go on."

Darcy drew a breath. "It concerns an agreement made between our fathers—yours and mine. Shortly before my father's death, they signed a marriage contract…an arrangement between our families. I became fully aware of it only recently, after arriving in Hertfordshire. Your father was the one who told me about it."

Elizabeth stared at him, frowning. "A marriage contract? And Papa has known about it all these years?"

"Yes," he said, stumbling a little over the word. "It seems our fathers agreed that—we should marry with the understanding that it must be something we both want."

There was a silence. Elizabeth's expression was unreadable.

"I want you to know," he added quickly, "that I would never enforce it. I have no intention of compelling you, nor would I expect you to accept such an arrangement without full freedom of choice."

"I see," she said slowly, her tone cool. "So, you would offer marriage not because you wish to, but because our fathers arranged it, and you feel duty-bound to honour our father's wishes. Did you pay attention to me for the same reason? To ease the way?"

Darcy's brow creased. "No—well, not only because of that. I mean—it was unexpected, certainly, but the arrangement aligns with what I…" He trailed off, clearly flustered.

Elizabeth's voice turned sharp. "With what you what, Mr. Darcy? With what you find convenient? Honourable?"

"No! That is not—" He stepped forward. "That is not what I intended."

"Then *what* did you intend?" she demanded, her voice rising. "From where I stand, it sounds very much like you are offering me a proposal out of obligation. Out of loyalty to your father, not out of regard for me."

His mouth opened, but no words came in the face of her anger. While he had known she would not accept him for mercenary reasons, he had thought she had liked him, at least a little.

She stared at him, furious and wounded, then turned on her heel. "Excuse me," she said, flinging open the door behind her.

Bennet and Colonel Fitzwilliam looked up as Elizabeth stormed into the room, her cheeks flushed.

"Papa," she said sharply, "is it true? Did you and Mr. Darcy's father arrange a marriage between us without ever speaking to me about the matter? Was I ever to know of it, or was I supposed to enter the church one day and simply accept someone whom I did not know at all? Was it merely chance that brought Mr. Bingley to Hertfordshire and Mr. Darcy with him, or was this merely some scheme of yours?"

Bennet blinked at her sudden entrance, but he only nodded calmly. "Yes, Mr. Darcy's father suggested the marriage contract, in large part to protect his son from those of his family who would attempt to force or cajole him into a marriage he did not want. You were only fifteen at the time."

Elizabeth gave a disbelieving laugh. "I was practically running this estate for you then before you decided to take an interest in it. In all the time we have spent together speaking of estate business, you might have mentioned it! You certainly ought to have done so once Mr. Darcy visited."

"I might have," he agreed. "But I did not—because it was never meant to be a command, only a possibility. There is an addendum that allows us to nullify it should you have wished to marry another. Again, Lizzy, it was mostly done in an effort to protect Mr. Darcy from relatives who had ill intentions towards him."

"I do not understand. You make it sound like some sort of transaction," she said bitterly, "while he makes it sound like…like a duty."

Colonel Fitzwilliam rose from his chair. "Miss Elizabeth," he said gently, "I feel quite certain Darcy did not mean it as it sounded." He glanced towards the door, where his cousin had just entered behind her—looking flustered, pale, and not a little stunned by the vehemence of her response.

"If he has made a muddle of it," the colonel continued, "I suspect it is not because he does not care for you—but because he cares rather more than he knows how to say."

Bennet gave his daughter a pointed look. "Shortly after Mr. Darcy arrived in Hertfordshire, I informed him of the contract—due to some circumstances he shared with me. At the time, he asked me not to speak of it to you."

Elizabeth opened her mouth, but Bennet raised a hand to forestall her.

"He wanted to tell you himself, once the two of you had come to know each other better. If the two of you did not suit, there was no reason to burden you with it at all. But he came to me again today, asking if he might explain—not only the existence of the contract, but the reason I told him about it in the first place. He wanted *you* to be the one to decide."

Bennet arched his brow. "I rather think you did not give him the chance. Likely, you got your back up the moment he said the word 'contract.'"

Elizabeth flushed but said nothing.

"Now," he said, not unkindly, "do not punish the man for speaking clumsily when you would not allow him the time to speak fully."

Elizabeth stood frozen for a moment, her heart thudding. She looked towards the sitting room door, and saw Darcy standing there, looking at her in confusion.

"I see," she said finally, her voice softer now.

"Elizabeth—please, may we finish our conversation?" Darcy asked, his voice low but firm, offering her his hand.

Elizabeth nodded and accepted his hand, allowing him to lead her back into the small sitting room. Once inside, he guided her to a settee and gently helped her sit before taking the seat opposite her.

Almost at once, Darcy rose again, restless. He crossed the room, paused, then turned and came to stand before her. For a moment, he seemed to struggle with the tumult of his thoughts. Then, realizing how he towered over her, he dropped to one knee in front of her—not in dramatic supplication, but as though drawn down by the urgency of his own heart.

His breath was uneven. His voice, when he spoke, was low and even.

"I spoke poorly before," he said. "I know I did. But you must understand—my request was never about duty. Nothing in our acquaintance has ever been. The contract…it means little to me, except as proof that my father once hoped for a match between us, which I already knew from his words to me when we visited Longbourn all those years ago. I told you about it, not to justify anything, but because I wanted to be honest with you and allow you to choose. You deserve nothing less. I never intended it to shape your answer—or compel your regard. Perhaps I was too honest, but I did not want you to misunderstand my intentions."

Her eyes flashed. "Then why mention it at all, if not to give weight to your proposal?"

"Because I would not have you think—" He faltered. "I would not have you believe my affection was insincere, or that I approached you under false pretenses."

Elizabeth replied, her voice far quieter than it had been in the study. "And what are your feelings, Mr. Darcy? I confess, they have become rather difficult to interpret."

Darcy straightened from where he knelt in front of her, sitting beside her and taking her hand in his. "I care for you, Elizabeth. Deeply. Not because our fathers wished it, not because you are clever or accomplished—though you are—but because you are wholly yourself. I admire your mind, your wit, your courage. I should have said so clearly from the start."

Elizabeth regarded him for a long moment.

"Tell me, sir," she said at last, "what are *your* wishes in this matter? As you have explained it, neither of us is bound unless we choose to be. So why raise the subject now?"

Darcy hesitated, struck silent by the directness of her question. She watched him closely as he stood and paced as he attempted to search for the right words.

At last, he spoke—quietly, but with growing resolve.

"Perhaps it is too soon to speak of affections," he began. "And yet, I find my desire to be in your presence deepens each time we meet. I cannot yet name what I feel—not fully—but I believe I felt the first stirrings of it when we first met that day in the fields, and it has only grown since."

He paused, closed his eyes briefly, steadying himself before continuing.

"My purpose in telling you of the contract was not to bind you to it, but to gauge whether you might…be amenable to such a match, should your feelings ever incline that way. There are things you do not yet know—matters I must still explain—but before I burdened you with them, I needed to be honest about what compelled me to speak at all."

His voice softened as he drew nearer.

"My uncle would have me make a match elsewhere—a match I cannot accept. But you…" He met her eyes, and something vulnerable flickered there. "You are not a duty, Elizabeth. You are—if I may say it—a lifeline. A hope. A treasure I did not expect to find when I joined my friend to visit his estate. I knew *of* you, of course, but even then, I did not expect to find a…a partner."

He returned to the seat beside her.

"It was not my intention to propose—not yet—but I could no longer keep the existence of the marriage contract from you. Not while my feelings for you continue to grow each day."

He paused, gathering his thoughts before continuing.

"I wished to speak openly about the matters that trouble me, to show you that part of myself, so that you might make an informed decision about whether a life with me is something you want. As I told your father, I am certain of my choice—but I would not ask for your regard without first offering you the truth in full."

Elizabeth nodded slowly, absorbing all he had said. "Then please, Mr. Darcy," she said gently, though her voice remained even, "tell me what you believe I should know, so I can understand everything clearly and make a thoughtful decision about what lies ahead."

"Let us rejoin your father and my cousin, and I will explain all," Darcy said. "They are both aware of the details and I believe they can fill in any parts of the story that I miss."

She lingered for a moment, her eyes searching his. "Thank you for trusting me with this—and for letting me stand beside you. I hope it will always be so."

For a moment, Darcy could do nothing but stare at her. "You are decided, then?"

A slow smile curved her lips as she rose to her feet. "I, too, know what I wish," she said. "But I will hear you out and allow you the advantage of your sex—which is to ask." She tilted her head, eyes bright with mischief. "And then I shall claim the privilege of mine, which is to answer."

Turning, she moved back towards the study, with Darcy slowly following behind her.

CHAPTER 25
A Tentative Understanding

Upon Darcy and Elizabeth's re-entering the study, Bennet ceased his conversation with Colonel Fitzwilliam and turned towards his daughter with an affected sigh.

"Well, Lizzy," he said, "if you are quite finished shouting at everyone, perhaps now you will sit and speak to us like a rational creature."

Resisting the childish urge to stick out her tongue at him—for both the remark and the concealment of the contract—Elizabeth took her customary seat with as much dignity as she could muster. Darcy claimed the nearest chair, drawing it slightly closer so he could meet her eyes as he spoke.

"Your father informed me," he began carefully, "that one of the original purposes of the contract was to shield me from the ambitions of my uncle—my mother's brother—who, as you know, is a peer."

Elizabeth's expression shifted from wary to curious.

Darcy went on, describing his increasingly strained relationship with Lord Matlock, his recent confrontation with the earl, and at last, Georgiana's near-elopement in Ramsgate the previous summer. He spoke plainly, though not without evident discomfort, and when he had finished, a silence lingered for a moment before Elizabeth broke it.

"Do you believe your uncle was involved in Mr. Wickham's attempt to elope with Georgiana?" she asked.

The three gentlemen exchanged a brief glance as though the thought had crossed their minds more than once. Bennet and the colonel looked faintly surprised by her swift deduction, but Darcy merely smiled—his expression touched with admiration for her perspicacity.

"Why do you ask?" Colonel Fitzwilliam said after a moment.

Elizabeth leant forward slightly, her tone calm but incisive. "Because a scheme like that would have been conducted with the utmost secrecy. If the truth did not come from a servant—which, as you have said, seems unlikely—then someone must have known in advance. It is hardly plausible that Mr. Wickham would approach Lord Matlock directly. Far more likely, the earl knew of the attempt beforehand—perhaps even arranged it himself."

She paused, then added quietly, "Such silence suggests foreknowledge. It is possible he intended it all along—as leverage to force you into compliance, Mr. Darcy."

All three men stared at her.

Darcy was the first to recover. "That is precisely what we suspect," he said, a note of admiration in his voice, "although none of us put it quite so succinctly."

"She does have a habit of being uncomfortably perceptive," Bennet said, with a sideways glance at his daughter. "It is a trait she inherited from her mother, I believe—though heaven help me, Lizzy possesses far better timing and a sharper wit, particularly in matters unrelated to securing husbands."

Elizabeth gave him a look, but her expression softened as she turned back to Darcy. "What do you mean to do about it?"

Darcy met her gaze. "That," he said quietly, "is what I was hoping to decide—with you."

"What does Lady Matlock know of her husband's attempt to blackmail you?" Elizabeth asked.

"I spoke with her yesterday, and I believe Richard spoke to her this morning," Darcy replied, glancing at his cousin for confirmation. At Fitzwilliam's nod, he continued, "She mentioned that her father's money was keeping the Matlock estate afloat. At the time, I thought little of it—but now, I believe we must better understand what she meant."

Elizabeth glanced towards the door. "She's in the drawing room. Why not ask her now?"

Fitzwilliam grimaced. "To do so openly might raise suspicion. Thus far, we have kept the earl's threats from Georgiana, and I fear how she might react if it comes out abruptly."

Elizabeth arched her brow. "Tell me, Colonel—how well has shielding Miss Darcy from adversity served your family so far? I met her only today, and yet I would wager she is far stronger than any of you give her credit for."

Darcy opened his mouth to respond, but no words came. He simply stared at her, as though seeing something in her that left him momentarily undone.

Colonel Fitzwilliam let out a slow breath, then inclined his head. "You are not wrong, Miss Elizabeth. We have protected Georgiana out of love, but perhaps also out of fear—fear that she might break under pressure. You see strength where we see fragility."

"Because you look at her and remember the child she was," Elizabeth said gently. "I look at her and see a young woman who will rise to the occasion, if only someone would give her the opportunity."

Darcy finally spoke, his voice low. "You understand her already."

Elizabeth met his gaze. "I understand what it is to be underestimated due to my sex."

There was a beat of silence.

Bennet cleared his throat. "Well then, since Lizzy has neatly put us all in our place, shall we determine what is to be done?"

Darcy straightened slightly. "We need to speak to Lady Matlock—to find out what she knows or may suspect. She is not happy with her husband, and the two rarely reside under the same roof anymore. Perhaps for a few weeks during the Season they are forced to do so, but even then, they often avoid each other as much as they are able."

"When we return, we should suggest a walk," Elizabeth offered. "The suggestion of a quiet stroll in the garden would draw no attention. She has already indicated she wishes to speak further with me, and it is a pleasant day for conversation. It would not seem odd for her to join us, would it?"

"The countess is fond of the outdoors," Fitzwilliam replied, chuckling slightly. "She would likely be the first to accept the invitation."

"Then once we are outside, I will ask her to speak privately, and we can wander towards the small wilderness to the west of the house. Colonel, can you keep the others occupied and away from our conversation?" Elizabeth asked.

Fitzwilliam nodded and stood, but before anyone could depart, Darcy said, "And what should I do?"

"You should join us, Mr. Darcy," Elizabeth said with a pert smile as she also rose to her feet. "After all, I see little point in pretending that this is anything other than what it is. While I know enough, I doubt that the short version you have told me is the whole of your relationship with the earl. There is much that I cannot know, and it is best you are there to ask any additional questions about what the countess reveals."

Darcy stared at her for a moment. "That is very wise of you, Miss Elizabeth."

"I have my moments," she shot over her shoulder, teasing him with a glimpse of her smile.

Slowly rising to his feet, Darcy continued to stare after the woman who had so thoroughly captured his attention—and was swiftly stealing his heart.

Bennet chuckled at the stunned expression on his young friend's face. "In the span of a few minutes, you have learnt two valuable lessons about my second daughter, Darcy," he said, joining him as they moved towards the door. "First, she has a quick temper when she feels underestimated—or when she believes something important is being kept from her. It flares fast and hot, but she will usually listen once she has had a moment to cool."

Darcy gave a quiet laugh and pinched the bridge of his nose. "I believe you are right, sir. I muddled both my explanation of the contract and any attempt I might have made at a proper proposal. She has not answered the question regarding her interest in me—though, in fairness, I am not entirely certain I ever asked," he added with a wry shake of his head.

Bennet's smile widened. "That is the second lesson, son. She is intelligent—sometimes disarmingly so. Whether it is from her experience helping with the estate, her natural wit, or something less easily named, she often sees matters from an angle I would never consider. She is not always right—but when she is wrong, she will admit it… eventually."

He paused, then added with quiet fondness, "She is young, but in many ways, I have long thought her older than her years. When you marry—since I have no doubt you will get around to asking the all-important question—you would do well to listen to her."

Darcy turned to him, both humbled and heartened. "Thank you," he said simply before both men joined the rest of the company in the drawing room.

Darcy promptly introduced Bennet to his sister and his aunt, and a few minutes later, Elizabeth suggested a walk in the garden to extend the visit. When Mrs. Bennet attempted to dismiss the younger party—leaving the matrons and Miss Horatia Bingley to converse indoors—Bennet intervened, insisting that everyone, himself included, ought to enjoy the fine afternoon. Within moments, they had all donned their outerwear and were prepared to make their way outside.

The company quickly separated into smaller groups. Bennet chose to follow behind Jane and Mr. Bingley, having resolved to keep a closer watch on this particular daughter and her suitor. Although Bingley seemed to have matured somewhat during his time in the country, Bennet remained uncertain whether the young man's attentions would endure, especially given his sister's evident disdain for all things connected to Longbourn.

As in the drawing room, the younger girls stayed together, carefully shepherded by their companions. When Mrs. Bennet would have lingered with the countess, both Horatia Bingley and Mrs. Hurst appeared to sense a shift in the atmosphere and, with mutual understanding, began to ask her questions about the gardens.

As the gardens were among Mrs. Bennet's few undisputed triumphs, she was delighted to oblige. If any of them found Colonel Fitzwilliam's decision to accompany them curious, no one remarked upon it.

SPORT FOR OUR NEIGHBOURS

This arrangement left the countess, Elizabeth, and Darcy. Seizing the opportunity, Darcy promptly offered his arm to both ladies. With Elizabeth's direction, he led them towards the small wilderness at the edge of the grounds—the very path she had suggested earlier, in the study.

"Why do I think this whole matter has been carefully arranged?" the countess asked after a few moments of silence.

"Aunt, yesterday we spoke about the earl's threats, and you mentioned that he relied on money from your father to fund his home, at least in London. Can you tell me more about that?" Darcy asked.

"Why?" she replied, narrowing her eyes. "And why is Miss Elizabeth privy to a conversation which concerns family? You have not made her an offer, have you?"

"Would it trouble you if he had?" Elizabeth retorted. "We have known each other for several weeks now, and our families have been known to each other longer than that. If my father and his approve of the match, why would you not?"

Darcy gently released his aunt's arm and brought his free hand to rest lightly over Elizabeth's where it still lay upon his other elbow. "Elizabeth," he murmured.

Just as swiftly as her anger had flared, it faded at his calm touch.

"No, Aunt," he said, turning to Lady Matlock, "I have not yet made an offer. But I did speak with Elizabeth this morning to inform her of the contract. We discussed how best to deal with my uncle—particularly in light of the fact that I, at least, know who I wish to marry, and it is most certainly not the viscount's daughter."

Lady Matlock's brows drew together. "The two of you are engaged?" she asked, clearly displeased at this news, particularly in light of her conversation with her nephew the day before.

"We are not," Darcy replied smoothly, "although the contract signed by our fathers still exists. Were it only up to me, I would have little hesitation in announcing the engagement. But I will not do so until Elizabeth is ready and until I can be certain that no scandal or threats will endanger my sister, Elizabeth, or Elizabeth's family."

"Then you would do well to avoid referring to her by her Christian name in company," the countess said with a huff. "Very well. I see your mind is made up, and I know too well that arguing with a Darcy man rarely yields results."

"What was it you wished to know about your uncle?"

Darcy's tone sobered. "We are trying to understand why the earl might resort to blackmail—and why he or the viscount would need access to my funds. When you mentioned yesterday that your father was regularly sending money to support Matlock, it raised questions. The estate should be profitable enough on its own. So why would your husband require an outside contribution of capital?"

Lady Matlock's expression tightened at this question, her lips pressing into a thin line in her displeasure. For a moment, she said nothing, and then she exhaled slowly, deliberately releasing her tension.

"You are correct to question it," she said at last. "Matlock *should* be profitable. For many years it was. But my husband has made several poor investments of late. He would rather bleed us dry than admit to mismanaging the estate. There is something else that is draining its funds, but I am less certain what that may be. As you know, we rarely speak, and he would never dream of confiding in me."

Her tone was clipped, each word carefully measured as she went on.

"My father offered assistance when things first began going poorly several years ago," she continued. "Like myself, he believed it a temporary matter—an unfortunate stretch of misfortune that would soon correct itself. But it did not. The funds he gave were never repaid, and he has continued to send money regularly. I cannot say why he has

SPORT FOR OUR NEIGHBOURS

not simply stopped the payments, but as far as I know, he continues giving money to my husband quarterly."

Darcy's jaw clenched. "Does the viscount know of this?"

She hesitated. "I cannot say for certain. As I told you yesterday, I was unaware the two were even on friendly terms. Of course, they know each other since they both serve in the House of Lords, but we have never socialised with them or attended events with them. The viscountess died several years ago, and the daughter was sent to school not long after. As I understand it, she is quite a wilful girl. I suppose she must be Georgiana's age."

There was a beat of silence. Then Elizabeth, still holding Darcy's arm, spoke gently. "I thought you said she was still a child, only twelve or thirteen?" she asked Darcy.

"That is what I thought as well," he replied. "Little is known of her since the viscount has kept her hidden from society."

The countess pursed her lips. "I recall the announcement of her birth taking place a little before Georgiana's. We were in town then, as was your family, Darcy, since Lady Anne had been weakened by her pregnancy, and George wanted his wife in London where medical care could be more easily obtained. I remember seeing the viscountess a time or two out and about, which was, of course, quite scandalous, given her condition and the proximity to her giving birth."

"Does the earl know her age?" Elizabeth asked.

"He ought to," the countess sniffed. "I remember much being said when the viscountess gave birth to a daughter, rather than to a son. The viscount is quite old, and his wife was much younger than he. When she died a few years later, many speculated the babe must have died in childbirth, but that was never confirmed."

"What will happen when Mr. Darcy informs the earl that he will not give in to the blackmail and refuses to marry the viscount's daughter?" Elizabeth asked.

Lady Matlock's eyes met hers—sharp, intelligent, and slightly weary.

"I am afraid he will do whatever he feels he must, regardless of if that endangers the family's reputation," she said flatly. "He is a proud man and not easily thwarted. When he finally comes to the realisation that Darcy will not give into his plans, he will take steps to cause problems."

"I am not afraid of him," Darcy said.

"No," she agreed. "But perhaps you should be cautious all the same. My husband will not be so easily rebuffed, and you are not the only one who might be in danger. You already suspect that he was behind George Wickham's attempt to elope with Georgiana, and do you doubt that he would not attempt to cause harm to the lady who has ruined all his plans for you, Darcy?

She looked away briefly, then added, her voice low and bitter, "Miss Elizabeth, if your connection to my nephew becomes widely known, you will need to be far more cautious. I fear that if my husband is willing to endanger Georgiana's reputation, he would think little of ruining yours—and perhaps even placing you in actual danger. If he cannot get to you, he might attempt to do something to another member of your family."

Elizabeth met the countess's gaze directly. "I cannot think that anyone in our local society would consider harming me, but we have an entire regiment of militia soldiers presently staying in Meryton. It was my understanding that your son will be working with the militia colonel during his time here, so perhaps he can help keep an eye on these newcomers. My father insists that a footman or groom join me each time I leave the house, but it is possible we can find a second man to join me."

"I can certainly spare one or two footmen for your use," Darcy interjected. "Many of mine are retired soldiers—men Richard recommended—and they train regularly. In fact, I shall send to London for several more, as I suspect Georgiana may require protection as well."

He paused, then added with a glance towards Elizabeth, "While I would prefer to ask that you not leave Longbourn unaccompanied by your father or by me, I suspect that, despite the brevity of our acquaintance, such a request would not be well received."

Elizabeth struggled to contain an unladylike snort. "Five years ago, I would have fought with you over the suggestion that I needed anyone to accompany me on my walks about the estate and beyond. However, I have learnt better, and if you tell me you are serious about the potential threat to me, I will agree to be accompanied by two footmen on all my rambles. If you wish to join me as I visit our tenants, you are welcome to do so."

Darcy smiled at her easy acquiescence. "Thank you, Elizabeth," he murmured, his voice so low that Lady Matlock could not catch the words.

Her smile was answer enough.

CHAPTER 26

Realisations

Upon returning to Netherfield, Darcy met his cousin in the sitting room adjoining their chambers to recount what had been said in the garden. The Netherfield party had departed from Longbourn shortly after they all returned indoors, and Elizabeth had promised Darcy that she would inform her father of the countess's revelations.

"We must uncover the nature of the connection between the earl and the viscount," Darcy said to his cousin once he had finished his account. "Why is it so essential to the earl that I marry the viscount's daughter—so much so that he would risk Georgiana's reputation to ensure my compliance? There must be something we are overlooking."

"I agree," Fitzwilliam said. "Tomorrow, I shall send for a few men I know—reliable fellows who will not object to a post in the countryside for a few months. As you know, I have been corresponding with the colonel of the regiment stationed in Meryton and intend to meet with him early next week once my leave is officially concluded. While there, I will take the opportunity to learn what I can about the officers and observe them closely. Since I will be helping with their training, I will have many opportunities to observe the men to see which ones might be susceptible to taking bribes."

He paused, his expression darkening as he met his cousin's gaze.

"If my father discovers your attachment to a woman here, he will not hesitate to send one of his lackeys to interfere—or worse. As much as I dislike admitting it, I no longer know what he is capable of. The man I knew as a child was cold and distant, yes, but the one who came to demand you marry a child while threatening his own niece? I do not recognise that man."

Darcy closed his eyes for a moment, reflecting on the day's events. "My conversation with Bennet did not go as planned. I must speak with him again, to learn whether he has received any further word from his brother in London. If he has not, it may be time to engage an investigator of my own to investigate both the earl and the viscount."

He opened his eyes, his voice resolute. "I shall call on Bennet first thing in the morning. Elizabeth promised that I could accompany her as she visits the tenants and that she will allow herself to be accompanied by at least two footmen whenever she leaves Longbourn. While I do not think there is anything to fear at this moment, I prefer to think that she will be well protected."

"Elizabeth, is it?" Fitzwilliam teased. "I did not think things had progressed quite so far."

Darcy shook his head. "We never had the opportunity to speak privately after I explained the terms of the contract. The matter of the earl soon took precedence, and I am determined to wait until I can assure her safety."

He fell silent for several moments, but the colonel, knowing his cousin well, simply waited.

At last, Darcy gave a quiet, self-deprecating laugh. "I have never met a woman like Elizabeth Bennet. Before her, I would have assumed that the mere suggestion of marriage to me would be welcomed—

expected, even. But Elizabeth was furious when she believed her father and I had conspired to coerce her into a match without her knowledge."

The tension was visible in his posture as he reached up and rubbed the back of his neck. "When speaking of estates, crop yields, and investments, I seldom struggle to express myself. But attempting to convey what I feel for Elizabeth Bennet?" He gave a rueful shake of his head. "I bungled it entirely."

He paused again, his voice quieter. "Even now, I am not certain what she feels for me. She leapt into the fray when it came to deciphering my uncle's intentions, and she was far more agreeable once I had explained everything fully. But still…"

Fitzwilliam chuckled. "I believe she feels at least as strongly for you as you do for her. It was plain enough in the way she held your hand in the drawing room."

Darcy's eyes snapped to his cousin.

"Oh yes, Darcy—do not imagine that moment passed unnoticed. Nor was it lost on me how disappointed she looked when you clarified that your conversation with her father was not a proposal, as she had begun to hope."

He leant forward slightly, his tone softening.

"Had you made your offer then, I believe she would have accepted it. And if I had to guess, I would say a portion of her anger this afternoon stemmed from the belief that your interest was merely a matter of duty, born of the contract. I saw her expression after you left. For a moment, she struggled to keep her composure."

"Damn and blast," Darcy muttered. "There are days I curse my father's interference in this matter—even if the contract may now prove a solution to one of my present problems."

Fitzwilliam chuckled. "Miss Elizabeth is the least of your troubles at the moment. My father is, without question, the greatest. And you know as well as I do that Lady Catherine will have her say in all of this."

Darcy groaned. "Do not remind me. I have told her often enough that her ambitions were in vain, but she refuses to hear it. She has a singular talent for disregarding anything that contradicts her expectations. Neither my mother nor my father desired for me to marry my cousin as evidenced by the contract he *did* sign, but my aunt will not let the matter alone."

Fitzwilliam laughed outright at his cousin's expression. "Well, at least she may be the easiest to handle, considering that the contract overrides her claim that she and your mother had an agreement that you would marry Anne. Mother is already coming around to the idea of your Miss Elizabeth—which is no small feat, given they only met today. Give her another day or two and she will be singing your intended's praises."

He paused, amusement dancing in his eyes. "Or perhaps you should simply marry her at once. If the knot is already tied, it will be that much harder for anyone to object or for anyone to threaten her since I doubt you will let her out of your sight."

Darcy turned on him with a scowl. "You suggest we do what—marry in secret?"

Fitzwilliam leant back in his chair, arms crossed, thoroughly enjoying himself as he baited his cousin. "Why not? You are clearly devoted to her. She all but declared her feelings in front of half the drawing room when she hid your joined hands underneath her skirts. Had the others in the room seen the interaction, particularly her mother, she would have proclaimed your engagement to the entire room. I am afraid that the only people unaware of your attachment are those who choose not to see it."

Darcy gave him a withering look. "Marriage is not a matter to be rushed through like a battlefield dispatch, Richard. Elizabeth deserves better than to marry in secrecy and haste. She deserves a proper courtship, a proper proposal—and the freedom to refuse, if she wishes. I would not have her bound to me against her wishes."

"Of course you would not," Fitzwilliam said mildly. "I am only suggesting that time may not be on your side. If my father is half as determined as we believe—and if he suspects your feelings are fixed—he will do something. It is likely he will not act with the same regard for Elizabeth's well-being that you possess."

Darcy's jaw tightened. "Then I must act first, but not with deceit. If I am to marry her, it will be openly and with her full consent."

"I never suggested anything else." Fitzwilliam studied him for a moment, then gave a short nod. "Then do it soon, before the earl does more damage. After today, your Miss Elizabeth already knows your intentions. Ask her properly and let the rest of us deal with the fallout as you celebrate your bride."

After recounting her conversation with the Countess and Mr. Darcy to her father, Elizabeth withdrew to her room. The day's visit had been a whirlwind of highs and lows—Mr. Darcy's near-proposal, followed by the painful suspicion that his interest stemmed merely from a long-standing contract between their fathers, and then the moment of clarity when he had spoken—quietly but deliberately—of his feelings and his desire to marry her.

He had not said he loved her, but he had made it unmistakably clear that he cared.

Lying back on her bed, Elizabeth closed her eyes, letting the hush of her room soothe her while her mind returned to the conversation in the sitting room. In essence, he had offered hope—if not a proposal, then a promise of one. And the thought left her both thrilled and deeply unsettled.

Their acquaintance had been short—they had only officially met at the start of the previous month—but their relationship had grown in a way that seemed to defy time. From the very beginning, the conversation between them felt effortless. The letters they exchanged, although they had not written directly to each other, had given them a level of familiarity with each other that would not have been possible otherwise.

With the echo of his words still fresh in her memory and the warmth in his eyes lingering in her heart, Elizabeth could no longer deny what she felt.

She loved Fitzwilliam Darcy.

If his words held the truth she believed they did, he might very well love her in return.

A gentle knock stirred her from her reverie. Jane's voice followed, soft and hesitant. "Lizzy? May I come in?"

"Of course, Jane," Elizabeth replied, lifting herself from the bed and going to the door to let her sister in.

"Lizzy, what did you and Mr. Darcy speak about with Papa today?" she asked.

"There were several matters of business that we needed to discuss," Elizabeth evaded. "As you recall, Mr. Darcy went to see him first, and then he called for me and the colonel to join them."

Jane nodded slowly, a frown replacing the smile she had worn upon entering. "Oh," she said, her gaze dropping to her hands. "Papa joined Mr. Bingley and me while we walked. I thought it strange since I would have expected Papa to remain inside or to accompany you and Mr. Darcy. He seems to rather like Mr. Darcy."

"Did it trouble you that Papa followed along with you?" Elizabeth asked, tilting her head slightly.

"It surprised me," she said, exhaling slowly. "Even though Papa has changed so much over the last five years, I am sometimes still astonished when he acts as he did today On occasion, I have seen him watching me converse with Mr. Bingley, but today his attention was more marked than usual."

"What are your feelings towards Mr. Bingley?" Elizabeth asked.

Jane sighed. "I like him, Lizzy, but I am uncertain if what I feel for him is more than that. Perhaps it can grow into more, but we would need to spend more time together first. Most of our conversations have been superficial, and I do not feel that I know him very well yet."

"You will come to know him in time," Elizabeth reassured.

"What of you and Mr. Darcy?" Jane asked her sister.

Elizabeth felt her cheeks heating. "I like him very much, Jane," she confessed.

"Do you love him?"

"I think I do, Jane," Elizabeth replied. "He is so very good and kind, and I have enjoyed talking to him so much since he came to Hertfordshire. We seem to never run out of things to say to each other."

Jane looked at her sister in quiet surprise. "You have not known him long," she said gently, after a pause. "Are you certain you can feel so deeply, so soon?"

Elizabeth smiled, a little wistfully. "It may seem sudden, but it is not quite as brief as it appears. Mr. Darcy may have only been in Hertfordshire these past few weeks, but I first met him in September—before he ever came to Longbourn for that brief visit. Papa had been corresponding with him since the elder Mr. Darcy passed away."

She paused, her expression thoughtful as she tried to explain as much of the truth as she could. "I often read his letters aloud to Papa—and more than once, I helped to draft the replies. Over time, we even began adding brief personal notes to the ends of Papa's letters. Through those small exchanges, I began to form a sense of him—not just the dutiful master or an attentive correspondent, but the man himself. He is reserved, yes, but also intelligent, steady, and far more kind than I once assumed. By the time we met in person, I already knew something of his nature, and I believe that familiarity helped me to understand him far sooner than I otherwise would have."

"I did…I did not know," Jane stammered. She dropped her voice and whispered, "You exchanged notes with Mr. Darcy without Papa's knowledge?"

Elizabeth laughed. "No, Jane, Papa was aware of everything from the beginning. There was nothing clandestine about it—we never corresponded in secret, and there was certainly nothing improper in the letters. They were mostly about estate management, but we did mention a thing or two about books or philosophy. Nothing more."

Jane tilted her head, clearly intrigued. "Truly?"

Elizabeth smiled, her expression wistful. "Yes, truly. It was nothing at first—comments about an essay he had read, or a passage from Locke or Addison that struck him. But over time, I came to look forward to those lines. They revealed much about him, and while I thought nothing would ever come of it, I enjoyed exchanging these little pieces of information with him."

Jane's eyes searched her sister's face. "And now?"

Elizabeth hesitated, then nodded slowly. "I still enjoy speaking with him. We still talk of books and philosophy, and all the same things we spoke of in our letters."

Again, Elizabeth chuckled softly. "We have even discussed estate management—both here and at Pemberley. He spoke of it with ease as though he trusts my opinion. While he has not yet said the words aloud, I believe he means to. I am quite certain he has spoken with Papa, and I expect an offer will be made before long."

Jane reached for her hand, her voice soft with concern, but touched with hope. "Then I am glad for you, Lizzy. In private, Mama has made a few comments that made me think she believes the connection is unlikely because of Mr. Darcy's status in the *ton*, but I am not surprised. Perhaps at the speed, but, my dear sister, if you are certain of his heart—as well as yours—then I shall be happy for you."

Elizabeth gave her sister's hand a grateful squeeze. "I did not expect it either. But somehow, it feels right, as though it were fated to be."

CHAPTER 27
Meeting Wickham

Shortly after breakfast the following morning, Mrs. Bennet declared that she required a particular item from the haberdasher's and insisted that her four daughters go into the village to fetch it. Elizabeth would have preferred to wait until the party from Netherfield arrived, so they might walk together, but her mother would brook no delay.

The resulting party consisted of the four Miss Bennets, their companion, and the two footmen Mr. Darcy had sent to Longbourn the previous evening. Upon their arrival, Bennet had outfitted the men in plain livery, not wishing to invite questions as to why his daughters were accompanied by footmen in unfamiliar colours.

As the group went about their errand, they became aware of a marked increase in red coats among the villagers. The militia had clearly begun arriving in earnest. Having been warned by their father to avoid too much familiarity with the officers, the young ladies made no effort to approach any of them and, indeed, took pains to keep their distance.

That proved more difficult than expected.

As they exited the haberdasher's shop, they were met by none other than Sir William Lucas, who appeared to be introducing several militia officers to young men from the neighbourhood. Upon spotting the Bennet sisters, his face lit up.

"Ah! Before you, gentlemen, are some of the jewels of our county," he cried. "Come, Miss Bennet, and allow me to present you and your sisters to these fine officers of His Majesty's militia. You shall see much of them, I imagine—they are to be quartered here for the winter, and I am certain they will be attending many of our neighbourhood's events."

Reluctantly, the young ladies stepped forward, followed closely by their footmen whose watchful eyes did not waver from the officers.

Sir William beamed with importance as the young ladies approached. "Ah, splendid timing, ladies! Gentlemen, may I present Miss Bennet, Miss Elizabeth Bennet, Miss Mary Bennet, and Miss Catherine Bennet—four of the loveliest young ladies in all Hertfordshire. They are accompanied by their companion, Mrs. Graham."

He turned to the officers with a flourishing gesture. "Ladies, this is Captain Richard Carter, and Lieutenants Jonathan Sanderson and George Wickham."

Captain Carter and Lieutenant Sanderson bowed politely, murmuring appropriate pleasantries.

Lieutenant Wickham, however, took a step forward and offered Elizabeth a particularly warm smile as he singled her out for his attention. "Miss Elizabeth," he said, his gaze lingering, "a pleasure."

Elizabeth returned a restrained nod, her expression cool. "Lieutenant," she said evenly, her gaze flicking—just for a moment—towards the footman who had subtly stepped closer to her.

Sir William, oblivious to the shift in atmosphere, continued speaking with cheerful enthusiasm.

Behind them, the two footmen remained alert, their postures deceptively relaxed but their eyes sharp—especially on the officer who had so quickly singled out one of their charges.

"Did Sir William say your name was George Wickham?" Elizabeth asked, her tone light but unmistakably wary.

Wickham turned to her with an easy, bright smile, his posture effortlessly graceful. "Yes. Yes, he did."

He studied her face with interest. "Have we met before? I feel certain I would remember such a lovely face if we had."

Elizabeth's smile was polite at the fulsome compliment but remained distant and unaffected by his flirtations. "No, Lieutenant, I do not believe we have."

"Ah," he said, tilting his head. "Then perhaps it is merely that I feel I know you already."

Elizabeth arched her brow, unimpressed. "I cannot imagine how that would be possible."

Wickham let out a soft laugh as though she had said something delightfully clever. "It is only that your reputation precedes you, Miss Elizabeth. Sir William spoke of your wit and fine eyes before you arrived—and I can now say he did not exaggerate on either account."

Elizabeth did not acknowledge the compliment. "So, you are newly committed to the militia," she said instead, her tone returning to one of polite neutrality. "How do you expect to enjoy serving your country?"

Wickham nodded, sensing the shift in her tone but undeterred by her apparent disinterest. That, he was confident, would not last, for he had won over even more difficult ladies before.

"Indeed. I have only just joined the regiment here—Meryton is a welcome change. I was not always intended for military life, you know. I was once meant for the church." This he said as though inviting more questions, but when Elizabeth merely said nothing, he continued on with a light, self-deprecating laugh.

"However, things did not proceed as planned, and so—here I am. One learns to adjust and be happy in the face of difficulties."

His gaze lingered on her as he added, looking at Elizabeth in what could nearly be described as a leer, "The air, the quiet…this part of the world certainly has its charms."

Elizabeth's expression remained composed, though she inwardly shivered at his tone. "Are you already familiar with Hertfordshire, or is it all new to you?"

Wickham hesitated briefly, then shrugged, as if the matter were of little consequence. "Not particularly. I grew up in the north, in the Peak District. My path led elsewhere."

He cast a glance towards the horizon, his tone apparently reflective. "Hertfordshire is quite unlike Derbyshire, but I find it agreeable. A fresh start, in a peaceful place—there are worse fortunes."

She caught the careful phrasing but did not press him.

As the rhythmic sound of approaching hooves grew louder, Elizabeth glanced over her shoulder and saw Mr. Darcy and Mr. Bingley riding into the square.

Without hesitation, she stepped away, leaving Wickham without excusing herself, and moved directly into the path of the riders, forcing them to slow and dismount.

Darcy dismounted first and came to stand next to her.

"Mr. Darcy," she hissed, "I must warn you; George Wickham is here and has joined the militia that will be encamped here in Meryton for the autumn and winter."

Darcy stiffened at the mention of the name. "He is here? In Meryton?" he asked, his voice low and tight. "Did he speak to you?"

SPORT FOR OUR NEIGHBOURS

"Only briefly," Elizabeth replied. "He made a few vague remarks about past misfortunes, but—" she hesitated, clearly reluctant to say more, yet compelled to add, "I believe he singled me out quite deliberately. If I am not mistaken, he was attempting to flirt with me, or at least to ingratiate himself with me by flattering me."

Darcy's eyes flashed with anger, though his reply was measured. He gave a sharp nod. "I must inform Richard."

He turned—and at once caught sight of the remaining three Bennet sisters still engaged in conversation with Sir William where they were standing entirely too close to Wickham for his comfort.

From the expression on Wickham's face, it was clear he had seen Darcy. Judging by the smug curve of his smile, he had already guessed his presence would be unwelcome.

"Come," Darcy said, his expression darkening. "Let us see how he behaves now that he knows I am in the village. He will attempt to insinuate himself into others' good graces while casting me as the villain. While he fears Richard, I am afraid he has always seen me differently—perhaps because I once gave him too much grace, owing to our shared childhood."

He paused, his jaw tightening. "After Ramsgate, I warned him—if he crossed me again, I would call in every debt he owes. I confess, I am curious to see what he intends now," he added, his voice so low only Elizabeth could hear.

Offering his arm to her, he spoke with quiet urgency. "Bingley and I will escort you and your sisters home. I was already on my way to Longbourn to speak with your father—and now I must inform him of this as well. The merchants should be warned, and any father with daughters."

Glancing again towards Wickham, he murmured, "Richard can see to that. He is due to meet with the colonel of the regiment shortly. He did not accompany us this morning, but I must reach him before he encounters Wickham unprepared. It would be best if Wickham does not learn of his presence too soon."

With that, Darcy guided Elizabeth back towards her sisters. After exchanging a few quiet words with Bingley, he turned and began escorting the group in the direction of Longbourn. One of the footmen took the reins of both horses and, at Darcy's nod, mounted swiftly, riding ahead with Bingley's horse following behind.

THE REST OF THE PARTY HAD BEEN OBLIVIOUS TO THE TENSION Elizabeth and Darcy felt upon leaving Meryton. Only Mary noticed that her sister was uncomfortable in the presence of one of the officers, but she had not noted his name.

Jane and Catherine had been pleasantly conversing with Sir William and the other two gentlemen, while Mrs. Graham looked on. They failed to observe how Lieutenant Wickham had singled out Elizabeth, though the footmen, who had been instructed to keep a particular watch on her, had done so and remained cautious.

Regardless, Jane had been pleased with Mr. Bingley joining their group, and neither she nor Catherine had thought anything of it when Mr. Bingley offered to escort them home.

As the group made their way back towards Meryton, no one noticed that Darcy and Elizabeth had fallen slightly behind the others—or that the second footman followed the couple at a respectful distance, his attention sharply fixed on his surroundings.

The man's diligence allowed Darcy to relax somewhat, and despite the seriousness of their conversation, he found himself grateful for Elizabeth's company.

"I should very much have liked to see your sister," Elizabeth said softly, glancing ahead to ensure they would not be overheard, "but I am glad she did not accompany you today. It is better that she be forewarned about Mr. Wickham's presence."

Darcy exhaled heavily. "Indeed. Her presence would have made the encounter far more difficult. I am relieved he did not approach me directly, but the mere fact that he now knows I am here is troubling."

He paused, brow furrowed. "If, as we suspect, he and Lord Matlock are in league, then his arrival may not be a coincidence. He could have been sent—deliberately—to pressure me, to remind me of what is expected. Now that he has seen us together, I have no doubt he will report it to my uncle."

Blowing out a slow breath, Darcy took a moment to consider his words.

"Last night, Richard suggested that—were I already married—my uncle's threats would carry far less weight. But as we are not yet engaged, and have only touched on the subject briefly, I find myself uncertain how best to proceed."

He paused, then added in a rush, "I am not opposed to the idea—quite the opposite—but I would never wish to rush you or rob you of the sort of wedding you might have hoped for."

Elizabeth had stopped short in the middle of the lane, staring at him as he once again stumbled over his words.

"I beg your pardon?" she asked, utterly flummoxed by his statement.

Darcy briefly closed his eyes, feeling the heat rise at the back of his neck—no doubt turning his ears pink.

"Regardless of the contract our fathers signed, I am convinced that you are the only woman in the world who could truly induce me to marry. Others might serve as mistress of Pemberley, perhaps, but only with you can I imagine the joy, the partnership, the life I hoped marriage might bring."

He drew a slow breath before continuing, more carefully. "That said, I do not yet know what you feel. We have touched on the subject, but I had hoped to offer you the courtship you deserve—not one rushed, not one forced into secrecy. Certainly not a marriage we would be obliged to conceal."

Elizabeth blinked, her brow furrowed. "Why would we need to keep our marriage a secret? I do not understand your cousin's reasoning," she said. His words pleased her—but she could not quite untangle their meaning.

"I am not entirely certain I understood Richard's rationale for secrecy," Darcy admitted. "Perhaps he believed that if our marriage were not immediately known, we might observe the earl's actions to discern his intentions more clearly—and use that knowledge to neutralise whatever threats he might attempt against me or my family."

"Would not the announcement of our marriage be enough to stop his blustering?" Elizabeth asked. "Did you not say the countess would act to silence any rumours about Georgiana if necessary?"

Darcy nodded distractedly, murmuring, "I am not certain," before falling silent. At last, he turned fully towards her and took both her hands gently in his.

"Please, end my misery, Elizabeth," he said, his voice low but fervent. "This conversation has left me at sixes and sevens—we speak of marriage as if it is settled, yet as you rightly reminded me yesterday, you cannot answer until I have asked."

He drew a breath. "I am asking now—Elizabeth Bennet, will you marry me? Be my wife, the mistress of my home and of my heart. I…I love you. And I cannot imagine my life without you in it."

Elizabeth smiled, her eyes bright as she gently squeezed his hands.

"You wonderful man," she said, her voice warm with affection. "Of course I will marry you. Not because of any contract our fathers signed—but because I love you, too, Fitzwilliam Darcy."

Darcy pulled Elizabeth into a brief embrace, right there in the middle of the lane—unseen by anyone save the footman, who glanced away with a knowing grin.

After a moment, Darcy stepped back, but did not release her. Instead, he guided her hand to his arm and placed it gently at his elbow, covering it with his own. Their fingers twined together with quiet certainty, neither of them inclined to let go. Slowly, they resumed their walk towards Longbourn.

"My darling Elizabeth, you have made me the happiest man in all of England," Darcy said quietly.

Elizabeth grinned up at him. "So, how quickly ought we to wed?" she asked. "If we marry by common license, we can marry next week, and if need be, we can keep the matter quiet until you and your cousin feel it can be revealed."

Darcy shook his head. "If we marry in that way, we will be forced to be separated until it can be revealed. I would prefer not to wait to have you always at my side once you are mine. We can obtain the license as soon as may be, but we can wait to use it until it is necessary or you can plan the wedding you desire."

Laughing, Elizabeth stopped them again. "Certainly you know me well enough now to know that the details of the wedding are of less concern to me than they will be to my mother, Mr. Darcy. She is the one who would prefer to delay the wedding to make it into the grandest the village has ever seen. For myself, a simple wedding would do, with just my family and friends in attendance. I would like my Gardiner relations to be able to attend, but other than that, I think that all of those we hold most dear are already here."

Smiling broadly, Darcy gave Elizabeth's hand a tender squeeze before guiding them forward once more. "Yet another way you are ideally suited to me, dearest. However, I do have one small complaint to make."

He paused, waiting until she looked up at him again.

"My name is Fitzwilliam, Elizabeth—or William, if you prefer. My aunts call me Fitzwilliam, Georgiana calls me 'Brother,' and my male friends refer to me simply as Darcy. Only my mother ever called me William, and I think…I should very much like to hear that name from your lips."

"William," Elizabeth breathed, her voice soft as she tried out the new name.

Darcy drew in a sharp breath, as though the sound of it had struck him. It had been more than twelve years since anyone had spoken that name with such affection. Hearing it now, from her, was heady.

After a moment, he said quietly, "My only regret just now is that I proposed to you in the open where there is no place nearby for me to kiss you."

He glanced down at her with mock solemnity. "Perhaps your father might allow us the use of that little room beside his study once more. I would like to seal our promise in a far more agreeable way."

Elizabeth laughed, the sound light and happy. Darcy gave her a look of theatrical injury though his eyes danced.

"I love you, Elizabeth," he said again. "Promise me that you will always laugh, no matter what befalls us. I know that I can be far too solemn at times, but your laughter always improves my mood."

She smiled gently at him. "You have had to carry much weight, particularly since your father died," she said, seeing him nod in reply. "I would be delighted to bring happiness into your life, as well as, I hope, take some of your burdens. For years, I have done that for my father, and now I will do that for you."

CHAPTER 28

Discoveries

All too soon, the newly engaged couple arrived at Longbourn, and, instead of joining the others in the sitting room with Mrs. Bennet, they went directly to Bennet's study.

As soon as they entered, Bennet seemed to recognise what had happened.

"Ah, so you have finally gathered the nerve to ask, and I dare say, Lizzy has accepted," Bennet said by way of greeting. "However," he said again, looking at the pair, "I believe you have come to my study for more than simply that. Tell me, what occurred in Meryton for, as I recall, my daughters left not more than an hour ago and returned with not just one, but two gentlemen in tow."

"I will let William tell you everything, Papa," Elizabeth said. "I will go join the others so Mama does not speculate on the reason for both of us being in here with you."

Bennet raised his brow when Elizabeth referred to Darcy by his Christian name but said nothing. "I suppose it goes without saying that you have my permission to marry my daughter, much as I hate to lose her. Now, what is it that you need to tell me?"

"Wickham has joined the militia and is encamped here in Meryton," Darcy said without preamble. "He was introduced to your daughters this morning and singled Elizabeth out for his interest. She was uncomfortable with his attention, and she obviously knows he is not to be trusted. Richard will be working with Colonel Forster starting next week, but when I inform him of Wickham's presence here, he may wish to seek the man out sooner."

Darcy paused, his anxiety at this man's proximity coming back to him. "The additional footmen I requested arrived last night. With your approval, I would like to send additional men here for Elizabeth's protection. I understand you have sufficient staff, but mine are better trained—many of them are former soldiers, not typical footmen."

Bennet nodded at this. "Most of mine are younger men, the sons of my tenants or young men from the village and are solely trained as footmen. Perhaps, if you have enough men to teach some of mine some basic skills, all my daughters could be escorted wherever they go."

"We never had time yesterday to discuss what, if anything, you learnt from your brother in London," Darcy said. "I would like to understand what my uncle's purpose is in trying to force me to marry the viscount's daughter. My cousin suggested that, if I were to marry Elizabeth privately, and then let it be known, my uncle would have to back down, but I am unconvinced it can be that simple. While I would take Elizabeth as my wife as soon as you will allow it, I do not want to hurry it because of the threats. My uncle's obstinacy should not deprive Elizabeth of the wedding she wishes."

"Elizabeth will wish for a far simpler wedding than what my wife will feel necessary," Bennet said ruefully. "You would be doing both me and Elizabeth a favour to insist on a quick ceremony."

Darcy closed his eyes as he considered this. "Elizabeth said as much as well. When we leave, I will go straight to the church and obtain a common license. May I take the marriage contract with me to prove I have your permission, or would you prefer to simply write a note? Either way, I will ask your rector to keep the matter silent for now and inform him of the possible threat."

"I will write a note, lending credence to your request for secrecy," Bennet said. "While I write, read the letter I received yesterday afternoon from my brother and see if that tells you anything you do not already know. I also had a letter yesterday from Livesay, and he will arrive within a fortnight."

Accepting the letters Bennet handed him, Darcy settled into the comfortable chair beside the fireplace and began to read. He opened Livesay's letter first. It offered little beyond what they already knew though it did promise further explanation upon his arrival—expected either at the end of the week or early the next. Livesay was travelling with his younger son and his youngest daughter, a girl slightly older than Mary Bennet who had made her debut the previous spring.

Darcy remembered her well—a striking young woman with golden hair who had drawn no small amount of interest within the *ton*. Her dowry was said to rival Caroline Bingley's, yet Darcy recalled Miss Bingley declining her acquaintance, citing the young lady's lack of title and the modesty of her family's estate as reason enough to disregard her.

Shaking his head at the memory, Darcy turned to the second letter.

As he read, the colour drained from his face. The contents were troubling.

> *At present, Bennet, nothing can be confirmed. Whatever is taking place, it is conducted with such secrecy that few are privy to the truth. Still, rumours abound. Livesay may know more as the centre of activity appears to be near Lancashire. Much of it is masked as wool transport, which—as you know*

—is heavily regulated. Yet it seems there is something far more nefarious at play.

As I said, nothing is certain. My belief is that someone pays handsomely to keep it quiet—whether with coin or coercion. Most of my sources suggest the latter. Intimidation, it seems, is the currency of choice.

Bennet, I hesitate to put too much in writing, but there are whispers of something far beyond smuggling. It seems trade is being used as a front—wool and armaments, mostly—but some believe the goal is political influence, perhaps even control over military contracts. A few names have been mentioned, one in particular said to be facing ruin unless funds are secured in the new year.

If true, it explains the secrecy—and the intimidation. Those who ask questions tend to vanish from public life or quietly recant. Livesay may have more. For now, I urge caution. Keep your eyes open—and your daughters close.

Shaking his head as though to clear it, Darcy read through the letter a second time, much more slowly this time. When he reached the end, his jaw was tightly set and his fingers curled around the paper until he was forced to release them, so he would not crumple it.

"This is far worse than I anticipated," Darcy said quietly, noting that Bennet had finished writing and was now watching him closely. "If your brother is correct, we are facing more than a desperate bid for money. This is something else entirely—organized, deliberate, and, if true, not merely treasonous but a very real attempt to harm the monarchy."

He exhaled sharply, his expression grim. "I can only suppose that my uncle seeks to tie me to the viscount's family both to silence me and to gain access to my funds. Matlock is entailed—Pemberley is not. If he is as deeply involved as Gardiner implies, then my name and fortune offer both protection and legitimacy."

Darcy began to pace slowly towards the window. "Pemberley has flourished these past years, and my investments have yielded well. My uncle knows it. He may see me as a lifeline—one he means to secure through manipulation."

He stopped, arms folded tightly across his chest and stared out at the early twilight.

"Richard must be informed at once," he said, after a moment. "His suggestion that I marry Elizabeth quickly no longer seems rash—it may, in fact, be prudent. I know you have every reason to be protective of her. But if there is danger, I cannot remain at a distance. Not when I know she could be made a target."

He turned back to Bennet, his expression dark. "Wickham saw me today. He saw Elizabeth approach me, and he watched as I escorted her home. It will not take him long to deduce my feelings—and he will write to my uncle at once. As for Wickham…he would not hesitate to harm someone I care for if he believed it would injure me."

Bennet walked over to where Darcy stood. "Slow down, Darcy," he said. "What of the countess? Does she know any of this?"

Darcy shook his head. "No, she does not. I will ask her, if only to be certain, but if Lady Matlock knew anything of this, I believe she would have said so when we spoke to her earlier. Her father is the Earl of Coventry, and while I would not expect him to be directly involved, I do wonder if he understands where his money is going. He will not be pleased."

"This is a question for another day," Bennet replied, waving the matter aside. "What concerns me now is what you intend to do about Elizabeth's safety. With this Wickham fellow in Meryton and considering what he attempted with your sister last summer, I imagine you are just as worried for Georgiana."

Darcy rubbed a finger across his eyes, then pinched the bridge of his nose. "It would be far easier if all the relevant parties were in the same room at the same time as we discussed this. My aunt, my cousin, and Elizabeth all should be here—there is too much to coordinate and too much potential to miss critical details if we keep passing information back and forth. We must be careful; I am unwilling to speak at Netherfield, for there are too many ears there we cannot trust, but also, I do not want to raise suspicions if we meet here to talk. With neither option appearing without problems, I do not know how to have this conversation without fear of eavesdroppers—or unintended witnesses."

"Does your aunt ride?" Bennet asked.

Darcy raised a brow but nodded slowly.

"There is a cottage near the western boundary between Netherfield and Longbourn," Bennet said. "It has sat empty for years. My tenants know to leave it alone—Elizabeth and I use it from time to time when we need quiet. She often slips away there to read, always with a maid. I use it myself occasionally, when the house becomes…overfull."

Darcy narrowed his eyes. "What exactly are you suggesting?"

"Tomorrow morning," Bennet said evenly, "bring your aunt and your cousin to the cottage. I will bring Elizabeth. We can speak freely, out of sight and out of earshot, and decide what must be done. But for today—go home and tell your cousin about Wickham. From what I have seen of Colonel Fitzwilliam, I suspect he will handle the news better in private than in front of his mother and my daughter."

He gave Darcy a pointed look. "Let him cool his temper tonight, so that by tomorrow, we can all speak like rational creatures."

Chuckling at his wit, Darcy merely shook his head. "I will have to prise Bingley from your sitting room," Darcy said with a sigh. "For years, I have watched him flit from woman to woman. I fear that is what he is doing here and that, when another arrives, such as Miss

Livesay, his attention towards Miss Bennet will wane. I have warned him about this behaviour, and I specifically warned him against singling out any of the Bennet ladies and raising expectations he does not intend to meet. There have been too many other matters for me to broach this topic with Elizabeth. I will do so as soon as I am able, but I wanted to make you aware so you can decide what you wish to do."

"I am aware of his reputation and have been watching him when I can," Bennet replied. "My wife knows better than to push our daughters towards any gentleman, but I cannot vouch for what she says to her daughters in private. Before today is over, I will speak to both my wife and Jane and see what they have to say about the matter. Perhaps I ought to speak to Jane first to see what sort of impact this young man has already had upon her."

With this understanding, the two men moved together towards the sitting room and joined the ladies. Darcy had only a moment or two to whisper some private words to Elizabeth before he strongly encouraged Bingley that it was time to leave.

"Come, Bingley, let us return home," Darcy had said. "It would not do for us to outstay our welcome, and I have matters I need to discuss with my cousin."

Frowning, Bingley reluctantly agreed, but not without issuing an invitation to dinner on Monday. "My aunt suggested it but had not fixed a date before we left Netherfield. I will confirm that there is no difficulty with Monday night and send word to Mr. Bennet."

"Thank you, Mr. Bingley," Mrs. Bennet gushed. "We would be delighted to accept your aunt's kind invitation."

That done, the two gentlemen took their leave and turned towards Netherfield across the fields, deliberately avoiding the village of Meryton at Darcy's suggestion. Sending Bingley on ahead, Darcy paid a quick call to the Longbourn chapel, not far from the estate, to present Bennet's letter to the rector and begin the process for a common license for him and Elizabeth to wed.

CHAPTER 29

A Confrontation

When Bingley found his aunt and sisters gathered in the small sitting room near the music room, the scent of tea and Miss Bingley's perfume hung in the air, barely masking the chill that seemed to have settled between the ladies. His aunt was seated nearest the hearth, a bit of needlework untouched in her lap, her sharp eyes watching Caroline with something bordering on disgust, while Mrs. Hurst idly played with her bracelets, a habit of hers when she was nervous.

He cleared his throat and said, rather too cheerfully, "I have invited the Bennets to dine with us on Monday evening."

Aunt Horatia did not attend him at first. Then, with a resigned smile, she said, "Well, now that it is done, it would be awkward to withdraw. Monday night will suffice though I might have preferred a few more days to settle in. Still, Mrs. Nicholls is quite capable, and I believe we shall manage well enough between us."

Across the room, seated with her back too straight by the window, Miss Bingley let out an audible scoff. "I daresay whatever arrangements you make will be more than adequate—for *them*," she said, setting down her teacup with a deliberate clatter. "That family can hardly be accustomed to true refinement. They will likely be beside themselves simply to enter this house—again."

She tossed her head and looked out the window, her expression tight with disdain. Her voice dripped with petulance, and her meaning could not have been clearer.

Aunt Horatia's voice cut through the room like a snapped ribbon. "Caroline, that is quite enough."

Miss Bingley froze, then slowly turned in her chair, clearly startled by the censure.

Aunt Horatia continued, her tone cutting and brooking no dissent. "Once again, I will remind you that the Bennets are landed gentry. That places them *above* you in standing. What *were* they teaching you at that finishing school?"

Miss Bingley flushed at yet another reminder of her status. "I simply fail to see why we must *fawn* over a family so dreadfully provincial."

"You will see it, or you will *learn* it," Aunt Horatia said flatly.

Rising in a theatrical flounce, Miss Bingley adjusted her gown as though the mere presence of this conversation offended her sensibilities. "If you are all so fond of them, perhaps you should invite them to stay at Netherfield permanently," she muttered, and she swept from the room in a rustle of silk and wounded pride. "The countess will be so *delighted* with their company."

With that parting shot, she swept from the room.

"That girl," Aunt Horatia said sharply, watching the door swing closed behind her, "needs to be taken down a notch or two. But she will never learn if no one addresses her behaviour." She turned on Bingley. "Confine her to her room. Dock her allowance. Send her away if you must. But *do not* let her continue to spew that vitriol. I understand her motivation—envy—but she refuses to see reason. I have *seen* how you

SPORT FOR OUR NEIGHBOURS

look at Miss Bennet. Would you really subject her sweetness to that... that harpy?"

Mrs. Hurst, silent until now, folded her hands in her lap. "Our mother spoiled her terribly," she said quietly. "Caroline cannot bear being denied anything. She came here hoping to ensnare Mr. Darcy. When he made it clear he had no interest—none whatsoever—she grew spiteful. She pretends now that *he* is beneath *her*, but she cannot abide the thought of him preferring someone else. If he were to show true interest in Miss Elizabeth, I fear how Caroline will act."

"She may have been spoiled by your mother," Aunt Horatia replied coolly, "but your mother has been gone for years. My brother did her no favours in her upbringing. Neither of you," she added pointedly, looking between Mrs. Hurst and Bingley, "have done anything to correct her?"

Turning to Mrs. Hurst, she asked bluntly, "Did you know of this plan to entrap Mr. Darcy?"

Mrs. Hurst lowered her eyes. "I did try to dissuade her, but not as firmly as I ought. She was obsessed with the idea of becoming Mrs. Darcy. No argument would sway her."

"With the countess now here," Aunt Horatia said grimly, "Caroline would be wise to check her pride. That woman does *not* approve of your sister. It would take little for her to spread word in London about what she has seen—and heard. Even you must admit, Caroline is no better than a fortune-hunter. Mr. Darcy, I assure you, has learnt to spot such women with ease."

Mrs. Hurst gave another reluctant nod.

"She does not listen to me any more than she listens to Louisa," Bingley said, his voice low and sulky. "I tried speaking with her just last week."

"Then perhaps stop speaking and *do* something," his aunt said coldly.

"Establish rules. Deduct funds from her allowance. She has made a fool of herself—and of you—and still you hand her more money?"

"She asked for her quarterly funds in coin," Bingley muttered. "I gave her over two hundred pounds from the safe. She said she preferred coin to letters of credit. I assume she had her reasons, but I did not question her."

Aunt Horatia stared at him. "You gave her two hundred pounds without asking *why*?"

"She is entitled to it," he said defensively. "I could not see the harm in giving her what she wished in this case."

"Then open your eyes," Aunt Horatia snapped. "She disdains everything about this village. She scoffs at your guests. What do you imagine she needed *coin* for, Charles? To donate to the church? To spend money in Meryton's shops, which she thinks cannot possibly be the equivalent of those in London? Mayhap she means to return to London."

"She would never spend her own money to return to London," he muttered. "She says it is too vulgar to arrange one's own travel. Were she to return, she would insist upon a carriage from my stables."

"She did go into the village yesterday," Mrs. Hurst said quietly. "When we returned from Longbourn, I saw her just coming in—her pelisse slightly askew, her reticule clutched tightly. I asked where she had gone, but she said nothing. Her maid offered no explanation. But one of the grooms mentioned to Mr. Hurst that she was seen speaking to militia officers in the street."

Aunt Horatia's face turned to stone. "Why in God's name would she do *that*?"

"I do not know," Bingley said, bewildered.

"Although she thought I could not hear, she said clearly enough: if she cannot have Darcy, she will not let another woman have him either,"

Aunt Horatia said grimly. "Two hundred pounds is more than enough to bribe someone into a foolish—or ruinous—act. One sister compromised, and the others would bear the stain. Caroline may think such a scandal would be enough to turn Mr. Darcy's affection from Miss Elizabeth."

Bingley stared at her. "She may be unpleasant at times, but she would not go so far as to destroy another woman."

Mrs. Hurst coughed delicately. "She has whispered rumours in the past about ladies she feared might gain Darcy's interest—small insidious things, just enough to muddy their reputations."

"It is society's way," Bingley mumbled. "Ladies gossip. It is not the same as arranging…ruin."

"You are correct," Aunt Horatia said icily, rising from her seat. "They are not the same. It is far *worse* to arrange for the ruin of another."

Pacing the room, she considered the different possibilities. Her youngest niece had become vindictive and cruel, and if she would whisper rumours about a woman to deflect Mr. Darcy's attention, it would not be too much of a step to think of ruining someone. It would not take much to injure a family's reputation. Merely a whisper of wrongdoing could potentially harm the entire family.

"We need to discover which officers she spoke with," Aunt Horatia said after a few minutes. "Does Gilbert recall which groom?" she asked her elder niece.

Mrs. Hurst shook her head in response but said nothing.

"Charles, you must do something to ensure that Caroline cannot cause anyone actual harm," Aunt Horatia said. "I do not care if that means you must restrict her to her rooms until we discover what she is about, but she needs to be contained. Tell the grooms not to ready a horse or a carriage for her without notifying you first. Someone ought to watch her, to ensure she does not meet with any of the officers again in case she does intend to arrange something."

"She will be unbearable to live with if I do any of those things," Bingley sighed.

"If you do nothing, your inaction may well cost you Mr. Darcy's friendship," Aunt Horatia said sharply. "I will speak to the countess about what we have learnt so she may take whatever measures are necessary to protect the Misses Bennet. You may be certain she will inform Mr. Darcy and the colonel as well. Can you truly imagine how any of them will react if it becomes clear that you allowed your sister to deliberately harm innocent young women—and did nothing to stop her? At the very least, Mr. Bennet is a friend of Mr. Darcy's. Even if Mr. Darcy has no firm intention of offering for Miss Elizabeth, it is difficult to believe he would look kindly upon a man who stood by while the reputation of an entire family was ruined—particularly when he might have prevented it."

"What would you have me do?" Bingley asked again.

Aunt Horatia shook her head at her nephew's ineffectualness. "Start with informing the servants she is not to venture into the village unaccompanied. Tell the grooms they are not to saddle a horse or ready a carriage at her order. Who pays for her maid?"

"I do," Bingley answered.

"Then tell her you expect her to keep you informed of any of Caroline's actions," Aunt Horatia told him. "If you are paying her salary, she owes *you* her loyalty, not Caroline."

Bingley attempted another half-hearted protest. "She will be angry if she finds out."

"So?" his aunt retorted.

Hanging his head, Bingley gave in. "I will see what can be done without Caroline's knowledge. As you suggested, I will start by speaking to the grooms and save Caroline's maid for later. However, I doubt I will be able to get the funds back from her."

He exited the room, followed a moment after by Mrs. Hurst, who had been silent for the last portion of the discussion. *At least she seems to realise her own complicity in Caroline's behaviour,* Aunt Horatia thought as she watched her niece and nephew depart.

Scowling at her nephew's lack of resolve, she was faintly gratified to see him taking at least a few necessary steps to check his younger sister. To his credit, his first and most sensible act had been to relinquish the running of the household; she meant to discover precisely how that decision had come about. She suspected Darcy's influence though it seemed whatever firmness had prompted the change had since waned. Still, it was a beginning, however belated.

Settling back into her chair, Aunt Horatia fixed her gaze on the now-closed door. No one in the Bingley family had ever truly checked Caroline. She had been allowed whatever she wished, first by her mother, then by her father—whose indulgence stemmed from a misplaced guilt over the early loss of her mother. Charles lacked the firmness, and Louisa the inclination, to correct her. Unchallenged, Caroline had grown into a woman who mistook manipulation for charm and scorn for discernment.

She would have to be handled carefully. Public humiliation had made her vicious, and any further direct rebuke might drive her to reckless extremes. What Caroline required was someone who could take charge of her—someone capable of imposing limits she could neither ignore nor twist to her advantage. Removing her from society entirely might cause a minor scandal, but Caroline was not well enough liked within the *ton* for it to leave any lasting damage. Some might even applaud them for it.

Aunt Horatia decided she would need to speak to Mr. Darcy. She suspected he had been the impetus behind Charles's decision to invite her there and to install her as temporary mistress of Netherfield. Lady Matlock might also be enlisted—her title carried weight with her niece, and she had already demonstrated a lack of patience for Caroline's pretensions. If Caroline could not be made to behave, then she would simply be given no opportunity to behave poorly at all.

Her lips pressed into a thin, resolute line. She would not sit idly by while her niece jeopardised the reputation of one of the Bennet girls—and, by extension, the entire family. It was high time someone reminded Caroline Bingley what it meant to conduct oneself with sense—and to enforce consequences for her poor behaviour.

CHAPTER 30

Defensive Tactics

18 OCTOBER 1811

As planned, Lady Matlock joined her son and nephew on their early morning ride. The air was crisp and still, the last of the morning mist curling along the hedgerows as they made their way towards the small, secluded cottage that marked the border between Netherfield and Longbourn. It was not long before they spotted horses already tethered and patiently cropping the sparse grass while the footmen stood guard nearby, their eyes alert. One nodded at the colonel and Darcy in recognition.

The door opened before they could dismount fully.

"Good morning, Lady Matlock, Colonel, Mr. Darcy," said Bennet with a polite nod, stepping aside to admit them. "We arrived a short while ago. My men lit the fire and Lizzy has hot tea waiting as well as a few scones and pastries."

Once everyone was seated in the various chairs scattered around the room and had taken their choice of refreshments, Lady Matlock offered her appreciation. "Thank you, Mr. Bennet," Lady Matlock stated, smiling at the gentleman. "This repast was most thoughtful of you and quite fits our early morning conclave."

"Yes, well, it was Lizzy's suggestion," Bennet said with a laugh. "Such a thought would have never occurred to me as necessary."

"Then, thank you, Miss Elizabeth," Lady Matlock said with a gracious smile. "I have always said that a good hostess never relies on others to ensure things are arranged as they ought to be. You will make an excellent mistress of an estate one day."

Elizabeth smiled her thanks, flushing slightly at the praise, but before any more could be said, the colonel turned the conversation towards its intended topic.

"What do you know of Father's business dealings, Mother?" Richard asked curtly. "We have little time this morning, and I am reluctant to leave Georgiana alone too long—especially if Miss Bingley decides to attempt to confide some untruths to her."

The countess's expression hardened. "I know very little, I am afraid. My father cannot possibly know the extent to which Matlock is draining funds. If he suspected even half of what your father is rumoured to be involved in, he would sever all contact—and all financial support—at once. If he had any proof of treasonable activity…" She exhaled slowly. "He would not hesitate to see my husband hanged and damn the consequences."

Darcy crossed his arms, his voice cool. "That may be reassuring in principle, but it does little to help us understand *what* my uncle is doing—or *why* he feels the need to blackmail me into marrying the viscount's daughter. We need the specific details about what he is involved in so we can take steps to circumvent him."

Lady Matlock sighed. "I have written to the servants at Matlock House, the housekeeper and butler in particular, to see what they may know. My husband can be careless with his papers at times, but few are allowed into his study. Only the housekeeper enters that room to clean, and only for a certain few hours each week. It is possible she knows something but is too afraid to write to me directly."

"That is something, at least," Fitzwilliam said in a low tone.

"What about my uncle's blackmail attempt?" Darcy asked, taking Elizabeth's hand in his. "I have asked Elizabeth to marry me, Aunt, and while I wish to give her the courtship and engagement period she deserves, Richard suggested that a quick, secret wedding might thwart the plans of those who would cause us harm. If we were married, this scheme between my uncle and the viscount would be circumvented. However, we must consider that he might still take action against me or my family in that case, but my marriage to her will allow me to keep her safe."

"I will take steps to ensure he cannot harm you or Elizabeth," Lady Matlock said, her tone firm with resolve. "But we must also consider how to protect Georgiana. Any scandal tied to her name could be disastrous, not just to her reputation, but to her confidence. She is still recovering from the events of the summer. Should the details of Ramsgate be released, particularly anything that could construe her actions as scandalous, or, worse, exaggerations and outright ruinous lies, she would have to start the whole process of healing over."

After a moment of thought, she spoke again. "Once I make my approval of your match known in town, my husband will have little choice but to offer public support. To do otherwise would make him appear a fool—and he cares far too much for his reputation to risk that. We also may be able to pre-empt any rumours he attempts to spread about Georgiana before they take hold."

The room had fallen utterly still. A low fire crackled in the hearth, warming the cool room, providing the only sound in the heavy pause that followed her words. Darcy's brow furrowed in concern, but he still gave a short nod.

"As much as I dislike dissembling, we must do what we can to protect my sister from gossip," he said. "However, at the moment, I am more concerned about the potential danger presented by Wickham's presence in Meryton than the gossip my uncle may or may not spread in town. Richard—were you able to speak with Colonel Forster without drawing attention?"

Fitzwilliam's expression darkened. He leant forward, his voice low and grim. "Yes. I sent a note, and we met in secret. Forster has agreed to keep a close watch on Wickham. We plan to catch him off guard when I report to the camp on Monday."

Darcy's jaw clenched.

"Wickham's enlisting in the militia has consequences he may not have realized." Fitzwilliam continued. "He cannot leave the area now without facing punishment. If he disappears, he will be declared absent without leave. In that circumstance, I will see to it personally that he is found. The penalty could be the noose—or a firing squad." The look that crossed his face was ugly, and reminded those present that this man was a soldier who had faced more than anyone there could imagine.

A tense silence followed, the weight of the implications of his words settling over the group like a pall. Elizabeth, seated beside Darcy, drew in a quiet breath, her fingers tightening slightly around his.

Fitzwilliam's voice hardened. "Frankly, I consider both punishments far too merciful. I would rather see him sent to the Peninsula—into real battle. I would relish watching his bravado crumble under cannon fire."

Elizabeth drew in a quiet breath at this, seeking her intended's eyes. Their gaze locked, and after a moment, she again drew in a steadying breath before she spoke, her voice quiet but firm.

"That is surely possible," Elizabeth continued, "But I think we must first try to discover what he may be about and whether he is in contact with Lord Matlock."

"Richard, can you set a man whose primary responsibility will be to watch him?" Darcy suggested, drawing Elizabeth's hand to his lap and idly caressing it. "Perhaps even befriend him to see if he will reveal his plans in time."

"I will certainly enlist one of the officers to watch him, but it is possible that he has already notified Father not only of your presence here, which Father already knew, but also about your connection to Elizabeth. You said, Darcy, that you were not discreet when you spoke to her nor when you escorted her home, so Wickham is already aware of your preference for her," Fitzwilliam replied. "He will likely have already written to Father about it, if the two are working together as we suspect."

Bennet, who had been listening to this exchange and watching closely the interactions between Darcy and his second daughter, caught Darcy's eye before clearing his throat and looking pointedly at Elizabeth's hand enclosed within her intended's.

Seeing this, Darcy almost released it, but Elizabeth tightened her grip slightly which seemed to strengthen Darcy's resolve. Instead, he raised his brow at his future father and did nothing.

Leaning back in his chair, Bennet glared at the man a moment longer before shrugging his shoulders.

Having remained silent until this point, Bennet shifted in his seat and cleared his throat once more. "It seems this Wickham fellow leaves a trail of harm wherever he goes," he said, his tone more serious than usual. "I cannot pretend I understand the full extent of it, but you have told me enough, Darcy, that I am concerned about what he might try. He has only been in the area a few days, but it is possible from what you've said of him that he is already up to his usual habits and has begun to accumulate debts. Could we not use that to our advantage to find a way to muzzle him?"

He looked towards his daughter. "Given the connection between the Darcy family and our own, any harm done to one will inevitably reflect upon both. If there is a way to outmanoeuvre him and prevent any harm before it takes root, then the sooner it is done, the better for all of us."

Darcy inclined his head, his expression grave. "I could not agree more, sir. This is no longer a matter of family pride or personal grievance—it is a question of protection. Georgiana must be shielded, and so must Elizabeth."

He glanced towards his cousin, then to Lady Matlock, before his gaze returned to Bennet. "Whatever actions we take towards either Lord Matlock or Wickham, I refuse to act in haste—but I *will* act. He has had far too many opportunities to slip through the cracks. That ends now. Richard, what do you suggest we do?"

"You have already sent for some of your men from London to increase the guard around both Georgiana and Miss Elizabeth," Fitzwilliam said. "If Wickham tries to spread damaging stories about Georgiana, we need a way to quietly discredit him first. Bennet's idea of investigating his debts is a good place to start. Father may have given him some money, but Wickham never pays for anything he can charm someone into giving him. He likes to keep his cash for more indulgent uses—not for something practical like the well-tailored militia coat he has already bought."

Fitzwilliam continued with a sneer. "Wickham has always been vain and demanded the best, whether or not he could afford it."

Darcy nodded. "He has been in the area less than a week, but I have seen him fall into debt in even less time—especially debts of honour. He was a reckless card player at university and never knew when to stop. Some of the officers might demand coin, but many will be easily convinced he is good for it, especially if he has already begun his campaign against me."

Bennet leant in, steering the conversation in a new direction. "While we are keeping an eye on Wickham, my brother Gardiner is continuing to look into Lord Matlock's affairs. I will let you know as soon as we learn anything more from London. That said, Darcy, you mentioned hiring your own investigator which I think is wise. The more people involved, the better."

He turned to the countess. "Countess, I know you do not have much contact with your husband, but if word starts spreading in London about his activities—especially with the suspicion of smuggling—how badly would it affect your reputation?"

The countess frowned thoughtfully. "Less than it might have a few years ago. Those closest to me are well aware of how rarely I spend time with my husband, and how I detest his habits. No one would be surprised if I stayed with a friend, took up residence at Darcy House for the Season, or simply returned to my father's home for a time."

She paused, considering further. "If the worst were to happen, I could easily distance myself from him—and let it be known there has been a formal break between us. It would cause a scandal, of course, but it would also protect my reputation if he were to be charged with criminal activity."

"You can begin to let it be known that you are spending the autumn with me in Hertfordshire," Darcy suggested. "Perhaps even begin to lay the groundwork for my marriage to Elizabeth amongst your friends and let it be known that you approve of the match. If you could mention that Georgiana is with you, and has been since the summer, it would cause many to question anything that may be said about her. It is a small falsehood, but if people believe she has been with you all summer, it will be more difficult for any of the accusations about Ramsgate to land."

Lady Matlock nodded. "I have already taken a few steps towards that end. Although I never lied outright, I may have implied that I was in Ramsgate with Georgiana when I was visiting a friend not far from there. Darcy, did you ensure that neither Mrs. Younge nor any other of the servants would spread rumours about Georgiana?"

Darcy nodded. "Yes," he replied. "Those closest to her were well paid for their silence. Mrs. Younge knows that it would not be to her advantage if she were to speak out against my sister, no matter if Wickham might attempt to convince her otherwise. While, like you, Aunt, I try to stick as close to the truth as possible, I did employ a few small falsehoods to protect my sister's reputation. We must concern ourselves only with Wickham and any rumors my uncle might attempt to spread."

"Let us return to the matter of Elizabeth and Darcy marrying," Bennet said. "Darcy, would Mr. Bingley be able and willing to keep it quiet for now? If so, we could come up with a reason for Elizabeth to remain at Netherfield for a time. But if we want to keep the marriage secret, we must avoid discussing it in front of my wife."

Darcy shook his head. "I trust Bingley, but I cannot say the same for his sister. Miss Bingley is displeased with me and would make things as difficult as possible if she found out. If anyone in that household could be relied upon to keep the matter confidential, it would be Miss Horatia Bingley."

"She strikes me as a very matter-of-fact woman, and quite capable of keeping her niece in line," Lady Matlock said. "However, it will take time to bring a woman like Miss Bingley to heel. At present, I suspect something is stirring with Miss Bingley, given her persistent efforts to ingratiate herself with me and my family. Both Fitzwilliam and I have given her little encouragement, yet she continues in her attempts. I am almost as concerned about Miss Elizabeth spending time in her company as I am about her being near Wickham."

"Perhaps we should all remove directly to London, even Pemberley," Bennet suggested, with his typical sardonic humour. "Once Elizabeth and Darcy marry, we can all retreat to a location where none are there who wish us harm."

Darcy grimaced. "That does sound appealing, but it hardly seems fair to Elizabeth."

Elizabeth squeezed his hand, then shook her head firmly, her eyes steady and clear. "I have no objection to marrying William soon—

quietly, without all the spectacle Mama would demand—but I have no intention of hiding away as though we have something to be ashamed of. These people who would do us harm must be confronted—each one of them, individually if necessary, and their threats against us eradicated."

Fitzwilliam let out a low whistle and grinned. "You would have made an excellent soldier, Miss Elizabeth. Are you sure you have chosen the right Fitzwilliam? With you beside me, I would be promoted to general in no time, and you could bark orders to a whole regiment of men eager to obey your every word."

Darcy frowned at the jest, but Elizabeth only laughed, a warm, bright sound. "Tempting as that is, I am afraid your cousin has already won me over. Much as I might enjoy commanding a regiment, or even a battalion, it is not quite enticing enough to cause me to abandon him for the glory of military life."

CHAPTER 31

Sweet Williams

The group spent the next half hour discussing further details surrounding Elizabeth and Darcy's impending wedding as well as plans to ensure the continued safety of both Elizabeth and Georgiana.

At length, they parted ways—Fitzwilliam escorting his mother back to Netherfield, while Darcy accompanied Elizabeth on the walk back to Longbourn, arm in arm. Bennet had ridden ahead, taking their horses with him, leaving the pair with a rare opportunity for private conversation.

"I know you have said more than once that you do not care how the wedding is conducted," Darcy began again, his brow furrowed as they walked, "but can you truly be content with a rushed ceremony kept secret from nearly everyone for an indefinite period of time?"

Elizabeth smiled, the amusement in her eyes softening the firmness of her voice. "It is not how I imagined it, no. But truly, the only part that matters is marrying *you*." A laugh slipped from her lips at the sight of his small smile her words evoked. "Of course, I would prefer something more open—and to live under the same roof once we are wed—but we both know there are matters to resolve first. Whatever the earl is entangled in is only part of it. Until things are settled, our marriage at least grants us some protection from the plots that appear to be surrounding us."

Darcy gave a groan, though the corners of his mouth tugged upward. "Must you always be so reasonable, Elizabeth? Must you give me hope precisely when I would prefer to dwell on the impediments?"

Her laughter answered him.

He continued, his tone more playful now, lightened by her laughter and presence next to him. "I had few expectations about marriage, but I certainly never imagined beginning it separated by three miles, forced to suffer in Miss Caroline Bingley's company, when all I wish is to lock myself away in my chambers with my wife."

His candour caught them both off guard. A blush rose on his cheeks as he realized what he had said aloud, and Elizabeth's colour deepened to match. The heat of it surprised her—not just from his words, but from the emotions they stirred within her.

She might have known only a little about what passed between husband and wife, but her Aunt Gardiner had been forthright with both her and Jane when they entered society. Now, with Darcy's desire plainly voiced, she found herself unexpectedly—and undeniably—eager for what lay ahead.

"If nothing else, there is always the cottage," she blurted, flushing again at the thought of arranging for an assignation, even if the man would be her husband. "Never mind that now," she said again, shaking off these thoughts, as she attempted to return to the subject at hand. "You have already arranged for the license?" she asked.

"I have."

"Then we can marry at the end of next week or early the following week," she replied. "It will be Papa's business to worry about what Mama might say or do, and he will need to keep her silent. While perhaps it does not matter, not really, if the people in Meryton know of our wedding, the more who know, the more difficult it will be to keep the news away from the two with whom we do need to concern ourselves."

"Yes," Darcy agreed. "It is imperative that neither Miss Caroline Bingley nor Wickham learn of it. That means I cannot tell Bingley either, but I believe Miss Horatia Bingley could be trusted to keep the matter a secret though I suggest we not tell her unless it becomes necessary for some reason."

"What of Georgiana?" Elizabeth asked gently.

Darcy exhaled, his expression tight. "I have been reluctant to tell her any of this, but I know I cannot delay much longer. It would be better for her to hear it from us directly than to be startled by a careless remark or stray bit of gossip."

He paused, then looked at Elizabeth. "Will you be with me when I speak to her? She will take it better with you there—or rather, you will explain it more clearly, and with less…unintended alarm. You have seen how easily I can make a muddle of things when I try to explain them."

Elizabeth laughed. "Yes, that is probably for the best," she agreed. "Perhaps tomorrow you and she can take a ride which ends at Longbourn. Or, I can meet the two of you at the cottage as we did this morning, accompanied by my minders, of course." This last was said with a teasing lilt, and Darcy smiled at her once again.

The rest of the walk to Longbourn passed swiftly, their conversation drifting between concern for Georgiana and the quiet joy of imagining the life that awaited them once their union could be openly acknowledged. Elizabeth found herself increasingly enchanted by her intended—not only by his evident devotion to his sister, but also by the flashes of dry humour that emerged when he allowed himself to relax.

He was, perhaps, a touch overprotective of Georgiana, treating her more like a daughter than a sister—a tendency likely born of their age difference and his deep sense of responsibility. But even before they were wed, he was already treating Elizabeth as his equal, listening to her thoughts with genuine attention. With time and her influence, she felt certain he could learn to treat Georgiana more as a sister, bridging the years between them with affection rather than solemn duty.

In some ways, it felt strange, and yet utterly natural, to speak of a future together—as husband and wife, partners in every sense. She caught herself smiling often as she considered this. If this was only the beginning, she could hardly wait to see what came next for them when they would arrive at Pemberley, whenever that would occur.

As Longbourn came into view through the thinning trees, Darcy slowed his steps. Then, quite suddenly, he released their linked arms and instead, grasped her hand and gently drew her off the main path, behind a small copse of trees that stood just far enough from the house to shield them from view.

He turned to her, still holding her hand, and she saw the intensity in his gaze shift—no longer just thoughtful, but openly tender.

"My dearest, loveliest Elizabeth," he said softly, his voice low and slightly roughened, "we have been engaged these four and twenty hours, and I have yet to kiss you as I wish."

Elizabeth felt her breath catch. There was something unguarded in his words, a glimpse of the longing he had been holding back. She recognized it—because she felt it, too.

Smiling, and feeling strangely breathless, she teased gently, "Have you been suffering terribly?"

He stepped closer, his eyes fixed on hers. "You have no idea."

His hand lifted, his fingertips brushing lightly along her jaw before curving behind her neck, reverent and unhurried. She seemed to feel his touch everywhere though his hand barely moved; she felt the steadiness of his breath, the warmth of his palm, the slow, inevitable closing of distance between them.

When his lips met hers, they were not hesitant nor timid. His kiss was reverent, a promise and a confession. Elizabeth leant into him, her free hand rising instinctively to rest against his chest where she could feel the rapid thrum of his heartbeat under her palm.

The world slipped away. There was only the quiet rustling of leaves overhead and the dizzying sweetness of his mouth on hers.

When they finally parted, it was only by a breath. His forehead rested gently against hers, and she realized she was smiling—helplessly, joyfully.

"I've imagined this moment often," he murmured, his thumb gently tracing the curve of her cheek. "But I never dreamed it would feel like this…my Elizabeth."

She pulled back just enough to meet his gaze, her voice soft, filled with quiet wonder. "Nor did I…my William."

His smile deepened, as he whispered in reply. "Yes, dearest Elizabeth. I am yours."

The family was seated at breakfast when they entered, met by nothing else than a raised brow from her father at the lateness of their arrival and obvious glow on her cheeks. Elizabeth shrugged slightly at him, and while he seemed to glare behind her at Darcy, he still did not say anything.

"Mr. Darcy," Mrs. Bennet said a moment later, unaware of the exchange between father and daughter. "Mr. Bennet said he and Elizabeth encountered you on their ride and that you would join us for breakfast this morning."

She looked at the couple expectantly, but they did not satisfy her curiosity.

"Thank you, Mrs. Bennet," Darcy replied. "Did you intend to call at Netherfield today? I believe I heard my aunt and Bingley's speaking of your coming, but perhaps I am mistaken, and it was tomorrow."

"Oh," she gasped, before collecting herself and continuing, "Yes, well, I had intended to return their call soon. I had not thought about going today, but if you say it is expected..." she trailed off, her surprise clear on her face.

"My aunt was quite complimentary of Longbourn yesterday," Darcy replied before seemingly running out of praises himself. He turned to greet the rest of Elizabeth's sisters and soon found himself seated next to Elizabeth at the table, a plate full of food in front of him. Without a word, Elizabeth prepared him a cup of coffee, exactly as he liked it, and sat it in front of him.

Under the table, he squeezed her hand, showing his appreciation.

"Mama is beside herself," she whispered. "She has seen enough to suspect something, particularly Papa leaving the two of us behind to return to Longbourn on foot, but she knows that he will not appreciate it if she speaks out of turn."

"What will he tell her?" he asked, following her lead and keeping his voice low.

"I am not sure," she admitted. "I will speak to him after we finish eating and explain what we talked about." She paused, her cheeks warming as she dropped her gaze. "Well...perhaps not *everything* we talked about," she added, a quiet giggle escaping her—just enough to draw the attention of her father and Jane.

"What, may I ask, is so amusing, Lizzy?" Bennet enquired, eyeing the growing flush on her cheeks. He looked at Darcy with a raised brow.

"Mr. Darcy was simply recounting an amusing story from his childhood," she replied quickly, lifting her teacup in a valiant attempt to hide her face.

Bennet eyed the couple speculatively, but he allowed the moment to pass, turning the conversation towards the events recounted in the newspaper he had only been able to scan that morning. Darcy answered him intelligently, with Elizabeth interjecting here and there, and even Mary spoke up a few times, something she had been loath to do during most of Darcy's previous calls.

Darcy rewarded her participation with a brotherly smile, and he reflected on the fact that he and Georgiana had never had a conversation such as this one. It was something else he needed to remedy, and he began to wonder if he truly had harmed Georgiana by allowing her to be so sheltered.

He pushed that thought aside as he returned his attention back to the conversation.

When the meal was finished, Darcy accompanied Bennet to his study. Elizabeth would have followed, but Mrs. Bennet insisted she join her instead, and plied her with questions about Darcy's attention.

"What can your father be about, Lizzy, allowing you and Mr. Darcy to walk together as he did this morning?" she demanded.

"It was only a short walk, Mama, and you know how much I enjoy the exercise when I can," Elizabeth explained.

"What did the two of you speak of?" she asked, trying again to discover what was going on between her second daughter and the wealthy gentleman. While she might believe Jane was better suited for such a wealthy gentleman who was connected to the nobility, he had paid that daughter little attention.

"We spoke about his estate and some of the changes he's made there," Elizabeth said. "As you know, he and Papa have corresponded since Mr. Darcy's father passed, often exchanging ideas about managing their land. We were simply discussing how some of those improvements were received at Pemberley and how the response from his tenants compared to those here."

Mrs. Bennet scowled. "That is hardly the way to make him fall in love with you and offer you marriage one day," she huffed. "Perhaps, though, he enjoys that, for he continues to seek you out for conversation. I cannot understand it. Will anything come of your friendship with the man?"

"What do you mean, Mama?" Elizabeth asked, attempting to not answer by asking her own questions.

"Will the man offer you marriage, Lizzy? Is that not your purpose in seeking him out as often as you do?" she asked, leaning forward as though she could entice the information she sought from her most obstinate daughter.

"No, Mama, it is not," Elizabeth replied. "I do enjoy Mr. Darcy's company, but I will do nothing to induce him to offer for me. While I cannot deny that I do seek out his company, I cannot suppose any and every man who speaks to me will necessarily offer for me. If he wished to marry me and made me an offer, I would answer in the way that would guarantee my happiness. I know that Papa has told you the same about all of your daughters."

Mrs. Bennet sat back in her chair with a huff at this response. "You would feel very differently were you forced to ponder a life in the hedgerows."

Elizabeth shook her head. "You know that none of us are destined for the hedgerows. Papa has ensured that we will all be provided for if something happens to him, and Mr. Collins inherits before my sisters and I are wed. There is the dower house, and we all have funds set aside for our futures."

This time, Mrs. Bennet scowled at her daughter although there was little she could say to contradict her. Elizabeth knew far more about the estate and its dealings than she ever would. Even what her husband had attempted to explain she had not understood, and, frankly, she had not cared to. Her husband had forbidden her from speaking of their daughters' dowries, not that he had told her the amounts.

Unsatisfied, Mrs. Bennet picked up her sewing from the basket and was determined to punish her second daughter by refusing to speak to her for the rest of the morning.

Relieved that her vague answers had gone unchallenged, Elizabeth retrieved her embroidery basket and took up the handkerchief she had started not long after first meeting Mr. Darcy. Almost without realizing it, she had begun stitching Sweet Williams into the fabric—a choice that now struck her as both ironic and fitting.

The flower, after all, symbolized gallantry and admiration—qualities she had come to see more clearly in him over time. Once she noticed, she had resolved to finish it and had been working on it diligently when she could. Now, as her needle moved through the cloth, she considered adding his initials and, perhaps, offering it to him as a token of their engagement.

CHAPTER 32
Further Discussions

Aunt Horatia had risen early that morning and heard Lady Matlock, Colonel Fitzwilliam, and Mr. Darcy depart for their ride. She attended to her duties as mistress while she waited for their return, sipping tea while she contemplated what might be done about her niece.

The afternoon before, she had interviewed the coachman and groom who had accompanied Miss Bingley to Meryton. This interview revealed a few more details, including the meeting with Lady Lucas and the conversation with members of the militia.

"Two of the gents were officers, already wearin' their red coats," the groom replied. "The third one was dressed like a proper gentleman, miss, but he said he'd joined the militia." The groom was still just a lad—son of one of Netherfield's tenants, hired on to help in the stables while the estate was let.

"Did you hear any of their conversations?" Aunt Horatia asked.

"Miss Bingley, that is, Miss Caroline, was talkin' about the Bennet ladies," the coachman replied. "I was not close enough to hear the entire conversation, but I do believe she mentioned that Miss Elizabeth Bennet was prone to wandering the estate without an escort. The third gent, he spoke to Miss Caroline in a lowered voice, and both looked very pleased with the other after they spoke."

Aunt Horatia gasped. "She intends for the men to compromise Miss Elizabeth," she voiced her suspicion aloud. "Was any more discussed?"

"No, ma'am," the coachman replied. "But I was in the village yesterday morning, and that one fellow, the one who wasn't wearing a red coat on that day, he was wearing it then. He stopped me as I passed through and held out a note for me to give to Miss Caroline's maid. When I arrived back at the estate, her maid met me in the stable and demanded the missive. Like her mistress, that one is demanding and haughty and insisted that I not wait even a moment to give her what she wished."

Scowling, Aunt Horatia nodded and thanked the two. "My nephew, he spoke to you, did he not?" At the confused looks on their faces, she went on, "He intended to inform you that Miss Caroline Bingley is not to travel into the village without her brother's knowledge. You are not to prepare a carriage or saddle a horse on her order but are to confirm any such requests with him."

"No, madam," the coachman said slowly. "We were given no order like that."

Her frown deepened. "Has she left the estate again since that morning?"

"Yes, ma'am," the groom said. "She came to the stables yesterday mornin' and asked me to saddle a horse. I offered to ride along and accompany her, but she said she'd manage on her own. Rode off towards Meryton and didn't come back for a good two hours."

Aunt Horatia pursed her lips in displeasure. "Miss Bingley is not to leave the estate without an escort, regardless of what she may claim. Even if you have to follow her without her knowing, someone must do it. If she meets with that militia officer again, or if she or her maid receive another letter, I want to know about it immediately. Confirm any order for a carriage with her brother but notify me as well."

"Yes, ma'am," the two said almost in unison before leaving the room.

When she heard steps in the hallway, she remembered where she was and stepped out to see who was approaching. Seeing the colonel and Lady Matlock, she quietly indicated that they should join her.

"Did Mr. Darcy not accompany you this morning?" she asked.

Lady Matlock smiled. "Yes, but we met with Mr. Bennet and Miss Elizabeth, and Darcy accompanied them to Longbourn. He will return later."

Aunt Horatia returned the smile. "Is something brewing there?"

Laughing, the colonel replied before his mother could. "Much has happened there, but I will tell you in confidence that Darcy and Miss Elizabeth are engaged. Her father approves the match, as did his, but there are other details that must be resolved before any public announcement is made. Darcy will not even tell his friend, not yet, so I ask that you keep this between us."

"That is probably wise," Aunt Horatia replied with a grimace. "Caroline has entirely too much influence over my nephew, and what he knows, so does she. In fact, she is why I asked the two of you to join me, for I have news to report."

"What is it?" Lady Matlock asked, suddenly concerned.

"I fear Caroline may be attempting to influence one of the militia officers to at least damage Miss Elizabeth's reputation—if not cause her true harm," Aunt Horatia said gravely. "At present, I have only fragments to go on—second-hand accounts of secret meetings and whispered suggestions—but it appears she told a group of officers that Miss Elizabeth often walks alone. It may have been an attempt to encourage a situation that could lead to compromise."

She went on to recount the rest of her conversation with Bingley and the Hursts from the afternoon before.

"Miss Elizabeth no longer walks or rides out alone, and in fact, has not done so in above five years," the colonel replied, his brows furrowing as he wondered which men Miss Bingley might have spoken with. "However, due to the presence of one militia officer in particular, and other potential threats, Miss Elizabeth is now to be accompanied by two footmen whose sole responsibility is to protect her. Do you know which officers she spoke to?" the colonel concluded.

"I do not, but I know that one of the men had just joined when she spoke to him, for he did not have his red coat yet," Aunt Horatia answered.

Scowling, the colonel leant back into his chair. "Wickham," he said in a near growl, causing both women to stare at him.

"I would stake my pay for the next year that she spoke with Wickham," Fitzwilliam replied to their unasked question. "That would explain his attention to Miss Elizabeth when he met the Bennet sisters in Meryton, and he would think ruining a young lady a lark. Now that he knows the lady Miss Bingley wishes to have ruined is the same one in whom Darcy has shown interest he will be even more determined to follow through with it."

"That does present a problem, but, Richard, you said just this morning that you will assign a man to follow Wickham," said Lady Matlock. "You should do it now instead of waiting until Monday."

Fitzwilliam nodded in acknowledgement, but he did not speak for several moments. While the ladies spoke about Miss Bingley and her ambitions, Fitzwilliam was thinking.

Finally, Fitzwilliam muttered, "Perhaps it is best if we let him think he has won."

His mother looked up sharply. "What do you mean?"

"Wickham," he said grimly. "If we wait until after Miss Elizabeth and Darcy are married, we can stage a situation where Wickham believes he has a chance to catch her alone and ruin her. But we will be watching—he will not get near enough to do any real harm. It would be enough to trap him and put an end to at least one of the problems we are facing in Hertfordshire."

Lady Matlock narrowed her eyes. "You mean to arrest him for attempted assault, then have him tried for conduct unbecoming by a military court."

Fitzwilliam nodded. "Exactly."

"And the second problem?" she asked. "You are speaking of Miss Bingley, are you not?"

"I am," he confirmed. "If she is aiding Wickham—even if we cannot bring formal charges—it will be enough to destroy her socially. Her reputation will be in tatters, and I can promise Darcy will never speak to her again."

Lady Matlock scoffed. "If she is assisting that miscreant—whatever her motives—I will see to it she is unwelcome in every drawing room in England. The only life left to her will be across the ocean."

"She is my niece," Aunt Horatia said with a heavy sigh, "but I cannot say she doesn't deserve it. I had thought to help her. But if she is conspiring to harm another, then there's nothing left to do but hold her to account."

She tilted her head in thought. "Why would this Mr. Wickham still accost her after she and Mr. Darcy are wed?"

With a grin at his mother, Fitzwilliam replied jauntily: "Oh, we had not mentioned the wedding. Miss Elizabeth and Darcy will marry late next week. At present, we do not want my uncle, Wickham, or Miss Bingley to learn of it, so they will marry in secret at the Longbourn chapel. Once these threats have been eliminated, then they will announce it publicly."

Aunt Horatia raised her brows at this. "Let me know what I might do to assist," she stated. "Although I have only seen Mr. Darcy and Miss Elizabeth in company together a few times, I have rarely seen a couple more in harmony with each other."

Lady Matlock pursed her lips. "I confess that I had hoped for a different sort of woman for him, but you are correct about the pair of them. They will be happy together, and these trials will only make them stronger."

She paused, then asked, "What does Mr. Bingley say about all this—about his sister? You have not mentioned his reaction."

Aunt Horatia grimaced. "He insists she could not possibly mean to harm anyone. We spoke yesterday morning, and I thought he agreed to speak to the servants—make it clear that Caroline was not to be allowed to leave without permission. But it seems he never followed through. I had hoped, by inviting me here, he meant to take a stand against her. Now I suspect he expected *me* to do it for him."

Fitzwilliam scowled. "I have always said he was a puppy, but perhaps it is worse than that. He is strong only when someone stronger is backing him. On his own, he is helpless, at least where she is concerned."

"I am afraid you are right," Aunt Horatia said with a sigh. "It would take something significant to change his mind. If he marries someday and Caroline is still living under his roof, he will need a particularly strong-willed wife to stand against her. Frankly, that is an unfair burden to place on any woman."

"What about the Hursts?" Fitzwilliam asked.

Aunt Horatia considered this. "Louisa has always followed Caroline's lead, but I have noticed she has begun to pull away—subtly, but noticeably. As for Gilbert, he remains detached. But if Caroline were to pose a serious threat to the family's reputation, I believe he would act. She is not his responsibility, after all. If it came to it, I suspect he would take Louisa to his family's estate and leave Caroline and Charles to fend for themselves."

"So far, he has said and done nothing," she concluded, "but that does not mean he never will."

"Let us not find out," Fitzwilliam replied. "As I said, all this is to be kept a secret from the rest of your family. Darcy is not pleased that his marriage will begin in this way, but I am hoping we might find a way to offer him a day or two of seclusion. Do not be surprised if he is suddenly called to London soon."

Lady Matlock elbowed her son. "That is hardly appropriate to discuss in mixed company," she said. "However, I do think that we may be able to do something for them before we toss them back into the fray. We will likely need your help, Miss Bingley."

"Please, Lady Matlock, call me Horatia, at least in private," she replied. "It will be easier since my niece is known by that name."

"And you should call me Lady Elaine," the countess responded, surprise in her voice at the other lady's temerity.

CHAPTER 33

A Dinner Party at Netherfield

21 OCTOBER 1811

For the next two days, things in Meryton were quiet. Heavy rain kept everyone indoors on Saturday, and on Sunday, those at Netherfield encountered the family from Longbourn only briefly at church.

At Bennet's invitation, Darcy had attended Longbourn chapel each Sunday he had been in the area, but this was the first morning the rest of the Netherfield party joined him.

Darcy and Georgiana sat beside Elizabeth in the Bennet pew, much to Miss Bingley's displeasure. Although he returned to Netherfield with the rest of his party and made no effort to seek out Miss Bingley's exclusive company, she took some comfort in the fact that he had not visited Longbourn or spent another day with Miss Eliza.

Even so, the countess's pointed treatment of her, along with the sharp remarks she had endured from both that lady and her own aunt, left her unusually subdued. She offered only a few small comments, mostly remarks about how fortunate she felt to be spending her time in what she termed "superior society."

On Monday morning, Darcy and Georgiana set out early on horseback and met with Elizabeth during their ride. After acknowledging Elizabeth's footmen, they rode the last little bit to the cottage, where Darcy and Elizabeth began to tell Georgiana all that they had discussed over the past few days.

"Mr. Wickham is here?" Georgiana asked, her voice trembling as the colour drained from her face at the mention of his name.

"He is," Elizabeth replied gently, placing a comforting hand on the girl's arm. "But you need not be afraid. Your brother and cousin have taken every precaution to ensure that neither of us will come to harm."

Georgiana closed her eyes, visibly shaken. "This is all my fault," she whispered, breathless. "I should never have spoken to him in Ramsgate. If I had not, none of this would be happening."

"No, Georgiana," Darcy said firmly, his tone brooking no argument. "This is not your fault. You had no way of knowing what kind of man Wickham truly was—that failure lies with me. I should have warned you about what he had become. I know you tried to distance yourself from him and that Mrs. Younge encouraged you to receive him. She was complicit in all of this, and you were misled."

He paused, his expression tight with guilt. "Richard and I kept you too sheltered, thinking we were protecting you. But in doing so, we left you vulnerable. I should never have left you alone in Ramsgate. Still, that is not the full story."

He drew a slow breath before continuing. "Although I cannot prove it, I suspect our uncle, Lord Matlock, was involved. I believe he orchestrated the situation to create leverage over me—to force my compliance to his wishes. If that was his intent, he will be sorely disappointed. I will not yield to his demands."

Darcy's expression darkened as he spoke, and he rose abruptly, beginning to pace the small cottage with measured, agitated strides, while Elizabeth and Georgiana watched him.

"Richard and I are doing everything in our power to protect both you and Elizabeth," he said, repeating Elizabeth's previous assurance. His voice was tight with suppressed fury; his fists clenched at his sides. "Wickham will not come near either of you."

"Calm yourself, William," Elizabeth said gently, rising to her feet and stepping beside him. She took his clenched hands in hers, and after a moment's hesitation, he let go of his fists and folded his fingers around hers instead.

She watched as Darcy drew in a slow breath through his nose and exhaled sharply, a visible attempt to calm himself before he turned to face her.

"I will not yield to my uncle," he said firmly.

She held his gaze. "William, I know you will do all you can to protect your sister and me—and all my sisters—from whatever Lord Matlock or Wickham might attempt."

Darcy sighed heavily. "I do not believe I have mentioned what my aunt told me about Miss Bingley, have I?"

Elizabeth lifted her eyebrows. "No…you have not. What did she say?"

He released her hand to run his through his hair in frustration, his fingers lingering for a moment at the back of his neck before he dropped his arm. "It appears Miss Bingley may have been meeting with Wickham."

Elizabeth drew in a sharp breath, her expression shifting from confusion to alarm. "With Wickham? Why?"

"Although she claims to understand that I will never offer for her, she has been overheard suggesting she would rather see you ruined than allow you to marry me," he continued bitterly. "She has been furious with me since arriving at Netherfield. I embarrassed her, in her view, by ignoring her, and, as she put it, choosing a 'low country chit'—her words, not mine."

Elizabeth's brows rose, but she said nothing.

"For years, she has believed she is the ideal woman for me, when in truth, she merely wants my name and my wealth. She considers you unworthy of the position and has not liked that I have paid you attention while ignoring her. In fact, since coming here, I have made it very clear that I would never marry her, regardless of what she tried, and I suspect that has pushed her to act outrageously," he concluded.

"You mean—even if she compromised herself?" Elizabeth asked quietly.

Darcy nodded. "Even then, I made it clear that nothing would induce me to marry her. According to her aunt, she went into Meryton without her brother's knowledge the day after my aunt's arrival when we were all at Longbourn. Richard believes she intended to spread rumours about the Bennet family. She was seen speaking with Lady Lucas, then several militia officers. Nothing is confirmed, but Richard suspects the one she spoke with the most was Wickham. That may be why Wickham seemed to have targeted you when you first met."

His voice lowered. "We now have an officer shadowing him—his task is to gain Wickham's trust and uncover whatever plans he may have."

Elizabeth's eyes widened in alarm, her voice trembling. "I knew Miss Bingley disliked me—but to conspire with Wickham? Was she content to destroy my reputation, or…or was something even more terrible intended for me?"

Darcy's expression darkened. "We do not know yet. That is what we must find out—and quickly. Whatever they are planning, we need to be ahead of it."

Elizabeth stepped forward and slipped her arms gently around Darcy's waist. The unexpected gesture caused Georgiana to gasp.

Darcy turned, surprised by both the embrace and his sister's reaction. Elizabeth followed his gaze, her arms still loosely encircling him.

"Forgive me," Georgiana said softly, her voice tinged with hesitation.

Chuckling lightly, Darcy loosened his grasp on Elizabeth and turned to face his sister. "Apparently, we have told you so many things, but what we have forgotten to tell you is that Elizabeth and I are engaged. Her father knows, as do our aunt and cousin—but very few others. For now, we have chosen to keep it a secret. If Wickham finds out, Lord Matlock will know soon after. And I am not certain what Miss Bingley might do with the information or how she may react."

Georgiana nodded solemnly. "I will not say a word. But Elizabeth—may I tell you how glad I am to know we will soon be sisters?"

Elizabeth's expression softened as she moved from Darcy's embrace to pull Georgiana into a hug. "You may, and you may call me Lizzy, if you like. My sisters do. It is only your brother who insists on using my full name with such frequency," she said with a grin.

"That is true," Georgiana said before giggling. "Just a few days ago, my aunt scolded Miss Bingley for calling me by my Christian name. She has often tried to make it seem as though the two of us were closer than we are. I never returned the liberty—I never called her by her name—but she would slip mine into conversation whenever she could as if we were the best of friends. She particularly did it when we were in company."

Elizabeth laughed. "I would have liked to see your aunt put her in her place."

"It was rather satisfying," Georgiana admitted.

"Miss Caroline Bingley clearly looks down on everyone in Meryton," Elizabeth added. "I have no doubt she believes I am unworthy of marrying your brother. But it does not matter—he has chosen me, and I am quite content to be that choice."

Elizabeth turned to her intended, mischief dancing in her eyes. "I am certain she will not be the only lady disappointed by your choice." Her smile widened when she noticed the tips of his ears turning pink.

"There may be a few disappointed ladies," Darcy replied, his tone gruff, but his eyes betraying his humour.

Elizabeth leant in, eyes bright. "And I daresay there will be many who are quite put out that you chose me instead of them. After all, you are *very* wealthy, and Pemberley is rather grand, is it not?"

She pressed a playful kiss to his cheek, drawing a scowl from him—half-hearted and full of affection. His eyes, warm and steady on hers, betrayed no real annoyance.

Elizabeth laughed and leant lightly against his arm, her heart full.

Georgiana, watching quietly, felt a smile tug at her lips. It warmed her to see her brother so unguardedly happy.

At last, the three realized how long they had spent tucked away in the small cottage and agreed it was time to part ways.

"I am loath to leave you," Elizabeth said, "but we must go. I am glad we will see you again tonight at dinner. Miss Bingley, or, rather, Miss Horatia Bingley, has invited the Lucases, so it will be…an interesting gathering."

She smiled. "We will say nothing of our engagement, of course, but I intend to spend as much time with you as I can. I am certain the Lucases approve of our match—even if Miss Caroline does not."

With a small laugh, she continued, "I am particularly glad to see my friend Charlotte again. It has been too long—other visitors have been keeping me far too busy of late."

Darcy chuckled and walked them outside to where their horses were tethered. He helped Georgiana mount first, then turned to Elizabeth. Before he lifted her into the sidesaddle, he lingered for a moment with his hands on her waist, pressing a gentle kiss to her forehead.

Once Elizabeth was in the saddle, and after ensuring the footmen assigned to guard Georgiana and Elizabeth were ready, he gave a final nod.

The party then separated, heading to Longbourn or Netherfield and their respective breakfasts.

THE BENNETS WERE THE FIRST TO ARRIVE AT NETHERFIELD FOR THE evening's dinner party. They were shown into the drawing room, where the Bingley party awaited them, and after a few polite greetings were exchanged, everyone began to settle into smaller conversational groups around the room.

As was his custom, Charles Bingley immediately crossed to Jane and led her to a comfortable grouping of chairs. He seated himself beside her, speaking in low, cheerful tones, seemingly unaware of the rest of the gathering. Colonel Fitzwilliam joined Bennet nearby, both listening as much as they were speaking, while Mrs. Bennet made her way to a sofa occupied by Lady Matlock and Horatia Bingley, launching into spirited conversation with her usual enthusiasm.

Mary and Catherine soon found Georgiana and took seats near her. The three spoke quietly, occasionally glancing around the room under the gentle supervision of their elders.

In the far corner, Darcy and Elizabeth found a quieter spot, removed just enough to speak in relative privacy. For a few precious minutes—no more than ten—they enjoyed the rare luxury of uninterrupted conversation.

Then Caroline Bingley entered the room.

Her absence when the Bennets had arrived had gone entirely unnoticed. Now, as she stepped into the room, both her aunt and Lady Matlock looked up. Neither spoke, but their eyes followed her as she moved, without hesitation, straight towards the corner where Elizabeth and Darcy sat.

Without so much as a glance towards anyone else in the room, Caroline crossed the drawing room with affected poise, her gown, which was more suited to a night at the theatre than a country dinner party, shimmering in the candlelight. She stopped beside Darcy and offered him a practiced smile.

"Mr. Darcy," she said sweetly, holding out a sheaf of music, "I thought I would play for everyone to pass the time before dinner and am in need of someone to turn the pages for me. Might I impose upon you to assist me?"

Darcy turned to look at her, distaste clearly written in his eyes. "Perhaps your brother would be more appropriate. I am occupied at present."

Miss Bingley's smile faltered, momentarily, but she quickly recovered. "But I would far prefer your company at the pianoforte. I recall you were always so precise with timing."

Before Darcy could answer, Elizabeth spoke, her tone polite but firm. "I am sure Mr. Darcy is flattered, Miss Bingley, but we were in the middle of a conversation. Perhaps another time?"

With a huff barely concealed beneath a thin veneer of composure, Miss Bingley turned from the couple and swept away to the pianoforte. She launched into an elaborate concerto that was complex and demanding. Although her technique was undeniably polished, the performance lacked the warmth and expression that had made Elizabeth's playing so captivating when he listened to her before. The instrument, positioned uncomfortably close to where Darcy and Elizabeth sat, now filled the room with sound, making further conversation between them all but impossible.

Darcy grimaced at Elizabeth, and leant closer to speak directly into her ear. "I prefer to listen to your playing."

SPORT FOR OUR NEIGHBOURS

Elizabeth smiled in return but said nothing. For the next several minutes, the couple sat together, his hand wrapped around hers, hidden from sight in her skirts, as they listened to the music.

Soon, Miss Bingley's playing was interrupted by the arrival of the remainder of the guests. Darcy and Elizabeth took the opportunity to move away from the pianoforte as they went to greet Charlotte Lucas. After a few words were exchanged, and before anyone could settle back into their seats, the butler arrived and announced that the meal was served.

It did not take long for everyone to move into the dining room. Darcy escorted Elizabeth and Charlotte and followed closely behind their host and hostess. As soon as they entered, they noticed the confusion on the faces of all the guests.

Aunt Horatia's eyes narrowed as she surveyed the dining table. The place cards were not as she had left them—that much she was certain. As she moved around the table, reading each name, her jaw tightened. Someone had deliberately rearranged them. Although irritation simmered beneath her composed exterior, she maintained her calm.

"Everyone, please sit wherever you like," she said clearly, her voice firm and carrying. "It appears a mischievous child has been at the table. Do ignore the place cards."

Then, she began guiding the seating of a few. "Mr. Bennet, if you would sit to my right. Sir William, please take the seat to my left. Caroline, do sit beside Sir William."

Her voice, which had been filled with warmth when speaking to the rest, was cold when she mentioned her niece's name. Miss Bingley only glared at her aunt, but she complied with the command, unwilling to push her aunt too far.

The remainder of the meal passed pleasantly enough for most. The youngest girls—Georgiana, Mary, and Catherine, together with Maria Lucas—were seated together near the centre of the table, chatting easily about their lessons, music, and recent attempts at watercolours. Their laughter occasionally drew fond glances from their companions and the others nearby.

At the far end, Bingley and Jane remained content in each other's company, speaking in low tones and exchanging quiet smiles, seemingly oblivious to the rest of the table. The colonel sat near them and occasionally joined in, but as was his wont, he mostly listened.

Close to the head, Elizabeth and Darcy were seated near Lady Matlock, Lady Lucas, Mr. and Mrs. Hurst, and Mrs. Bennet. The conversation there was more general, touching on the weather, the improvements at Longbourn, and the celebration in Meryton that would be held on Guy Fawkes Day next Monday.

"I am told the musicians for the event are much improved," Lady Lucas said, reaching for her wine glass. "At the last assembly, they were off-pitch."

"I only hope they are not quite so fond of the hornpipes this time," Mrs. Bennet added with a dramatic sigh. "It is terribly hard to carry on a proper conversation over such noise."

"I believe you will be delighted to dance that evening," Lady Matlock said with a teasing glance towards her nephew. "Will you not? I know that dancing is not among your favourite activities, but I believe it has become more acceptable in your mind."

Darcy raised an eyebrow, his tone dry. "I have always enjoyed dancing but not conversing with a partner who can say nothing that is not about the weather or fashion."

Elizabeth smiled, unable to resist. "Yes, I can believe you are particular in regard to your partners."

"Only with the ones I intend to remember," he said, casting a glance her way.

A faint, pleased flush rose on Elizabeth's cheeks, which did not go unnoticed by Mrs. Hurst, though she chose—for once—not to comment.

CHAPTER 34

Caroline Bingley Plots

At the far end of the table, Caroline Bingley sat in simmering silence, her eyes fixed on the other end where Darcy and Elizabeth were seated. Every interaction between them tightened the knot in her chest.

Nothing had gone according to plan.

Her attempt to lure Darcy to the pianoforte failed; he refused to turn her pages, depriving her of the chance to whisper subtle criticisms of Miss Elizabeth's manners under the guise of polite conversation. Nor had she succeeded in securing the seat beside him at dinner.

She had planned to place Catherine Bennet on his other side, hoping the girl's lack of conversation would drive Darcy towards her. Miss Bingley had not spent much time with Catherine Bennet, but what little exposure she had was enough to judge her dull and easily ignored—a perfect buffer, or so she had thought. But none of that had come to pass due to her aunt's interference.

Nothing—not her charm, her schemes, nor her carefully laid plans—had thus far drawn his attention away from Eliza Bennet.

But something might.

After her second meeting with Lieutenant Wickham, she had begun to question the plan he had laid out. As much as she disliked Eliza, Miss Bingley had not been certain she wanted to go as far as Wickham evidently planned. Ruining a rival's reputation with gossip was one thing—she had done so before, and without remorse. But what Wickham proposed was something else entirely.

It was a seduction—a trap.

With Miss Bingley's assurance that Elizabeth was often unaccompanied, and Wickham's confident claim that he knew precisely how to handle the matter, he had insisted it would be simple. He asked for two hundred and fifty pounds—paid upfront—as a guarantee of his intentions. He had not spoken the threat aloud, but the implication was unmistakable: he would ruin Elizabeth Bennet completely. Once that was done, no respectable man would ever consider marrying her.

Miss Bingley had not yet agreed. But neither had she said no.

At first, she had balked at the idea—at the thought of orchestrating something so permanent. A ruined woman could not simply fade from memory; she would become a scandal, a warning, a shadow trailing every conversation.

But after tonight, Miss Bingley was determined to follow through with his plan. She would meet with Wickham on the morrow as arranged and give him the funds to have him ruin that *awful* Eliza Bennet.

The following morning, Miss Caroline Bingley rose far earlier than was her custom. After dressing in a dark green riding habit, she slipped out of the house and made her way to the stables where the groom saddled a horse at her request.

She declined his offer to accompany her and remained oblivious to the fact that, once she had ridden out, he saddled a second horse and followed at a discreet distance as instructed. He was the only one about at that hour, the others being occupied, so he hoped the mistress would not be upset with him for not sending word to her.

Miss Bingley rode for just over half an hour before drawing her horse to a stop near the outskirts of the militia encampment, Wickham's current post. He was not there, having paid an enlisted man named Farley to take his watch. Miss Bingley, however, had not been informed of this arrangement, and now sat impatiently atop her horse, fuming at the delay.

It was less than fifteen minutes later when Wickham finally appeared. Upon spotting her, he murmured a few words and dismissed Farley.

"Miss Bingley," Wickham greeted her with his usual polished charm, as though he were not late and she had not come to pay him for the ruination of a young woman. "A fine morning."

"I have your money," she said curtly in reply, her voice low and sharp.

Wickham raised an eyebrow, clearly surprised. "Capital," he said smoothly. "Then I shall begin making arrangements straight away. But tell me—what has this young lady done to deserve such a fate?"

Stiffening, she haughtily replied. "She has turned the head of a man who, had it not been for her interference, would have proposed to me. She has no fortune, no breeding, no business being in his company. I want her out of the way."

Wickham studied her for a moment, the faintest hint of amusement curling at the edge of his mouth. Then he nodded. "As you wish. Would you like me to send you word once the task is done?"

"Of course," she replied. "Send a note to my maid as you did before."

"And who is this man," Wickham asked, feigning curiosity, "that would drive you to such lengths to eliminate your competition?"

Of course, he already knew the answer—it was Darcy. He also knew, with certainty, that no matter what Miss Bingley did, Darcy would never marry her.

The irony amused him.

For the modest sum of two hundred and fifty pounds, he would be ruining the woman Darcy clearly loved. Miss Bingley might pretend otherwise, but Wickham saw the truth plainly enough. Despite her wishes, she had no real claim on Darcy.

Nor did the Bennet girl have much to recommend her, at least in society's eyes—no fortune, no connections, no notable dowry beyond the five thousand pounds to be divided upon her mother's death. Some suspected there was more, but nothing was mentioned with any surety.

Regardless, she had captured Darcy's attention in a way Caroline Bingley never had. The estate that she supposedly would inherit was something, but that was not guaranteed, merely speculation, and Wickham thought he had heard something said about an entailment.

Wickham acknowledged that the young lady was very attractive. The elder Miss Bennet was beautiful, but it seemed that this Miss Elizabeth had a spark that her sister did not. It would be fun to tame her, Wickham thought, particularly when he would get to sample the delights that Darcy would never taste after Wickham was finished with her.

That his actions would benefit him as well was a source of no small satisfaction. For destroying the chit Darcy held in regard, Lord Matlock had promised to secure his future. Wickham had every intention of making the most of it.

From his concealed position nearby, Lieutenant Sanderson quietly observed the exchange. The evening before he had informed

Colonel Fitzwilliam of Wickham's use of an enlisted man to stand in for him at his post—a blatant dereliction of duty for an officer. Now, having overheard this latest conversation, he had even more to report.

When Colonel Fitzwilliam had first tasked him with befriending the newly commissioned officer, Sanderson had been wary of spying on a fellow lieutenant. But after several days of close observation, his doubts had vanished. It was plain that Wickham had no business wearing a militia uniform; in truth, the man posed a danger to nearly every honourable person in Meryton—and likely well beyond.

Although still relatively new to the militia himself, Sanderson had served long enough to recognise the type: a man who viewed the uniform not as a symbol of service, but as a means to advance his own interests. Wickham was charming—quick with a smile, fluent in flattery—but it was a shallow charm, calculated for manipulation. Like the night before, he had once again shirked responsibility, relying on others to carry out duties he was unwilling to perform himself.

Once Wickham moved out of sight, Sanderson slipped from the shadows and made his way towards where Colonel Fitzwilliam awaited him. He did not know what the colonel would do with the information he now carried, but he hoped it would be enough to stop the scheme unfolding before his eyes—and deny Wickham and his accomplice what it was they sought.

Hidden nearby, the young groom who had followed Miss Bingley had also heard every word of the exchange. Miss Elizabeth was well-liked amongst the tenants of Netherfield, having done much over the last several years to improve their lives and the estate they worked on.

As soon as he saw Miss Bingley begin to depart, he hurried back to where he had hidden his horse and quickly made his way to Netherfield, hoping to avoid her notice.

The stable master was displeased to see the groom returning with the horse so obviously exhausted. "What the devil do you think you are doing, boy, to treat a horse that is not your own in this way?" he bellowed.

"Miss Bingley, the master's aunt, told me to keep an eye on the other Miss Bingley in case she rode out—as she did this morning," the lad explained. "That Miss Bingley is plotting to cause harm to Miss Elizabeth."

His brow furrowed, the stable master stared a moment longer at the lad.

"Aye, we mustn't allow that to happen. The young Miss Bingley has set her cap for Mr. Darcy who has been courting Miss Elizabeth—or so I have heard from the servants up in the house. Very well, son, I will take care of this beast while you wash up before telling the mistress what you heard. Mr. Darcy and the colonel will be eager to hear the news as well."

The boy did as he was commanded and went up to the main house, entering through the kitchen where he washed his hands and face before seeking out Miss Horatia Bingley.

He was shown into the small study, where he found her sipping tea with Lady Matlock. It was still early, and they were the only ones awake and within the house.

"Excuse me, mistress, but I have news to tell you," the lad said upon entering. He then proceeded to tell the women all he had seen and heard that morning.

"Thank you," Aunt Horatia replied when he had finished.

"What is your name, young man?" the countess asked.

"John, my lady," he replied nervously.

"Thank you, John," the countess said, smiling at him. "My son and nephew will ensure you are amply rewarded for your service."

"It is not needed, my lady," the boy said, his head held high. "I like my job here—but mostly, I did it for Miss Elizabeth. Miss Elizabeth is kind and caring, and no one at Netherfield would stand by and allow her to be harmed."

Colouring slightly at having given such an impassioned speech in front of the women, the boy dropped his eyes to the ground.

"No need to be ashamed, John," came the gentle reply of the countess. "It is admirable that you think so well of the young lady. I will ensure she knows of your defence of her."

"Oh, please don't do that, my lady," he cried.

"Whyever not?" Aunt Horatia asked.

"That Mr. Darcy is a rather big fellow, and I don't imagine he'd think too well of another man offering his lady such praise. I'd hate to lose my position."

He was surprised when the two ladies laughed.

"Trust me, my boy, after what you have done for our family, you are in no danger of that," the countess replied, still chuckling softly.

Still not understanding their laughter, the boy allowed himself to be dismissed and returned to the stables, setting about his duties for the day.

CHAPTER 35

Countermeasures

Darcy was livid after hearing the reports from both his aunt and cousin later that day. The one from his aunt had nearly convinced him to leave Netherfield with his sister and never again associate with any member of the Bingley family.

However, Lady Matlock forced him to calm himself. "You and Elizabeth will be wed in just a few days, Fitzwilliam," she said, halting his pacing. "Allow my son to do what must be done so that both Mr. Wickham and Miss Bingley may be held accountable for their actions. Regardless of what else may happen, she is finished in society."

"I wish to be able to celebrate my engagement to Miss Elizabeth openly, but due to the jealousy of two—perhaps three—individuals, we are forced to hide our attachment from those who would rejoice with us," Darcy complained. "Richard ought to work faster."

Despite his tirade, Darcy remained furious when Colonel Fitzwilliam returned to Netherfield after visiting the militia encampment that morning.

"Sanderson has reported to me," he said without preamble. "Miss Bingley handed Wickham the full two hundred and fifty pounds and is now waiting for word that the task has been accomplished. I have an idea that will take care of both our problems at once, but it will require the cooperation of both you and Elizabeth."

Darcy scowled. "The entire point of this scheme was to protect Elizabeth, and now you want to involve her further?" he asked incredulously.

"Hear me out, Darcy," the colonel replied. "Better yet, let us discuss it with your lovely intended. I suspect she'll be far more likely to appreciate the brilliance of my plan," he added with a laugh, clearly amused by the thunderous expression on his cousin's face.

"Tell me now," Darcy demanded. "Whatever plan you've concocted will undoubtedly anger me, and I would prefer to have my argument prepared in advance."

"I think not," Fitzwilliam said with a chuckle, further provoking his cousin. "Come, I sent word to Longbourn earlier asking Mr. Bennet and Miss Elizabeth to meet us at the cottage. If we do not depart immediately, they will arrive before us—again."

Without giving Darcy a chance to respond, Fitzwilliam strode out of the room. Darcy followed a moment later, hot on his heels.

"You intend to ride in those?" Fitzwilliam called back, gesturing at the soft house shoes Darcy still wore.

"Damn you, Richard," Darcy muttered, turning back towards his chambers. Entering his dressing room, he found his valet waiting and quickly changed into boots and attire more appropriate for riding through dusty fields.

A short time later, though longer than he would have liked, he arrived at the stables to find his horse already saddled, but his cousin nowhere in sight. Mounting, he cursed Fitzwilliam once more before spurring his horse into a canter, directing it across the fields towards the cottage.

SPORT FOR OUR NEIGHBOURS

Three horses were already tethered nearby when he arrived. He dismounted, silently acknowledging the guards stationed at a reasonable distance, all the while muttering invectives against his cousin as he approached the door.

To his surprise—and utter delight—the door flew open, and Elizabeth rushed outside and into his arms.

"Oh, Elizabeth," he groaned, wrapping his arms around her waist and drawing her closer into his embrace.

"Colonel Fitzwilliam has been telling Papa and me what he knows," she said after a moment of simply resting in his arms. "While I know—or think I know—what their motivation is, I simply cannot understand what would make either of them willing to go so far. Your cousin says he has a plan to hoist them on their own petard, but he refused to share any details until you arrived."

"Yes," Darcy replied darkly, "he said as much to me earlier as well. He also implied the plan would anger me, which is likely why he waited to explain it until you were here. He believes your presence will temper my reaction."

"Will it?" she asked, drawing back to look up at him more fully.

"I am uncertain," he admitted. "He implied the plan depends on your participation which I cannot like. But," he added with a wry grin, "with you here, he knows I will be less inclined to resort to violence and strike him for proposing something that places you in further danger."

Elizabeth gasped, then dissolved into giggles at the exasperated expression on his face.

"Come, dearest," she said, slipping out of his arms and taking his hand in hers. "Let us go in and hear his plan."

"Absolutely not!" Darcy nearly bellowed, the force of his voice echoing off the stone walls of the cottage. His fists clenched at his sides as he stared down his cousin, his entire posture radiating fury. "You cannot seriously expect me to allow Elizabeth to be used as bait!"

"But it is perfect, Darcy," Fitzwilliam insisted. His tone remained calm but resolute as he spread his hands in what he hoped would be a placating gesture. "We will be able to bring Wickham up on multiple charges this way—conduct unbecoming an officer, conspiracy, and kidnapping. With the evidence we have already gathered, this will guarantee he faces a firing squad. He will not have the slightest chance of escaping justice."

"Elizabeth will be at risk," Darcy said through gritted teeth. His stance was rigid as though only sheer will kept him from exploding further. Had Elizabeth not been there, he would have.

"She will not," Fitzwilliam replied, more emphatically now. "We will have men stationed throughout the area, including inside the cottage itself. For the charge of kidnapping to hold, yes, he will have to make physical contact. But he will not get far. The moment he lays a hand on her, he will be restrained."

Darcy turned away abruptly, his chest heaving as he tried to rein in his rising anger. He closed his eyes and took several slow, measured breaths, his shoulders tight with tension. The thought of Elizabeth anywhere near Wickham, of her being touched by him, even for a moment, was nearly unbearable.

A tender touch grazed his cheek, gentle and grounding. His eyes flew open in surprise.

"Do you not trust me, William?" Elizabeth asked softly, her voice a balm against the fury swirling inside him. She stood close, unconcerned by the others in the room, her gaze steady and full of quiet resolve as she looked directly into his eyes.

"Yes, but—" he began, his protest dying in his throat as she pressed her fingers gently to his lips.

"Do you trust your cousin?" she whispered again, her expression unwavering.

"Of course, but—"

Again, she silenced him, this time with a small shake of her head. Her fingers dropped from his lips, and she stepped closer.

"Yes, there is some risk," she admitted, "but the risk is minimal. You know that. If this is the only way to truly stop him, then I am willing to face it."

Darcy stared at her, torn between dread and admiration. He wanted to shield her from every possible danger, yet here she stood—strong, unflinching, and determined to be part of the solution. It both terrified and awed him.

"Like you, I wish to begin our married life without conflict. If this is what we must do to accomplish it, then so be it," she said firmly.

Through all of this Bennet had remained silent, but now he stood and joined the couple. "Darcy, I am afraid that my Lizzy has her mind made up. As you are not yet her husband, you cannot forbid her from doing this. Perhaps I could, as her father, although I do not doubt she would find a way to participate regardless."

With a heavy sigh, Darcy reluctantly nodded. "When?" he asked, his voice sounding resigned.

"It depends upon Wickham," Fitzwilliam replied. "You still have several days until your wedding, and if we can eliminate that threat before your wedding, then you will not have to hide your marriage. The most likely avenue for Father learning of it would then be eliminated."

Darcy nodded again. "Very well," he said after a moment.

"We need to make Wickham think Elizabeth is alone when she wanders the fields," Fitzwilliam began. "If she is on foot, so much the better. Sanderson reported this morning that Wickham is lazy, assigning his watches to an enlisted soldier so he does not have to rise as early. We will be able to get the guards in place well before Wickham rises from his bed."

"How will you know where he will attempt to accost her?" Bennet asked.

"Sanderson," was Fitzwilliam's reply. "He will 'encourage' him to attempt to take her here, near the cottage. It offers so many more possibilities, and, as you recall, Wickham is inherently lazy. He will do the least amount of work possible, and the cottage is simply a convenient option for him."

Darcy's fists clenched at the thoughts these words evoked. He wished to be a part of those protecting Elizabeth, but feared that if he saw Wickham touch her, he would wish to kill him. Already, just the thought of Wickham laying a finger on Elizabeth had him ready to pummel someone, most likely his cousin.

"What if Wickham is successful, and he does manage to abscond with Elizabeth?" Darcy demanded, his words sharp. "What if this Sanderson is not as reliable as you think, or if Wickham gets wind that something is not as it should be and changes tack in the middle? So many things could go wrong, and using Elizabeth in this way puts her at risk."

"William," came Elizabeth's soft voice. "More than one person will be watching me to ensure that I will be well. Wickham will not be allowed to harm me."

He reached out and drew Elizabeth into his arms, not caring about their audience. Her touch calmed him, and he let out his breath slowly. "It is difficult for me to willingly submit to someone I love being in danger," he whispered into her ear. "Forgive me for my stubbornness in this matter; it is simply that, now that I have found you, I do not want to run the risk of losing you."

"It will be well," she whispered back, her own arms encircling his waist

"While I cannot prevent Elizabeth from doing this," Darcy said finally, his cheek resting atop Elizabeth's head. For a moment, he simply closed his eyes and breathed her in. "I wish to be nearby, perhaps one of the men in the cottage. I may have an easier time of it if I am not watching things progress, but I *will* be near to wherever this occurs."

Fitzwilliam nodded, watching the two lovers almost jealously. "Yes, I will put you in the cottage with Elizabeth's two guards. A footman will accompany her, but he will need to allow himself to be 'knocked out' by Wickham to make the scheme more believable to Wickham. He has already seen that she is rarely completely unaccompanied, so he will need to think that he can easily overpower whoever is with her."

Darcy nodded his agreement. "One of my grooms looks younger than he is. He is stronger than he looks, and I think he could easily deceive Wickham into believing he has been overpowered. Starting tomorrow, he can accompany Elizabeth when she walks out. Another man can follow at a distance in case Wickham approaches her sooner than we think."

"That is wise," Bennet agreed. "Colonel, please send word when all of this is to take place. Like Darcy, I also wish to be near enough to see that all is well, but not so near that I am at risk of doing anything foolish."

"That can be arranged," Fitzwilliam replied. "Sanderson will send word when Wickham is ready to move, and we will finalise our plans then."

"Very well," Bennet said. "Darcy, would you please escort Elizabeth home? Her footmen are outside, but she wished to visit one of the tenants at Netherfield. I need to return to Longbourn."

"Of course," Darcy replied, releasing Elizabeth from his embrace. "Richard, we will speak more on this later."

"Of course," Fitzwilliam echoed, with a wink at Elizabeth. "I would have expected nothing else."

CHAPTER 36

The Confrontation

25 OCTOBER 1811

The next few days were tense—at least for those awaiting word on when Wickham might make his move against Elizabeth. Although there had been some discussion about delaying the wedding, it was ultimately decided that Elizabeth and Darcy would marry on Tuesday of the following week. Mrs. Bennet would be informed the evening before, but Mrs. Hill had been told that morning so she could begin preparing an intimate wedding breakfast for the couple and their carefully chosen guests.

The previous evening, a dinner was held at Lucas Lodge. During the gathering, Lieutenant Sanderson discreetly delivered a note to Colonel Fitzwilliam. It contained the news they had been waiting for: Wickham intended to approach Elizabeth the following morning.

Sanderson would accompany him—ostensibly to assist—but in truth, he hoped to accomplish the opposite. At the first safe opportunity, he would turn on Wickham and prevent any harm from coming to Elizabeth, without drawing Wickham's notice.

When Fitzwilliam quietly relayed the contents of the note to Darcy later that evening, Darcy's jaw tightened. He had already been reluctant to part from Elizabeth that night—but now, knowing what was planned, it took all of Fitzwilliam's reasoning to convince him not to act prematurely or to abscond with Elizabeth himself and carry her off to Pemberley. However, he allowed his cousin to send a note to Mr. Bennet to inform him that their plans would be put into effect the following morning.

Before the sun rose, Darcy and two of his footmen were ensconced in the little parlour of the cottage. Other of Darcy's footmen and a few trusted officers were hidden in the edges of the woods, and all were waiting to see what would happen. It had taken a significant amount of discussion, but Bennet had finally agreed that it was best for him to remain at home and wait for word about the events of the morning.

For Darcy, the morning dawned in what felt like an interminable fashion. He paced the length of the small parlour, glancing out the window every few steps despite the fact that it was too dark to see anything. Not long after their arrival, he had tossed his greatcoat and hat haphazardly over a nearby chair, gripping his gloves tightly in his hand while his expression remained grim. There was no fire, no candles lit, and he did his best to move through the room without crashing into any of the sparse furniture.

If his companions were aggravated by his constant movement, they did not show it, for they were equally anxious. The air in the room was thick with tension from all three men who waited to see what would happen.

As the sun was peeking over the hills, three short raps on the backdoor—the agreed upon signal with Colonel Fitzwilliam—made them all freeze. One of the footmen stepped to the door, opening it slowly.

Fitzwilliam entered and spoke quietly. "Miss Elizabeth is in place as are the guards. The scout reported that Wickham is on his way; he and Sanderson were seen leaving camp not ten minutes ago. Sanderson is keeping their pace slow, giving our people time to adjust as necessary. They all know Miss Elizabeth is not to be harmed, Darcy. You have my word that she will be well."

Darcy nodded once, sharply. "I want eyes on her every moment. If he so much as harms a hair on her head—"

"He will not get the chance," Fitzwilliam interrupted. "Stay sharp. It will all be over soon."

Darcy's hand tightened around the hilt of the small pistol tucked into his coat pocket. He prayed it would not be needed, but he was prepared to do whatever it might take to protect Elizabeth.

He watched as Fitzwilliam slipped back out of the cottage and found his hiding place nearby. The dim morning light provided cover, and Fitzwilliam wore a dark great coat to cover his brightly coloured regimental coat as did the handful of officers who were concealed as they waited for Wickham to act.

Unbidden, images of his sister crying over Wickham entered his mind. His sister's image soon shifted to Elizabeth, but in these, she was battered and bruised. Darcy had to shake his head to clear his mind of these thoughts. "She will be well," he muttered to himself.

Both of the men turned briefly to look at him, but apparently, the look on his face made them turn back. Darcy waited impatiently for several moments longer, and then finally, his patience was rewarded. Wickham had come.

He could not see Wickham's face clearly from his position, but Darcy could easily imagine the smug smile that would appear the moment he realized Elizabeth was seemingly alone, or at least, unprotected. His hands clenched into fists at his sides. Every instinct urged him to abandon the plan, to charge forward and drag Wickham from his horse—finally delivering the beating he had long dreamt about. But he forced himself to remain still. He had to wait.

While the confrontation likely only lasted a minute, for Darcy, it felt as though hours had passed between the moment he first spotted

Wickham approaching Elizabeth and when Fitzwilliam led him away in shackles.

Elizabeth paced slowly at the top of the hill, her hands clasped tightly in front of her to still their nervous energy. The early morning light cast long shadows across the landscape, and though the cottage below was partially obscured by trees and mist, she could still see its outline. She remained within sight of it, feeling the comfort it provided her. The knowledge that her intended was one of those watching made her slightly less nervous about what would come next.

A single footman stood at a distance, keeping her in view. He had been dressed plainly, his youthful appearance meant to seem unthreatening—especially to someone like Wickham.

From her vantage point, she spotted Colonel Fitzwilliam slip through the back door of the cottage. Before he knocked, he lifted one hand in a subtle signal—Wickham was coming.

Elizabeth took a steadying breath. Then, trying to appear casual, she turned and began walking slowly towards the path that led past the cottage as though she were simply out for her usual morning walk. She resisted the urge to look back, forcing her steps into a relaxed rhythm.

She had just passed the cottage when the sound of hooves reached her ears. Looking up, she saw two men in red coats approaching, their uniforms crisp against the pale light. One of them, unmistakably, was Wickham.

Her breath caught when she recognized him. Wickham sat easily in the saddle, his expression relaxed, almost smug as he approached, giving no sign that he knew he was walking into a trap. The officer beside him—Lieutenant Sanderson, presumably—rode slightly behind, his posture less at ease, eyes scanning the path ahead, looking for the men he knew were hidden there.

Elizabeth forced herself to keep walking. Her heart pounded, but her face remained composed, even pleasant. She could not afford to look afraid. Wickham would see that and press his advantage. No—if she was to play her part, she must seem unaware, unguarded, a young lady on her morning walk, meeting a recent acquaintance quite by chance.

"Good morning," Wickham called out. "It is Miss Elizabeth, is it not?"

"Do I know you, sir?" she asked, pretending to have forgotten him.

"We met in the village a few weeks ago," he replied smoothly, affecting a look of surprise. "You have forgotten me already? But then again, Darcy approached shortly after, and I think your attention was firmly fixed upon him, wasn't it?"

"My father has been careful to protect me and my sisters from men we do not know well, such as militia officers about whose characters and personal histories we know nothing beyond that which they claim," Elizabeth said.

"Ahh," Wickham replied. "That is extraordinarily foresighted of him. My old friend Darcy did not issue any warnings?"

"What if he did? Mr. Darcy and my father have been friends for many years, just as my father was friends with old Mr. Darcy," Elizabeth replied, her chin jutting forward in defiance. She had been warned not to antagonise Wickham, but she could not seem to help it.

"Do you walk often?" Wickham asked, attempting to turn the conversation to one that would help him charm her. While he could take her by force, he preferred not to have to and wished to make her willing.

"Not as much anymore," she replied. "I ride out daily, but my horse had a slight injury a few days ago and needed rest. Since I often rise early, I find it pleasant to walk in the early morning light, before too many people are about."

"I could not agree more," he said, dismounting smoothly. "However, I would say that quiet mornings are best enjoyed in good company. Might I join you?"

His tone was friendly, familiar—but his eyes flicked towards the trees beyond her, searching. He saw the single footman who had come a little closer upon seeing his charge with the officers, but, to Wickham, he appeared weak and easily overcome, particularly since he had Sanderson on his side.

Elizabeth stood still, allowing him to come closer, though every instinct in her screamed to step back. She was clearly wary, which she thought suited such a chance meeting.

Wickham noticed this and indicated the boy to Sanderson, who began to move in that direction as the two had arranged.

Elizabeth's stomach twisted in anxiety as she noticed this.

Returning his attention to Elizabeth, he now stood only a few paces away. His smile had shifted—no longer merely charming but sharpened by something colder. It was confident, calculated, and appeared almost predatory.

"Miss Elizabeth," he said in what he thought was a seductive tone, "you are looking particularly well this morning. The early morning light suits you, and the exercise has done wonders for your complexion."

Elizabeth met his gaze, her chin lifting slightly as she attempted to repress the shiver the look in his eyes caused.

He stepped closer still, his voice dropping into a murmur as he offered more hollow compliments. Rather than softening her, the words only made Elizabeth's spine stiffen with unease. Then, without warning, he reached out and seized her arm with a firm grip.

"Won't you come with me, my dear Lizzy?" he said, his tone falsely sweet, his expression dark with triumph. He believed the game was his—believed she was now entirely at his mercy. The idea that she might resist only thrilled him further. In his mind, it would make her eventual submission all the more satisfying; that and the idea that he was, again, taking something away from Darcy.

But before Elizabeth could respond—before she could twist away or strike him—a sharp whistle cut through the quiet morning air, rising from the trees behind them.

Wickham froze, recognising the signal for what it was.

In that moment, the woods seemed to come alive—footmen and officers emerging from their hiding places, surrounding him before he could even reach for the pistol he had tucked into his coat.

Elizabeth stepped back, breaking Wickham's hold upon her arm, her heart pounding in her chest, not from fear now, but from sheer relief. She had expected them but had still felt a moment of fear when he had grasped her arm.

Colonel Fitzwilliam strode forward, his voice clipped and firm. "George Wickham, you are under arrest for attempted kidnapping and conspiracy to cause harm to a gentlewoman. That will be added to the charges of dereliction of duty and conduct unbecoming an officer."

Wickham's expression twisted, the mask of charm falling away in an instant. Fury contorted his features.

He reached for Elizabeth again, but she had already stepped back. Darcy was only a few strides away, moving fast—but still, Wickham lunged.

"I will tell everyone I have ruined her!" he shouted, desperation and rage mingling in his voice.

"Silence!" Fitzwilliam commanded, his tone sharp. "You will have your chance to speak—but not here, and not now. You are under arrest."

Elizabeth watched, trembling but steady, as Wickham was disarmed and restrained. Only then did she allow herself a breath—a full breath—her hands still clenched at her sides.

Darcy appeared at her side a heartbeat later, his coat brushing against hers as he stopped. His expression was unreadable, composed on the surface, but his eyes searched her face with urgency, his focus never straying from her as he examined her carefully.

After a moment, he drew her into his arms without speaking, holding her tightly as if anchoring them both. Elizabeth did not resist. She let herself lean into him, feeling the steady rise and fall of his chest, the tension in his frame slowly beginning to ease.

Finally, he pulled back just enough to see her face. "Are you hurt?" he asked quietly, his voice tight with concern.

She shook her head, her voice soft but sure. "No. I am quite well."

He exhaled, then released her only to take her hand, gripping it firmly in his own. "It is finished."

Elizabeth's gaze drifted to where Wickham was being led away in shackles, flanked by two officers. Then she turned back to Darcy, her brows drawing together.

"Yes," she said, a small smile breaking through for the first time that morning. "It is." But then her smile faded. "At least this part is. We still have Miss Bingley to contend with."

Darcy's jaw tightened, and he pulled her gently back into his arms. "We will deal with her later this morning," he said, his voice low. "I can only hope her brother is willing to acknowledge her part in this and act to ensure she cannot do this again."

CHAPTER 37

Bingley Finds Out

It was still early when Darcy and Elizabeth arrived at Netherfield. Inside, Lady Matlock and Aunt Horatia were already awake and seated in the smaller sitting room they frequented each morning while they waited on the rest of the Bingleys and the Hursts to wake and come down for breakfast. A silver tea service sat between them, steam curling gently from the spout.

Lady Matlock sat upright in her chair, hands folded too tightly in her lap to be at ease. While she maintained a composed expression, her eyes flicked repeatedly towards the door. Her son had shared the barest outline of the plan with her the night before—only after she questioned him about his visible agitation following the dinner. She had not slept soundly, filled with worry as she considered various scenarios that might result in injury to either her son or her nephew —or the girl who would soon be her niece.

If Horatia Bingley noticed her companion's agitated state, she did not mention it.

When Darcy and Elizabeth were shown in, unaccompanied, both

appearing wind-worn but whole, the ladies said nothing of the unusual arrival. If either were surprised, they did not let it show.

"Good morning, Mr. Darcy. Miss Elizabeth," Aunt Horatia greeted them. "Would either of you care for coffee or tea?"

Elizabeth returned the greeting, her voice calm despite the faint flush in her cheeks. Both she and Darcy requested tea, and Aunt Horatia rang the bell. A maid appeared almost instantly, and upon receiving her instructions, she hurried away, closing the door behind her with a quiet click.

As soon as they were alone, Aunt Horatia turned to Elizabeth. "Tell me, my dear—how is it you find yourself at Netherfield so early in the morning?"

The question was delivered mildly, but Elizabeth could sense the curiosity behind it. She did not hesitate to provide an explanation.

"Colonel Fitzwilliam and Mr. Darcy arranged a plan to trap Mr. Wickham," she said. "He has long troubled the Darcy family, and this morning, at last, he was caught. This time, he will face the consequences of his actions."

Lady Matlock leant forward slightly, her gaze shifting between them. "All is well, then? No one was hurt? Everything went according to plan?"

Elizabeth nodded. "Yes. All is well. Word has already been sent to my father, and Wickham is on his way to face a court martial."

Darcy, who had been silent until now, suddenly straightened, unable to hold back any longer.

"Miss Bingley—" he began, then paused before speaking again. "Miss Bingley, is your nephew awake? I must speak with him at once; Hurst, too, if it can be managed."

He shook his head as if trying to clear it of the morning's events. "You should hear what I have to say, as well—but I would rather not repeat it. If it is not too much trouble, would you please send for both of your nephews?"

Aunt Horatia gave a small, decisive nod. "They ought to be awake. If either is not, I will instruct his valet to rouse him and have him presentable as soon as may be."

She rose and moved towards the door. "I suspect whatever you have to say will be neither pleasant nor suited to delay."

Without waiting for a servant, Aunt Horatia nodded and left the sitting room, giving the others a few moments of privacy. While the maid delivered a second tea tray and refreshed the first, Horatia made her way up the stairs to her nephews' chambers.

She knocked quietly on Bingley's door. After a short pause, his valet opened the door, blinking in surprise to see her standing there so early. Without raising her voice, she instructed him to wake and to have his master downstairs and presentable as quickly as possible.

From there she moved to Hurst's room, finding him already awake and in the process of dressing.

"Meet us downstairs in a quarter of an hour," she said quietly. "Mr. Darcy wishes to speak with Charles, you, and me without delay."

He nodded without argument and began dressing in earnest.

Nearly thirty minutes later, Bingley entered the sitting room, adjusting the cuffs of his jacket, his expression still drowsy but curious, particularly when he noticed the way the door was opened by one of Darcy's footmen who shut the door again as soon as Bingley entered. His gaze immediately turned to Elizabeth, who was seated beside Darcy.

"Miss Elizabeth," he said, blinking in surprise. "What brings you here so early?"

"She arrived with me," Darcy said, rising to his feet, his voice calm but firm as he faced the two gentlemen. "Bingley, Hurst—there is something you both must hear."

Darcy began to recount the events of that morning: Wickham's planned approach, the trap set to catch him in the act, and Elizabeth's role in drawing him out. Each word he spoke was precise, stripped of unnecessary emotion but clear in its urgency and in the danger that Elizabeth faced.

Then, his voice tightening, he shared what Lieutenant Sanderson had reported—of the meeting between Wickham and Caroline Bingley, and the sum exchanged in return for Wickham's promise to compromise Elizabeth. Sanderson had told Fitzwilliam more about what Wickham had said about the Bennets, including the rumour that Elizabeth would one day inherit Longbourn.

The room fell silent.

"That cannot be true, Darcy," Bingley said at last, his voice thick with disbelief. "Caroline may be thoughtless—vain and selfish, even—but she would never…she could not…that is *not* possible."

"She did," Darcy replied, his tone colder than it had been all morning. "There is no doubt since at least one witness heard her very clearly. I suggest you speak to her maid, for she was also involved in the plot."

"Charles," Aunt Horatia began, "we warned you that something like this was not only possible but likely. I questioned your giving her her full allowance and told you that she was heard muttering on several occasions that she would do whatever it took to ensure Miss Elizabeth and Mr. Darcy would not wed. Can you truly be that shocked that she would go to this extreme, particularly after seeing how upset she was after the dinner party Monday night?"

"Caroline would never do as you have suggested," Bingley said again.

"Bingley, are you truly so foolish?" Hurst bit out, tired of hearing his brother by marriage excuse the younger Bingley sister. "Caroline is vindictive and cruel and would have no qualm about causing harm to someone who was in her way. She has always wanted Darcy, and, despite her recent insistence otherwise, she would have never given up on him, not until he was married and perhaps not even then."

Bingley merely shook his head. "I cannot believe it of her," he reiterated.

"One of the grooms followed Caroline when she rode out the morning after our dinner party with the Bennets and Lucases," Aunt Horatia told him. "He told me the same thing that Lieutenant Sanderson told Colonel Fitzwilliam. If you recall, I warned you several days ago that you must do something about your sister. You neglected to act by speaking to the grooms or coachman about not allowing her to leave the grounds."

"And I told you, Bingley, about her trip into the village one day last week," Hurst interjected.

"The matter of your sister is no longer yours to manage, Bingley," Darcy said, his voice sharp, cutting through Bingley's protests. He looked squarely at the man he had called a friend for years, disappointment etched in every word. Bingley had always been too quick to excuse his sister's behaviour, and now Darcy wondered if he would ever see her clearly.

Bingley stared at him, stunned. "What are you saying, Darcy?"

It was Lady Matlock who answered, her voice cool and commanding as she spoke for the first time since the gentlemen had entered.

"You have two choices, Mr. Bingley," she said. "Your sister's actions were not merely improper—they were criminal. If you choose to shield her or turn a blind eye, I will see to it that word of her involvement spreads throughout every drawing room in London. You and your sister will be thoroughly disgraced."

Bingley paled.

"If, however," she continued, "you acknowledge the gravity of what she has done—if you condemn her conduct—then I will leave it to Miss Bennet and Mr. Bennet to determine what consequence should follow. But do not mistake my meaning: one way or another, your sister *will* be held accountable."

Bingley turned to look at Elizabeth. "Surely you must realise that she did not truly understand what she was doing," he said, his voice pleading. "She did not know of the connection between Darcy and this Wickham fellow and did not realise the extent to which he might act."

"Does that truly matter, Mr. Bingley?" Elizabeth asked, her voice steady as she tilted her head slightly, fixing him with a calm but piercing gaze. "Were your sister's actions somehow less abhorrent because she may not have known the full extent of what Lieutenant Wickham intended?"

Bingley opened his mouth to respond, but no words came.

Elizabeth continued, her tone still composed but sharpened by the weight of the truth. "If the situation were reversed—and I had paid a man to ruin your sister, extending to your entire family—would you be so quick to excuse it? Would you feel no anger? Would you not expect me to be held accountable for what I had done?"

Bingley continued to stare at her, still unable to speak.

Darcy stepped in then, his voice cold and controlled, each word deliberate. "Bingley, if Wickham had succeeded, it would not have ended with a kiss, or some trivial scandal to be quietly forgotten. His intent was clear—to render Elizabeth unmarriageable."

He paused, allowing the words to sink in before adding with steel in his voice, "That is what your sister wished for. She even lied to Wickham, telling him that Elizabeth would likely inherit Longbourn one day, offering him an extra incentive to go as far as he dared. She did not act out of ignorance. She acted with cruel intentions. She wanted Elizabeth ruined, and she wanted her to suffer. All because she wanted what she could not have—me."

"Darcy," Bingley began, but Darcy waved his hand, cutting him off.

"Unless you intend to acknowledge your sister's faults, I do not want to hear it. I refuse to hear any more excuses for her behaviour," Darcy said harshly.

Bingley turned instead to Elizabeth. "What would you see done to her?" he asked softly.

Elizabeth drew in a slow breath through her nose, then let it out just as slowly. "I do not know at present. My father will no doubt have some ideas about what ought to happen, and I will need to discuss it with him and William before we make any decisions. At the very least, she has no place in polite society—although banishment seems too easy since one man will hang for his part in it, after all. However, I am not certain that she deserves to go to Newgate for what she has done. The conditions there are so inhumane that I can hardly imagine sending another young woman there despite what she has done. I am torn," she admitted.

Bingley stared, glancing back and forth between Darcy and Elizabeth. "You called him William," he said, his tone accusing.

"We are engaged," Darcy replied, cutting off anything his friend may have said after that. "Mr. Bennet has given his blessing, and, for what it is worth, so did my father. It is a long story and not one I intend to share at this moment. We have kept the engagement a secret from all but a few due to this threat from Wickham and your sister."

"But Caroline was so certain..." Bingley was cut off, but this time it was by Colonel Fitzwilliam entering the room.

"Then your sister is every bit as much of a fool as you are," Fitzwilliam replied. "Darcy would have never married your sister, and it has far less to do with her connections to trade than his desire to not tie himself to a termagant. If you truly thought Darcy would one day give in and marry your sister, then you are blind, not to mention deaf, for my cousin has made his stance very clear."

Bingley let out a low groan and sank further into his chair, burying his face in his hands. His shoulders sagged under the weight of realisation of how far he had fallen.

"I do not know why I ever listened to her," he muttered, his voice muffled. "What am I to do with her now?"

Aunt Horatia stood, her gaze cool and unwavering as she looked down at her nephew.

"You begin," she said crisply, "by finding her a situation—somewhere far from town, far from temptation, and far from the society she craves. Then," she added, her tone sharpening, "you follow the example set by your friend and his cousin—and learn how to become a man. I suggest you escort her yourself to wherever she is going, and perhaps along the way, you can explain to her precisely where she has erred and how you have erred in not correcting her."

There was no malice in her words, but no softness, either. Bingley had no room to argue. "Miss Elizabeth," he said, raising his head to look at her. "Allow me to apologise for my sister's actions and for not checking her sooner. I am uncertain whether I could have done anything to prevent this, but I ought to have made the attempt. Please inform me when you and your father have made your decision about her punishment, and I will comply."

Elizabeth nodded. "Thank you, Mr. Bingley. I accept your apology, at least for your own actions. While you ought to have done something to check your sister long before now, you are not wholly responsible for her actions. She is quite old enough to know that what she did was wrong. However, I do not envy you having to inform her."

Darcy's gaze locked onto Bingley's, cold and unyielding.

"My family and I will remain under your roof, Bingley, but only on one condition; your sister must be kept under constant guard. A footman—one strong enough to restrain her, if necessary—should be stationed outside the doors to her chambers until she departs."

Darcy straightened slightly, his voice tightening. "Under no circumstances will I be in the same room as her. If she attempts to speak to me—or to any member of my family—I will leave Netherfield without a moment's hesitation. If you cannot agree to these terms, I will take myself to Longbourn until Elizabeth and I are wed and can return to London. Doing so may not be entirely proper, given my engagement to Elizabeth, but I do not care. I will not subject myself or those I love to your sister's presence. Nor will I hear her speak a word against Elizabeth or any other member of the Bennet family."

Bingley swallowed hard and nodded, his eyes dropping to the floor. He could not meet Darcy's gaze.

"You are correct," he said quietly. "Forgive me, Darcy. You have warned me before about her conduct and about my habit of giving in to her far too easily. Both you and Lady Matlock have spoken plainly about her atrocious behaviour, and I have done nothing. Even my inviting Aunt Horatia was done for selfish reasons and was another way for me to abdicate my responsibility for my sister."

He looked up, shame written across his face. "I have not been much of a friend to you."

Darcy looked at him harshly. "I cannot disagree, Bingley. Our relationship henceforth will be dependent on how you act in this situation and whether you can do as your aunt has suggested and learn to take responsibility for yourself."

Bingley nodded before quietly excusing himself and going to speak to the footmen about guarding his sister's room. Once that was done, he would speak to her himself and inform her that he knew of her actions and that there would be consequences.

"Come, Elizabeth," Darcy began. "I believe we are done here, and I confess that I prefer to be far away before Charles speaks to his sister. Richard, are you returning to the camp?"

He grinned. "No, in fact, I came to find you. I will accompany you to Longbourn and will tell both of you and Bennet at the same time what Wickham has said and what he attempted to claim."

"I do not think I can bear anything more today," Darcy muttered, pressing his fingers to the bridge of his nose, his weariness plain in the gesture.

Elizabeth chuckled. "Come, William, and after your cousin is finished we will sneak outside for a respite, and I will soothe the ache in your head," she whispered.

Darcy looked up at her, startled, heat creeping up his neck and turning the tips of his ears pink before he burst into laughter.

Elizabeth looked offended. "What about my offer was humorous?" she asked.

Still laughing, Darcy lightly patted her hand. "I love you, Elizabeth," he said, leaving Elizabeth still glaring at the *non sequitur*. "I will explain later, my dearest—after we are wed."

Perplexed by his answer, Elizabeth glared at him a moment longer before relenting and allowing him and his cousin to escort her to the stables.

CHAPTER 38

Decisions and Another Confrontation

Upon arriving at Longbourn, Colonel Fitzwilliam, Darcy, and Elizabeth were quietly shown to Bennet's study. To their mild surprise, the rest of the Bennet household had not yet come downstairs. A quick glance at the clock explained why—it was only half past eight. The family typically did not take breakfast until nine.

"If we hurry, we can finish speaking before Mama comes downstairs," Elizabeth said, raising her hand to knock. "She will question what is happening if Papa is not at breakfast on time, not that she will not have enough questions when she sees the two of you here so early."

At the sound of Bennet's call to "Come," the three of them stepped into the room.

"Papa," Elizabeth began, but before she could say more, her father had stood and embraced her.

"Dear Lizzy, I am glad to see you safe and well," Bennet said after a moment. "The footman Colonel Fitzwilliam sent gave a full report, but I am pleased to see you with my own eyes."

335

After a moment, he released her, and the four of them took their seats. Rather than settling behind his desk, Bennet chose one of the chairs near the fire. Colonel Fitzwilliam sat beside him, while Darcy and Elizabeth took the settee opposite, sitting close enough that their shoulders touched.

"We went directly to Netherfield after the arrest," Elizabeth began. "Fitzwilliam needed to confront Mr. Bingley about his sister's involvement." She paused a moment before continuing. "You already know of her part in the scheme?"

Bennet nodded solemnly.

"William told Mr. Bingley that her fate would be left to us," Elizabeth continued, leaning slightly into Darcy's shoulder, drawing strength from his presence. "As much as I might like to have her charged with a crime, I do not know if I wish for the notoriety of it, even if it only goes as far as Meryton. However, I feel certain that Miss Bingley would feel compelled to mention Mr. Darcy, dragging his name through the mud along with hers."

"Is it to be Bedlam, then?" Colonel Fitzwilliam asked.

Elizabeth visibly shuddered. "I have heard such horror stories about that place that I cannot imagine willingly subjecting anyone to it. Even Miss Bingley, who is clearly no friend of mine, does not deserve the treatment that I have read about. No, banishment seems most appropriate, but I am unsure how that is to be accomplished."

"Her brother cannot, or will not, control her. She would need a very stern keeper and limited funds, to guarantee she cannot escape. Personally, I would have liked to see her sent to Van Diemen's Land as a convict, but that may be difficult to do without formal charges. Still, I would prefer an ocean or some other significant body of water between her and any members of my family," Darcy said drily.

"I agree," Bennet said. "Is Ireland far enough, or the Outer Hebrides? The New World?"

"The New World amongst the natives?" Colonel Fitzwilliam interjected, a smile on his face. "Can you imagine how she would look down her nose at them?"

His attempt at levity fell flat amongst the others in the room.

"Ireland is, I believe, far enough," Darcy replied. "Not only that, but forcing Bingley to convey her there himself, not to mention arranging for a strict companion, guards, and the disposition of her funds to care for her, would be an adequate punishment for his unwillingness to put a stop to her behaviour before now."

"Where would he take her?" Elizabeth asked.

"While it would serve her right to live in a small cottage, it may be more difficult to ensure she is guarded by an adequate staff. Nor do I think it would do her any good to be housed in a Darcy holding, for she would certainly view it as something other than intended," Darcy mused.

"It ought to be her brother who takes on the responsibility of caring for her," Bennet stated firmly.

"Yes," Darcy agreed. "I will loan him two of my men, the same who have been watching over Elizabeth for the last few days. They can accompany him as far as Liverpool, but then he will need to make arrangements to have someone who can assist him once he boards the ship to take him across the Irish Sea."

"So, she is to be banished to Ireland then?" Fitzwilliam replied.

Bennet looked to Elizabeth for confirmation, and upon seeing her nod, indicated his own agreement with that plan.

"Yes, Bingley will need to set her up with a companion and someone to act as a guard, someone who will manage her funds and will ensure that she cannot ever return to England," Darcy stated.

"Then, it is decided," the colonel said. "Wickham has been charged as I indicated he would be and now awaits his court martial. He attempted to bribe me into releasing him by mentioning Georgiana, then stated that my father had sent him to Ramsgate to seduce her. He said the earl wanted something that he could use to blackmail Darcy into doing as he wished."

Darcy clenched his jaw, his anger simmering just beneath the surface as he closed his eyes, fighting the urge to unleash the torrent of curses pressing at his lips. Sensing his struggle, Elizabeth gently reached over and laid her hand atop his clenched fist, offering comfort.

After Darcy had calmed himself, the colonel continued. "When that did not work, he claimed that my father had sent him to Meryton to encourage Darcy to do as the earl demanded before attempting to lay the blame on Miss Bingley. It would almost be amusing to see the two of them in the same cell, just to see what accusations they would launch at the other. Regardless, Wickham will trouble your family no longer, Darcy."

Darcy acknowledged his cousin's words with a tight nod. He and Elizabeth had discussed the matter of Wickham on the ride back from Netherfield, and while Darcy felt some remorse for his former friend, he would do nothing to save his bride's would-be attacker. He opened his fist and clasped Elizabeth's hand in his.

Seeing that there were no questions, Fitzwilliam rose from his seat and continued, "I will return to Netherfield to inform the puppy of what has been decided and see how he takes it. Darcy, remain with your intended and enjoy your morning. After I speak to Bingley, I will escort my mother and Georgiana to Longbourn, so they can escape what will no doubt become a battlefield this day."

Bennet laughed. "Darcy, I invite you, your sister, your aunt, and your cousin to join our family for dinner this evening; in fact, I invite you all to spend the entire day at Longbourn."

Darcy lifted his lips in a slight grin. "I will gladly take you up on your offer, sir. You are correct; it is likely best that we are far from Netherfield today."

Despite the heavy conversation, the group was laughing as they exited Bennet's study. Fitzwilliam was able to slip away from Longbourn unseen by any other Bennets, and Bennet joined his wife and the rest of his daughters in the breakfast room, followed by Elizabeth and Darcy.

Once again, Mrs. Bennet regarded the couple with a speculative eye but managed, barely, to hold her tongue. That did not stop her from dropping several pointed hints throughout the meal. These were politely ignored by all present, even Jane who was aware of the couple's engagement but knew nothing of the morning's events or of Miss Caroline Bingley's role in them.

Shortly after breakfast, Lady Matlock and Georgiana Darcy arrived, accompanied by her companion. As suggested, they spent the entire day at Longbourn and had an enjoyable time in company with the Bennets.

When Fitzwilliam returned to Netherfield, he informed Bingley that the Bennets had decreed his sister was to be banished to Ireland. He and his sister would be expected to depart the area on Monday, allowing them a day to prepare.

"You say I must accompany her?" Bingley asked.

"Who else would?" Fitzwilliam replied, incredulous. "You will need to arrange for a place for her to live and set up accounts to cover food for her and her servants to eat and other necessities. Someone will need to be responsible for her funds, and one of the conditions is that she can never return to England. Either you will need to stay to ensure this is enforced, or you will need to hire someone to do it. How will you do this from a distance?"

Bingley hung his head. "This is my punishment, is it not?"

"Punishment?" Fitzwilliam said, eyeing the younger man with distaste. "Not a punishment, I would say, but your duty. Had you bothered to check your sister, it would not have become necessary to banish her, but since you did not, you must now resolve the problem you have created."

Bingley sighed heavily, having had time, and his aunt, to make him realise the error of his ways. "My aunt will remain in residence and can act as hostess for Darcy and your family. You will all be welcome to stay at Netherfield as long as you like. I imagine it will take several months to make all the necessary arrangements."

He sighed, as he took a moment to think. "Part of me wishes to ask Aunt Horatia or Louisa to come along. Aunt Horatia could manage my sister far better than I could, but that would not teach me the lesson that I am intended to learn, would it?"

Fitzwilliam remained silent, allowing the younger man to speak without interruption. He watched Bingley closely, and for the first time, wondered if this might be the catalyst that forced the young man to finally grow up. Dealing with his sister could either forge his character—or break it entirely. It remained to be seen which it would be.

After a pause, Fitzwilliam rose. "I will take my leave," he said, brushing an invisible speck from his sleeve. "My mother and cousin have been invited to spend the day at Longbourn, and I should not keep them waiting."

He paused at the door, then turned back. "But let me leave you with a final warning."

His voice dropped, hardening into steel.

"If Miss Bingley ever dares to approach a member of my family again—if she so much as speaks a word to them—she will not be the only one to suffer the consequences. Once she boards that ship in Liverpool, her feet should never again touch English soil."

SPORT FOR OUR NEIGHBOURS

The threat, calmly delivered, landed with unmistakable weight. Fitzwilliam's gaze held Bingley's, sharp and unrelenting.

Bingley, pale and stiff, managed only a nod. He had long feared crossing Darcy—but this was different. Colonel Fitzwilliam, a decorated soldier who had seen battle more than once, had the air of a man who did not bluff or make idle threats. Bingley had no doubt he would carry out every word he had spoken.

That warning still hung heavy in the air when Fitzwilliam departed, leaving Bingley to face the outcome of his sister's actions alone. As expected, the scene that followed at Netherfield was unpleasant for all involved.

Miss Bingley had been livid when she attempted to leave her room and discovered her path blocked by a broad-shouldered footman. She might have been even more enraged had she recognized him as the same man who had accompanied Elizabeth Bennet on more than one occasion—but Caroline rarely acknowledged servants and so failed to make the connection. Had she done so, she might also have remembered that he had once worn Darcy's livery which would have further increased her fury.

Instead, she found herself confined to her rooms, her attempts to leave met with firm refusal. Not long after, her brother appeared at the door. Already seething, her anger only deepened when he calmly informed her of what would happen in the coming days.

"Liverpool?" she nearly shrieked. "Why on earth would we travel to Liverpool? It is late autumn, surely it would be better to travel to London so we might prepare for the Season. And this nonsense about travelling to Ireland is utterly foolish. No, Brother, I refuse to accompany you."

"You do not have a choice, Caroline," Bingley said, already exasperated with her. "I am telling you; you will be travelling to Ireland as soon as it can be arranged. We will leave on Monday to go to Liverpool, and from there to Ireland."

"What do you mean, I do not have a choice? You cannot drag me all the way to Ireland," she demanded.

"Perhaps not, but if you do not accompany me, you will be tried for your part in that lieutenant's action against Miss Elizabeth Bennet. There are at least two witnesses who claim you paid Lieutenant Wickham to ruin Miss Elizabeth, even telling him that she would inherit her father's estate to encourage the man in his efforts," Bingley said slowly.

"You cannot believe that I would do such a thing," she said, her face red in her anger.

"Perhaps, but Darcy and Fitzwilliam both say it is true," Bingley said. "I would like to think that you are innocent of this, but they are adamant. If you can show me that you still have the two hundred and fifty pounds I gave to you and that you did not meet with Wickham, I might persuade them to relent. Can you show me the funds?"

Miss Bingley huffed. "I cannot," she said between clenched teeth. "I sent the money to London to pay for…a gown or two, and the rest I sent to one of the charitable endeavours I participate in. I had hoped to show Mr. Darcy how much better suited I am to be his wife than that Miss Eliza, but how can I do that if he thinks so poorly of me? You can convince him, can you not?" her voice had turned wheedling, hoping to convince her brother to act on her behalf.

"I cannot," he said. "I have been told that you are never to speak to a member of the Darcy family again. In fact, Darcy has said that he agrees to remain under the same roof as you only if you are confined to your rooms with guards to ensure you do no leave them. He will not relent, and Fitzwilliam might actually run me through if I attempted to ask him for leniency in this matter."

He straightened, his voice gaining strength as he spoke. "Your maid has been replaced and a new one has been instructed to pack your belongings. We are to depart first thing Monday morning—at dawn, Caroline, not whenever it pleases you to rise. And if you test me on this, I will have a footman carry you to the carriage in your bed clothes. Do not doubt me."

Miss Bingley huffed, clearly furious, but said nothing more. For now, she seemed to accept his authority—however reluctantly. Turning her back on him in silent protest, she moved to the window.

Bingley lingered only a moment longer, delivering his final warning.

"There will be a footman stationed at both doors to your rooms. You will not leave without my knowledge, and your maid has been ordered not to pass along any notes or messages. Louisa is fully aware of your actions the past few days and of your dealings with Wickham. She will not help you. Nor will Wickham—he is currently in a military gaol awaiting court-martial. And from everything I have learnt from Darcy, he will be far more concerned with saving himself than aiding you."

He closed the door just in time. A glass perfume jar crashed against the wood, shattering where his head had been moments before. He sighed—wearier than startled—then calmly turned the key in the lock, securing it with a quiet, resolute click.

CHAPTER 39

Preparations Begin

27 OCTOBER 1811

On Monday, preparations began in earnest for Elizabeth and Darcy's wedding the next day. When she learnt of it, Mrs. Bennet had been insistent that it must be delayed and listed the various reasons why it ought to be, but none of the parties involved would agree to the change in date.

Finally, Lady Matlock spoke, helping Mrs. Bennet to understand the urgency. "Mrs. Bennet, I know you feel that a grander ceremony is necessary, but truly, the marriage cannot wait. It has been kept secret for a good reason. If my husband, Lord Matlock, learns of the wedding, he will take steps to prevent it from happening."

"But…" Mrs. Bennet began again, but then the countess's words seemed to sink in. "Your husband…the earl, he would stop the wedding? Oh, does he disapprove of our family? But…"

"Lord Matlock has certain ideas about who our nephew should marry that have more to do with his own political aspirations than what is in Fitzwilliam's best interest," Lady Matlock soothed, cutting into the lady's nervous prattle.

"Do not worry, Mrs. Bennet; I will make it impossible for my husband to interfere with their marriage, but that is why the matter has been kept secret. There was an officer in the militia who was aiding my husband, but now he has been dealt with, and Miss Bingley has been sent away."

"What did Miss Bingley do?" Mrs. Bennet gasped.

"Nothing, Mama, or at least nothing of significance. Mr. Bingley has decided to escort her far from here for a time, to allow her an opportunity to reflect on her behaviour towards myself and Fitzwilliam. You do not need to worry," Elizabeth interjected, with a speaking look at Lady Matlock, who nodded her understanding.

Mrs. Bennet looked between the two, but before she could speak, she was interrupted by Mrs. Hill.

"Madam, there is a carriage approaching," she said. "I believe the master informed you that the Livesay family was expected today."

"Oh, yes, I had nearly forgotten about that in all of our excitement over the wedding," she exclaimed. "Does Mr. Livesay already know about the wedding?"

"I am uncertain," Elizabeth said, having not discussed the matter with her father. She knew that Mr. Livesay was expected, along with his daughter, but had not known anything else that may have been discussed between the men.

"It does not matter," Mrs. Bennet said dismissively. "Come, let us greet our guests, and we can inform them if they are unaware."

That said, Mrs. Bennet moved quickly to the hallway where her husband was waiting with Darcy. She moved next to her husband, while Elizabeth moved to stand next to her intended.

"Come with me, Elizabeth," Darcy murmured near her ear, his voice low and warm. "While your father greets his guests, we might steal a moment to speak about what comes after the wedding."

Elizabeth's cheeks flushed at once, her thoughts leaping to meanings he may not have intended. Still, she gave a quick nod and let him lead her away, opposite the direction of her parents.

Once they reached the music room and the door was drawn mostly closed behind them, Darcy turned to face her. He took one look at the vivid colour in her cheeks and the startled expression in her eyes and instantly realised her thoughts had run ahead of his words.

"No, Elizabeth—I fear I have spoken poorly again," he said, a rueful smile tugging at his lips. "While I certainly look forward to our life together after we are wed, I meant something rather more practical."

He reached for her hand, lifting it gently to his lips for a soft, chaste kiss.

"I only meant to ask what you would like to do after the ceremony. With the matter of Wickham and Miss Bingley finally behind us, we have a bit of freedom. We might spend a few days in London, or perhaps retreat somewhere quieter, just the two of us, before joining our families again."

"Are we not needed to confront Lord Matlock?" Elizabeth asked, tilting her head as she studied Darcy. She still held his hand in hers, unwilling to let go after the gentle kiss he had pressed to it only moments before.

"No," Darcy replied, his tone reassuring. "That is what your father and I were discussing while you were with your mother and my aunt. Your Uncle Gardiner is expected to arrive today, and while we are away on our wedding trip, he will meet with your father and Mr. Livesay. Together, they will review everything that has been discovered with Lady Matlock and Richard."

He paused briefly, then added, "They will all join us in London on Monday. Once we are reunited, we will confront Lord Matlock together and inform him of our marriage. Between them—and my cousin—they will ensure we are fully prepared when the time comes."

"Then, ought we go to London? What if your uncle learns we are there before we are ready for him?" Elizabeth asked.

Darcy hesitated for only a moment before speaking slowly. "I do not relish the idea of spending our wedding night in an inn," Darcy said. "It is too late to make many arrangements, and most places could not be properly aired and cleaned before we could arrive."

"What of the dower house?" Elizabeth suggested. "It is small, or at least, rather smaller than what you are used to, but it is clean, and if you were to borrow a few of the maids from Netherfield, it could be aired and freshened this afternoon. Mrs. Hill could send a maid or a footman to bring us our meals each day, and they can leave things that we can eat whenever we like."

Leaning down to press a quick kiss to Elizabeth's lips, Darcy found himself once again elated to have chosen such a brilliant bride. "That is the perfect solution, Elizabeth. We will be close by should someone have need of us, but we would not be sharing a house with any of our relations. I know we could have stayed at Netherfield, but I did not want to share a roof with my sister or cousin during the first day of our marriage or be forced to socialise with anyone apart from you."

Elizabeth laughed at his rare burst of exuberance. "You have chosen well, William," she said, grinning at the mock-affronted look he gave her in return.

"But we have been hiding long enough," she added, still smiling. "We need to greet Mr. Livesay and his daughter—before someone comes looking for us."

Darcy's expression shifted at once, a flicker of protest crossing his features.

"Just a moment," he murmured, pulling her into his arms.

Elizabeth's breath caught, but her gaze held steady. "I love you, William," she whispered.

He did not reply with words. Instead, his lips found hers in a kiss that was deeper, slower than any they had shared before. It held no urgency, only a quiet, smouldering promise wrapped in desire.

Elizabeth responded instinctively, her hands sliding to his chest, then upward, one drifting into the soft hair at the nape of his neck. Her fingers tangled there, holding him to her as the world around them slipped away. The warmth of him grounded her, the steady press of his body anchoring her against the many difficulties they had faced and would continue to face in the coming days. All of that was forgotten in the moment.

Their kiss deepened—slow, deliberate, filled with unspoken hunger. His hands settled along her waist, strong and possessive, drawing her closer until there was no space left between them. Every inch of their bodies seemed to touch and catch fire.

She melted into him. The kiss was enough to leave her flushed and breathless, her entire body tingling with awareness, every nerve attuned to the quiet, unmistakable truth of how much he wanted her.

When they finally pulled apart, Elizabeth rested her forehead lightly against his chest, her breath still uneven. Darcy's hand remained along the small of her back, holding her close, his thumb tracing a slow, thoughtful line along the fabric of her gown.

For a moment, neither of them spoke.

Then, in a voice barely above a whisper, he said, "You undo me, Elizabeth. Every time I believe I have regained control, that I can withstand your wit or your charm—you smile, or say my name, and I am lost to you all over again."

She looked up at him, her cheeks still flushed, her eyes soft but bright. "Then we are both undone," she murmured, her fingers lightly brushing the edge of his cravat. "And I find I do not mind it in the least."

He smiled then—a small, private smile meant only for her. "I was not prepared for this…for you, when I came to Hertfordshire in September. I thought I knew what love and marriage was meant to look like. But you have turned all of that on its head."

She tilted her head slightly, teasing. "You mean love is not meant to be inconvenient and rather impertinent?"

He chuckled under his breath. "It is meant to be worth everything. And it is. You are, dearest, loveliest, Elizabeth."

For a heartbeat longer, they simply stood there—holding, breathing, knowing that after everything, this was real. Then, reluctantly, Darcy stepped back and offered his arm.

"Shall we join the others, Elizabeth?"

Elizabeth took it with a quiet smile. "Of course, William."

When the couple entered the drawing room arm in arm, they were greeted with knowing smiles by the new arrivals. Darcy took a moment to introduce Elizabeth to Miss Amelia Livesay who he had met in town, and her brother, Frederick Livesay, second son to James Livesay.

"Darcy," the elder Livesay said warmly, rising to shake his hand. "I suspected you might be here, but Bennet tells me you and his Lizzy have been nearly inseparable since you met. So, when is the wedding?"

Darcy clasped his hand and gave a wry smile. "Tomorrow."

Livesay blinked, clearly caught off guard. "Tomorrow?"

Darcy chuckled at the stunned expression on the older gentleman's face. "Indeed. I believe Mr. Bennet related to you the troubles we have been having with my uncle. We thought to marry before he could do anything to prevent it. He knows I am in Hertfordshire, but expects me to return for the season and to marry the daughter of one of his political allies, Miss Harriet Sedgewick."

"Miss Harriet Sedgewick?" Catherine exclaimed. Nearly every eye in the room turned to her.

"Yes," Darcy replied.

"She attends Lydia's school," Catherine whispered.

It was Elizabeth's turn to be surprised. "Has Lydia mentioned her?"

"Yes," Catherine said, her voice soft and uncertain.

"What did she say?" Bennet asked, his eyes watching his second youngest daughter.

"She has…Lydia said she has recently been sent home from school," Catherine replied, unable to look at her father.

"Did she say why?" Bennet prodded again.

"The rumour at the school is that she is *enceinte*," Catherine said, her voice barely a whisper. "Lydia did not know for certain, but she often mentioned news of Miss Sedgewick. Lydia was not friends with her; Lydia said she thought she was so much better than all the rest of the girls and barely spoke to any of them. But more than once, Lydia said she was caught in places she ought not to have been and that there were tales about her having assignations with the grooms or even an officer in the militia stationed nearby. I had begun to believe she was a figment of Lydia's imagination, for surely the daughter of a peer ought to know better than to so flagrantly disregard the rules of the school and those of proper society."

"That is, unless she is the daughter of a viscount who has been indulged to the point that she believes she can do whatever she likes," Darcy said, anger creeping into his voice.

"But if she were with child, the viscount would not truly wish to delay the wedding so long unless she was too far along for him to wed her to a respectable man until after she had given birth," Livesay objected, Bennet nodding beside him.

"Or perhaps the viscount—or someone else—knows of the so-called remedies to rid a woman of an unwanted…complication," Lady Matlock said darkly, noticing the incredulous expressions of all those around her. "There are methods, yes—but none I would ever recommend, especially for a young woman. While they are intended to kill the babe," she continued grimly, "in more extreme cases, *if* the woman survives, they can also leave her unable to bear children ever again."

Several gasps followed the remark—this was not a subject typically spoken of in mixed company, especially not in the presence of younger women. Mrs. Bennet, visibly flustered, reached for the vinaigrette she kept in her reticule for just such occasions. She resisted the urge to wave her handkerchief about, a habit her husband had gently pointed out as more attention-seeking than soothing.

"Regardless, my husband and the viscount must have known the girl was ruined, and they sought to bind her to my nephew in a way that would leave him feeling he could not refuse," Lady Matlock continued. "It was a calculated attempt to secure a respectable match for Miss Sedgewick while ensuring access to the funds they desperately need."

She paused, then added, "But this is a matter for another day. Today we are preparing for Fitzwilliam's wedding."

Turning to Catherine, her tone shifted to brisk efficiency. "Miss Catherine, I need you to gather any letters you have that mention Miss Sedgewick and give them to me soon. Tomorrow is the wedding, so it can wait until the following day. I do not know if we have time to send a letter and receive a reply from your sister at school, but if you could write to her today and ask for any additional information, it would be most helpful."

"I can send a rider with the letter," Darcy replied. "He can wait for the reply and bring it to us as quickly as he gets it."

Still somewhat startled by the reaction to her news, Catherine quickly excused herself to carry out Lady Matlock's request, with Mary and Georgiana following close behind. The others remained behind to take tea and discuss the morning's revelations, soon settling into quiet conversations in pairs: Bennet with the Misters Livesay, Mrs. Bennet with Lady Matlock, Elizabeth with Darcy, and lastly, Jane and Miss Livesay.

Both young ladies listened to the earlier revelations without speaking, shocked at what they heard. Jane understood most of it and quietly filled Miss Livesay in on some of the goings-on of the last few weeks.

To the surprise of both, a few moments later, Colonel Fitzwilliam took the seat beside them. He had only barely been introduced to Miss Livesay, but after adding a few salient facts about the drama of the morning, he engaged the ladies by telling them some of the more amusing anecdotes from his time in military service.

CHAPTER 40

Mr. Collins Intrudes

The Livesays were not the only visitors to Longbourn that day. Shortly after their arrival, Mr. and Mrs. Gardiner were warmly welcomed, prompting the gentlemen to retreat to the study for private discussion while the ladies gathered in the drawing room to continue preparations for the following day's wedding.

It had been a pleasant and purposeful afternoon—until, precisely at four o'clock, an entirely different sort of guest made his appearance.

Mr. William Collins arrived at Longbourn, exactly as his letter had foretold.

Despite his cousin writing telling him to delay his visit, Mr. Collins, after consultation with his esteemed patroness, Lady Catherine de Bourgh, determined that such advice could only stem from excessive modesty. Confident in the correctness of his original intentions, he adhered strictly to his plan to arrive on the last Monday of October and saw no reason to trouble his cousin with further correspondence to inform him of this fact.

He was, therefore, distinctly disappointed to find that no members of the family were assembled to greet him upon his arrival as he had expected. Once again, he was displeased when he knocked and discovered that he was, in fact, not expected.

"The Master is not receiving callers at the moment. If you will leave your card, I will let him know about your visit," Hill said, standing in the door in a way that made it impossible for the clergyman to enter.

"But I am expected," Mr. Collins cried, "and I am family. Even if Mr. Bennet did not realise I would come precisely as I said, I should be allowed a room in the house that will one day be mine."

"You were not expected," Hill stated firmly, speaking with the confidence of one long in his position. "All the invited guests are here already, and every room in the house is occupied. I can see if the master will speak to you, but you will most likely have to stay at the inn."

Mr. Collins spluttered a response, but Hill ignored him, shutting the door in his face.

A few moments later, he returned with Bennet behind him. He opened the door, allowing Bennet to exit before shutting the door once again.

"Mr. Collins, I presume," Bennet said, his sardonic tone completely escaping his cousin.

"Yes, and you must be Mr. Bennet, my cousin," Mr. Collins replied with a bow. To his displeasure, it was not returned.

"Why are you here, Mr. Collins? You wrote to indicate you would come, but I wrote back and informed you that it was not opportune for you to visit my family at this time. We had already invited guests, and I am afraid to say, just as I informed you in my letter, we have no place for you to stay," Bennet replied.

"But I did not truly believe you meant it," Mr. Collins protested, his tone full of self-importance. "Surely, as the heir to this estate, I am at liberty to visit whenever I see fit, particularly when I come to offer you an olive branch as I mentioned in my letter. Indeed, I had fully intended to extend my generous offer to marry one of your daughters so that they might not be cast out of their home upon the occasion of your, ah, inevitable departure to your eternal reward."

"I have ensured that my wife and daughters will be well cared for when I die," Bennet said coolly. "They will not be reliant upon your generosity—or lack thereof. Furthermore, it is customary for one to wait for an invitation before visiting a near stranger, regardless of one's position as heir presumptive. I replied to your letter quite clearly, indicating that a visit at this time was not feasible, and asked you to delay it until the spring."

Mr. Collins's eyes widened, and he placed a hand to his chest in dramatic affront.

"My dear sir, I am quite distressed that you should take offense where none was intended. Lady Catherine always encourages me to act decisively in matters of family duty. Indeed, she often remarks that one must lead by example. It was under her wise counsel that I determined my visit would be both timely and welcome. After all," he added with an ingratiating smile, "what better occasion to solidify familial bonds than in the days surrounding a wedding? Particularly one so—ah—elevated."

He glanced around, clearly expecting some acknowledgment of the honour his presence surely bestowed.

"What is this wedding you speak of?" Bennet asked, eyeing the man with distaste.

"Why, that of your daughters to me," Collins proclaimed. "Given my status as your heir and my elevated rank, surely you could not object to my desire to marry one of your daughters, and bind our families together after so many years of, um, misunderstandings."

"Elevated?" Bennet scoffed. "You are a rector, not a duke, nor a bishop. Nor are any of my daughters presently engaged to you, nor will they be unless they wish it. Regardless of your expectations, you are not entitled to arrive at my home whenever you see fit, particularly when you have been informed that your visit is not welcome at that time. Now, excuse me, I am neglecting my invited guests."

"But..." Mr. Collins spluttered, his mouth opening and closing in helpless indignation.

Bennet, however, paid him no mind. Without another word, he turned and stepped through the door, pushing it firmly shut behind him. Collins could only gape at the now-closed portal as the soft click of the latch sounded, sealing him out—the conversation firmly over.

THE HACK MR. COLLINS HAD HIRED HAD LEFT PROMPTLY AFTER LEAVING him at his destination. He had little choice but to drag his trunk the entire mile into the village of Meryton, only to learn that the next mail coach would not arrive until noon the following day. Unused to such exertion, it had taken him more than an hour to walk the mile, and he was utterly exhausted when he arrived.

Mr. Collins had tried to have his stay charged to Longbourn, but the proprietor of the inn had refused, claiming that Bennet had not authorised anyone new to make charges on his behalf. When Collins had attempted to claim that it was his right as a "man of God," the innkeeper had laughed in his face.

Reluctantly, Mr. Collins had paid the amount requested for the night's stay at the inn as well as the additional fee for a meal and several pints of ale.

As he sat alone in the main dining room of the inn, Mr. Collins was thoroughly enjoying his meal—until a familiar name floated into his ears from a nearby table.

"Pardon me," he said, leaning towards the man seated at the next table. "Did I hear you mention Mr. Fitzwilliam Darcy?"

The man, red-cheeked and well into his second pint, turned with an amiable nod. "Aye, that's right. Miss Lizzy—one of the Bennet girls—is to be married tomorrow. To a Mr. Fitzwilliam Darcy, just come to the area a few weeks ago."

Mr. Collins blinked in disbelief.

"They announced the wedding at church yesterday," the man continued, oblivious to Collins's growing alarm. "Caught most of us by surprise, to be honest. Seems there was some reason for all the secrecy, but no one knows for sure. It may have something to do with the officer who was arrested, but nothing has been said for certain. Still, everyone's pleased. Miss Lizzy's well-liked, and it's clear the gentleman's taken with her and she with him. They make a fine pair, or so we've all said. From what I gather, Mr. Darcy owns a great estate up north somewhere. She'll be missed here, but we wish her well."

Mr. Collins paled, his mind racing. "You do not suspect a compromise?" he asked, lowering his voice, his tone tinged with self-importance. "Are you certain this Mr. Darcy is not…under some obligation to the lady?"

The man gave a shrug. "Far as anyone knows, it's a love match. And truth be told, even if it weren't, no one around here would speak ill of Miss Lizzy or suspect her of anything untoward."

But Mr. Collins was no longer listening. Fitzwilliam Darcy, the very same name his esteemed patroness, Lady Catherine de Bourgh, had declared was destined for her own daughter. And now—he was marrying a Bennet? The same family that had turned him out of his estate, or rather, the estate he would one day inherit.

Outrage and disbelief swelled in his chest. This was not just unexpected. It was unacceptable. He would have to find a way to stop it.

CHAPTER 41

A Wedding

28 OCTOBER 1811

Tuesday morning dawned clear and bright, the perfect day for a wedding.

Elizabeth dressed in her best day dress, a pale primrose colour that brought out the gold flecks in her hair. She had risen early in the morning, bathed and dressed, and was nearly ready before her mother entered her room to check on her progress.

Mrs. Gardiner had taken time with Elizabeth that morning, offering gentle, honest answers to the questions her niece still had about the marriage bed—especially after enduring her mother's rather alarming version of the subject the night before. That conversation had done little to reassure her, but Mrs. Gardiner's calm, practical explanation had eased her concerns. Before parting, she left Elizabeth with one final piece of advice: above all, she should trust her husband and allow him to guide the way.

"Communication is the key in this, as well as all things in your marriage," she had said. "If you and your husband can talk to each other, then problems will be solved much more efficiently and with fewer hurt feelings—for either party."

Elizabeth had nodded at this, but before she could reflect further, her mother had come bustling in.

"Oh, good, Lizzy, you are dressed," Mrs. Bennet said. "Come downstairs, your father wishes to speak to you. I suppose it is good you are not travelling to London yet," she said as she looked about the room. "You have hardly had time to pack all your things, and I suppose you must do that soon."

Mrs. Bennet paused and turned to face her daughter, her expression unusually solemn.

"You have made a very good match, Lizzy," she said, surprising Elizabeth with the seriousness in her tone. "Despite what your father always claimed, I used to worry you would have trouble finding someone willing to marry you, what with all that time he let you spend alone in his book room, saying whatever came to your mind."

She gave a small, almost sheepish smile. "But it seems Mr. Darcy likes you in spite of that…or perhaps because of it. He is a fine man, and from what I have seen, he truly enjoys your liveliness."

"Thank you, Mama," Elizabeth said, torn between amusement and gratitude. A smile tugged at her lips, but she kept her tone gentle. "That means more than you might think."

Mrs. Bennet sniffed, already blinking away the emotion threatening to betray her. "Well, it is no less than the truth. I daresay you'll do quite well as Mrs. Darcy. Just remember to write to your poor mother once you have gone off to that grand estate of his."

Elizabeth laughed softly. "I promise you shall hear from me often, perhaps more than you might like."

Mrs. Bennet huffed, though her eyes shone. "Nonsense. A mother can never hear too often from her children. I do understand why you kept your engagement a secret, but I wish I could have shared in your happiness for longer. Regardless, you will do well." She dried her eyes again. "Go, see your father but tell him to hurry. The

Gardiners and your younger sisters have already departed for the church and our carriage is waiting for us. Jane is downstairs as well."

Bennet had only a few words for his favourite child on her wedding day, and within a few minutes they had boarded the carriage and were on their way to the Longbourn chapel. As they approached, they were surprised to hear the sound of yelling.

"You cannot marry my cousin," they heard a strange nasally voice yell out.

The answer, in a more modulated tone, could not be heard. It only was a moment later when the coach stopped, and Bennet hopped down first, without waiting for the step to be placed. A footman arrived only a moment later, and Elizabeth, seeing her intended standing outside next to a tall, rather heavy-set stranger, followed behind him, displacing her mother.

Mrs. Bennet did not mind and allowed the footman to help her down last and went to see the melee.

"Mr. Collins," they heard Bennet mutter, and Elizabeth immediately closed her eyes in mortification at being related to the man, despite having never met him before.

"I am not engaged to my cousin, nor are you engaged to yours," Darcy stated, obviously not for the first time.

"Mr. Collins," Bennet said, approaching the group standing outside the church. "Why are you here?"

"I have come to stop this travesty from happening," he said. "Mr. Darcy cannot marry Miss Bennet when he is already engaged to Miss Anne de Bourgh, the daughter of my patroness."

"I am not, nor have I ever been, engaged to my cousin," Darcy said. "Would you like to see the marriage contract, signed by my father and Mr. Bennet more than five years ago? My father could not have signed two as I have already told you and Mr. Barington multiple times."

"I object to this wedding," Mr. Collins declared once more, puffing himself up with self-righteous indignation.

"Your objection is noted," said Mr. Barington, the rector of Longbourn Church, his tone polite but firm. "However, as it is without merit, we shall proceed. Miss Elizabeth is present and willing, her father has given his permission, and Mr. Darcy has shown that he is free to marry as he wishes. As a rector yourself, you know that is all that is required." He turned his back to the man and said to the rest. "If you would all make your way inside, we will begin the ceremony."

The guests began moving towards the church entrance, but Mr. Barington stepped to the side and held out a hand, stopping Mr. Collins in his tracks.

"Not you, Mr. Collins," he said, voice cool with restraint. "You have made your objection known, but as you have no valid grounds, you will not be admitted. I cannot trust you to remain silent, and I will not allow you to disrupt this wedding."

Mr. Collins sputtered with indignation, but before he could respond, one of Darcy's footmen—already positioned nearby—stepped forward. Once the final guests had entered, the man moved smoothly in front of the doors, blocking Mr. Collins with a quiet, unmistakable authority.

Realizing he had no further recourse, Mr. Collins could do little more than stand outside, muttering to himself about impropriety and ingratitude as the church doors shut firmly. Eventually, he left to return to the inn and plan for his return journey to Kent.

Half an hour later, the newly minted Mr. and Mrs. Darcy exited the church, making their way into Darcy's carriage. They were the last to exit, having accepted the well wishes of all their friends and family who had attended, after signing the registry.

It was a brief carriage ride, all too brief for the newly married couple. In Darcy's opinion, his lips had only barely touched Elizabeth's before the carriage was slowing before the doors to Longbourn where all their guests were waiting to celebrate with the couple at the wedding breakfast.

The next two hours felt interminable to Darcy. He wanted little more than to have Elizabeth alone, but it seemed rude to leave his own wedding breakfast too soon.

However, the first guests finally began to take their leave, and Darcy pulled Elizabeth into an alcove out of sight of the guests.

"When can we leave, Elizabeth?" Darcy asked, his exasperation clear.

Elizabeth glanced around, and seeing that they were truly alone, stood on her tiptoes and kissed him lightly. "How are we travelling to the dower house?" she asked.

"My carriage," he replied, leaning down to press a series of kisses along her jaw as he murmured. "It should be outside waiting for us, and I am certain the horses are nearly as anxious for their beds as I am."

Elizabeth laughed. "Then, seeing as we are not going far, and we will see my family again before we leave for London, I suggest we sneak away. Miss Bingley, Miss Horatia Bingley—really, we need to find a way to address her without visualizing the younger one—planned a dinner on Saturday for us and invited all my neighbours so they can wish us well."

Darcy groaned. "I suppose it is far less than what my aunt will plan for us when we are in London. As you are aware, I am not fond of social occasions, but I have done better when I have had you by my side. I need to speak to Georgiana, for I have neglected her of late, but she has had your sisters for company. She is very happy, I think, to have traded my company for that of your sisters. But, come, let us say a few words to a few people, and then we will leave."

Elizabeth laughed again at the aggrieved expression on his face, but it was not too many minutes longer before they sneaked out the door and had boarded the carriage for the short drive to the dower house.

They found the cottage warm and inviting with trays of fruit and cheese in the sitting room attached to the main bedchambers upstairs. It was obvious Darcy's valet and Elizabeth's borrowed maid had been there, for their night things were laid out, but on that night, they both agreed to eschew help from servants and rely on each other.

If there was a touch of awkwardness between them at first, neither remarked upon it. Instead, they laughed softly through the nervousness, hands gentle and unsure at first as they undressed one another. When at last there were no more layers between them, they chose to forgo nightclothes altogether, drawn by curiosity, affection, and growing desire.

What followed was quiet exploration—tentative at first, then more assured—as they learnt one another in the language of touch and breath, the closeness deepening into something both tender and intoxicating. By the end, any remnants of hesitation had vanished, replaced by the quiet certainty of mutual delight.

CHAPTER 42

Travelling to London

4 NOVEMBER 1811 - LONDON

Monday morning came all too soon for the newlywed couple. The dinner at Netherfield had been a success, and without Miss Caroline Bingley there to criticise, had been quite enjoyable for everyone present. Even the Hursts had been pleasant company, and Mr. Hurst appeared far more sober and talkative than usual. Elizabeth and Jane had enjoyed the company of Mrs. Hurst, speaking to her more often than they had done when her sister was there.

Several carriages met at Longbourn to begin the journey to London. To Elizabeth and Darcy's dismay, Bennet and Livesay both boarded their carriage, instead of riding with the Gardiners as had been expected. The reason soon became clear.

"I am certain your butler at Darcy House will have an interesting tale for you, but we had a visitor on Friday that may surprise you," Bennet began. "She was there for you, Darcy, but as a wedding gift, I decided not to send her your way."

Darcy steeled himself, knowing who the visitor likely was. "My Aunt Catherine was at Longbourn?" he guessed, groaning when Bennet nodded.

""Your father mentioned her once or twice in his letters, so I was prepared for a harridan—and she was exactly as I imagined," Bennet said drily. "She went to Darcy House first, expecting to find you there. When she did not, she came to Longbourn, ready to scold me, my daughter, and you—although you were conveniently absent—for the outrageous notion that George Darcy had signed a marriage contract with my daughter and not hers."

He shook his head, half amused, half exasperated. Elizabeth covered her laugh at the thought of the imperious lady being so disappointed.

"I showed her the copy of the contract which nearly sent her into apoplexy. She tried to tear it up until I calmly pointed out that it was merely a copy; the originals are safely stored and far beyond her reach."

His expression darkened slightly. "She was, let us say, enthusiastic in her disapproval. She instructed me to inform you, wherever you may be, that she is 'seriously displeased' and that she intends to 'carry her point.' With whom, I do not know or care. I told her, quite plainly, that the marriage is already made, and that there is precious little she can do about it now."

A brief smile tugged at the corners of his mouth while Livesay let out an amused laugh, seeing the look on Darcy's face at that pronouncement.

"In case you wondered how she knew, Collins informed her as soon as he arrived in Kent. She must have set off immediately and travelled without thought for her horses or her coachman," Bennet added.

"I suspected as much," Darcy replied, shaking his head, then looking at his new father-in-law with a grin. "Bennet, I am certain you put my Aunt Catherine in her place. I almost wish I could have seen that although I admit that I am glad you were subjected to her and not me. I had better things to do with my time."

Livesay leant forward in his seat, his tone thoughtful as he shifted the topic of conversation to one more serious. "Your uncle is aware of your marriage. With the countess already in London and spreading favourable talk about your 'love match,' he will be hard-pressed to oppose it without making an utter fool of himself. Even when he was the viscount, he was acutely conscious of both status and gossip and would not do anything to create a scandal. That is why his threat to spread rumours about your sister is so out of character."

Allowing a small smile, Livesay continued, "I received word from a few friends in town that Lady Matlock, bless her, has already begun to make the rounds among her friends and peers since returning to London the day after your wedding. She has been quite vocal about her attendance and has expressed nothing but delight in the match to everyone whose opinion carries weight."

He paused briefly, then added, "She also made a point of mentioning how much she has enjoyed having your sister with her since the summer."

Elizabeth grasped Darcy's hand more tightly. "She means to make it known that Georgiana has been with her so that any gossip can easily be refuted, should Lord Matlock still attempt anything," she concluded.

Livesay nodded, and then he and Bennet proceeded to fill Darcy in on what had been discussed over the last several days. More details had been discovered about Lord Matlock's involvement in the smuggling operation, along with that of the viscount, and Darcy's messenger had returned with additional details about Miss Sedgewick.

Armed with all of this information, they felt the confrontation with Lord Matlock would go in their favour, and of course, with Darcy's marriage already made and Lady Matlock ready to swear that Georgiana had been with her all summer, any attempts the earl would make to harm Georgiana's reputation would be easily refuted.

Still, Darcy preferred not to go that far, and he hoped that the confrontation with Lord Matlock would be more easily resolved than expected.

With so much conversation required along the way, the journey to London passed quickly. However, with others accompanying them the entire way, there had been little opportunity for intimate conversation or making plans for their time in town.

Still, it had all been necessary so they could be prepared for what would meet them in London.

After a brief stop to rest halfway through the journey, the seating arrangements changed once again. A rider from London had been waiting at the inn with fresh news from Lady Matlock, urgent enough that it required immediate discussion among the men.

Reluctantly, Darcy boarded his carriage alongside his father-in-law; his new uncle Gardiner; and Livesay. He watched with visible disappointment as Elizabeth climbed into the other carriage with Mrs. Gardiner, Miss Livesay, and the younger Mr. Livesay. However, he was not able to remain lost in thoughts of his bride for long.

"The colonel is already in London; apparently his mother sent him word early this morning to inform him that it was necessary for him to be present during the confrontation. Matlock is incensed with your Aunt Catherine's description of how your marriage came to be, doubtlessly tainted by her own impressions and those of her fool of a parson," Livesay said. "I know we have discussed it before, but I confess that I was shocked at his behaviour at the wedding. Of course, after meeting Lady Catherine de Bourgh, it was less so."

"What is my uncle threatening to do?" Darcy asked, unable to tolerate such unnecessary conversation at the moment.

"Lady Catherine arrived at Matlock House on Saturday, and the earl and the viscount spent all of yesterday at Devonshire House. When Lord Matlock arrived home late last night, he spent more than an hour in his study, rifling through papers before apparently falling asleep at his desk. Since waking this morning, he has attempted to gain entry to Darcy House, but your servants have kept him at bay," Gardiner said, repeating the information from the letter.

"What could he be looking for? And why would he want to get into Darcy House while I am not there?" Darcy wondered aloud, setting off another round of discussion.

While the men speculated, they were no closer to an answer when they arrived at Darcy House more than an hour later.

The Darcy carriage arrived first, and the men had just stepped down when the Gardiner carriage pulled in behind. Darcy moved swiftly to assist his wife, reaching up to take Elizabeth's hand as she descended with grace.

At the same moment, Livesay stepped forward to help his daughter alight, guiding her from the Gardiner carriage to the one that would soon take her on to their family's home. Mrs. Gardiner remained seated—she would be returning to Gracechurch Street to tend to her children—while Mr. Gardiner rejoined the group of men.

Darcy, still holding Elizabeth's hand, leant in and murmured against her ear, "This is not how I imagined you would first see Darcy House, dearest."

Elizabeth laughed softly. "You can give me a private tour another time, Fitzwilliam. For now, I suppose we must do what we can about your uncle." As they began ascending the steps, she glanced sideways at him, recalling the reason for their separation during this last leg of their journey. "Is there anything I ought to know before we go in?"

To her surprise, Darcy did not answer immediately. Instead, he paused at the top of the steps—then swept her suddenly into his arms and carried her over the threshold.

Elizabeth gasped, then laughed as he grinned down at her.

"We need all the good luck we can find," he said, his voice low and warm. "And I rather liked the excuse to hold you in my arms, particularly since we cannot be alone for quite some time."

After setting her down and introducing his new wife to his staff, Darcy led their party to his study. He nearly laughed upon seeing Colonel Fitzwilliam already in his study and seated behind Darcy's desk, his feet on top of it. Before Darcy could say a word, the colonel stood and greeted them all.

"Good afternoon, Mrs. Darcy, gentlemen," he said, jovially acting the part of host.

"Why are you here, Richard? You know how I feel about your sitting in my chair and placing your feet on my desk," Darcy said drily.

"I was here as protection against my father," he replied with a grin. "I knew my being here would stop my father from searching for whatever he might be looking for, or to keep him from placing something here that was not present before his arrival. Your servants are rather tenacious, however, and my assistance was not needed."

His expression turned more serious. "Regardless, we must speak of my father. A servant was dispatched to Matlock House as soon as you arrived to let Mother know. I expect that Father will 'discover' this soon enough and make haste to scold you."

"Do you or your mother have any idea what the earl might be looking for?" Livesay asked.

"No, I do not, but he was heard muttering about a contract," Fitzwilliam replied.

"Could he have a forged document about a marriage that he might use in an attempt to invalidate our marriage?" Elizabeth asked, her brow furrowed.

"If he had a marriage contract forged, he would not need to search for it," Gardiner said. "He would need to get inside Darcy House so it could be 'discovered,' but even then, he could do little about it now that the two of you are wed."

"Father would have never signed a contract with the viscount to marry me to his daughter," Darcy added. "He detested the man."

Any further conversation was ended by a knock at the door. "Lord and Lady Matlock are here to see you, sir," the butler said upon entering at Darcy's call. "Should I show them here or the drawing room?"

Darcy looked towards his wife, who shrugged. "I think we will be more comfortable in the formal drawing room. Please have a maid bring refreshments and then keep everyone away from this part of the house. Have them wait a few minutes while we get settled in that room so we can receive them properly."

The butler nodded and hurried to do as he was bid.

Five minutes later, the earl and countess were shown into the room where the others sat.

"Welcome," Darcy said in greeting, before drawing his wife nearer to him. Ignoring the usual practice, he began by introducing his wife to his uncle without asking for his permission.. "Uncle, allow me to introduce you to my wife, Mrs. Elizabeth Darcy. You know the rest, do you not? It has been many years, but I know you have met Father's friends, Mr. Thomas Bennet, my wife's father, and Mr. James Livesay. I am told you have also had business dealings with my new uncle, Mr. Edward Gardiner."

The earl scowled at these men, all of whom were far below him in consequence.

"I heard from Catherine that you had married some penniless nobody," the earl sneered. "Of course, I did not realise that you had tied yourself to the daughter of Thomas Bennet. He was useless at Cambridge, and I cannot believe that has changed much since then. I never could understand why your father befriended those men." He glanced between the others in the room disdainfully.

"Perhaps because my father valued character over status, a lesson he passed down to me," Darcy replied. "Now, you will either greet my wife properly, or this meeting is over before it has even started."

With a scowl, the earl turned to Elizabeth. "Did you target my nephew due to his wealth?" he asked. "Your father always was indolent and lazy, and the pittance he earns from his estate could not have enabled him to save much for your dowry."

"I fell in love with your nephew, and my dowry is of no concern to you," Elizabeth retorted. "Like your nephew, I prefer to look at one's character rather than their purse."

The earl scoffed, and Darcy stepped forward, standing directly in front of the earl. "How dare you treat my wife in such a way," he snarled, and was inwardly pleased to see the earl retreat a little.

"Enough, gentlemen," Lady Matlock snapped. "Come, all of you, and let us sit and see if we cannot have a civilized conversation. Husband, that is enough from you. As I have already told you, Mrs. Darcy is delightful and exactly what our nephew needs."

Grudgingly, everyone took a seat, with both Lady Matlock and Elizabeth doing all they could to keep up the appearance of a pleasant conversation. The butler showed in the maids with the tea tray, and after setting it in front of the new Mrs. Darcy, gave a nod to the master before shutting the door firmly behind him.

CHAPTER 43

Confronting the Earl

Once everyone had a cup of tea before them, more a gesture to allow a moment's composure than a reflection of actual need, Darcy broke the silence that had fallen upon the servants' departure.

"Uncle, I told you in September that I would never marry the viscount's daughter. Since then, I have learnt a great deal; most notably, that Miss Harriet Sedgewick was withdrawn from school earlier this summer after rumours surfaced of an affair with one of the grooms at the school she attended. It is also rumoured that she is with child although I suspect that the viscount intends to dispose of the child before forcing her to wed." He let the weight of the words hang for a moment, allowing them to sink in, and he saw the earl blanch. "Knowing that, even if I were not already wed, I would never have agreed to the match."

"Damn you, Darcy," the earl growled, his composure fraying. "Why could you not simply do as you were bid? A connection to the viscount would have secured your place in the House of Lords. As your father-in-law, the viscount could have petitioned the Regent to elevate you, perhaps even to an earldom if not higher. Instead, you had to go off to Hertfordshire, and not only have you married a nobody," he looked at Mrs. Darcy in distaste before turning back and paling further at the look on his nephew's face, "but you have dug into matters that you should not have."

Seated beside her husband, Elizabeth cast him a worried glance. His jaw was tight, lips pressed into a hard line, and his hand curled firmly over hers. The heat in his gaze left no doubt: he was furious.

Still, Darcy met his uncle's glare without flinching. "Because I did not want a title. Neither did my father, nor his before him. We have never chased titles or status beyond that which we already possess. There is nothing you could have offered that would have made me sacrifice my principles—or Elizabeth. I married her for love, and no pressure from you or anyone else would have changed that, once I met her."

The earl's face twisted in frustration, and his voice rose, cracking under the weight of something more than anger—there was fear there, too. "The viscount will ruin me! He has discovered my dealings along the Irish coast. He knows I have been importing more than livestock. Without your marriage to his daughter to keep him quiet, he will see me hanged!"

Lady Matlock, who had remained silent until that moment, turned sharply towards her husband. Her eyes narrowed as she glared at him, and her voice turned cold. "What dealings, Henry?" she demanded.

He faltered.

"What precisely have you been doing?" she demanded. "And why have you needed my father's money to keep the estate afloat?"

A tense silence followed Lady Matlock's question.

Bennet raised an eyebrow, his teacup halfway to his lips. "Smuggling, I presume," he said drily. "I doubt sheep are so lucrative as to inspire this level of panic. It would have to be something rather serious to inspire fear of hanging."

Gardiner said nothing, but his gaze sharpened, taking the measure of the earl, as he waited for the earl to reveal more.

"So, this is what it comes to," Livesay muttered, mostly to himself, recalling how often the earl, while still a viscount, had attempted to bully others at school; he found it interesting to see that he was now the target of a bully himself.

The earl, flushed and visibly sweating now, shifted in his seat. His eyes darted between the faces in the room—people he had viewed as his inferiors—and found no refuge in any of them.

"I had no choice," he said at last, his voice hoarse. "The estate was bleeding money, the tenants were struggling, and your father—" he shot a glance at Lady Matlock, "—refused to lend any further support unless I proved myself capable of recovering the losses. The trade routes along the Irish coast were already being used. I merely...made use of what was already in place."

"You trafficked in contraband," Mr. Gardiner said evenly. "What else? Spirits? Arms? People?"

The earl flinched at the final word.

Lady Matlock's expression darkened. "Henry. Tell me now."

The earl looked away, shame creeping into the lines of his face. His voice, when it came, was low and bitter.

"Merely spirits at first. French brandy, Irish whiskey—nothing worse than what half the peerage keeps in their cellars. But it was not enough." He swallowed hard. "Then came untaxed tobacco, rare silks —anything we could move quickly and sell high."

Lady Matlock's knuckles whitened around her teacup, but she said nothing.

"I told myself it was temporary," he continued, the words coming faster now, as if their weight would crush him if he did not speak them quickly. "Until the harvests improved; until the rents stabilized;

until I could repay your father. But then the viscount found out. Rather than report me, he made demands of me."

He finally looked at Darcy, his eyes bloodshot, his voice cracking. "He wanted an alliance. He said if I arranged a match between you and his daughter, he would keep my secret and even help expand the operation under his protection. That was the price of my survival, and I—"

He broke off, breath ragged. "I agreed. I saw no other way."

Lady Matlock sat in rigid silence, but her voice, when it came, was deadly calm.

"You allowed a criminal enterprise to grow under your stewardship, endangered your family's name, and tried to barter your nephew's future like coin in a ledger," she said, her voice growing in anger with each mention. "Worst of all, you attempted to have Georgiana ruined to guarantee Fitzwilliam's compliance, did you not?"

"You sent Wickham to Ramsgate," Fitzwilliam said, standing and facing his father directly for the first time during this confrontation. "You knew Georgiana was there, and you paid him to entice her to an elopement to give you leverage over Darcy." Up until this moment, he had been content to watch, but seeing his father seem to shrink with each accusation only served to make him angrier.

"I expected to help my estate and family survive," the earl snapped, his desperation apparent. "I expected my family to stand by me as I strove to make it stronger. But you have brought these strangers in, these men who do not matter, and feel that you can stand here and condemn me? What happened to family loyalty?"

Darcy rose to his feet, his expression cold and resolute, his hands clenched tightly at his sides. "You made your choices, Uncle, and now, you will answer for them. Shall we send for the magistrate?"

"You cannot," the earl cried. "I would be hanged."

"What else would you have me do?" Darcy asked. "I cannot condone your actions. You would have forced an unwanted marriage on me, you attempted to ruin Georgiana for your own purposes, and I can hardly imagine what would have happened had I not prevented that knave from absconding with her."

"Darcy," the earl pleaded, but a slash from his son's hand prevented further words.

"I do not wish for a public scandal," Fitzwilliam said to his father. "And I have spoken to my brother. He has already spoken to the Regent to see if all of this can be handled quietly."

"Handled how?" the earl asked, shock clearly written on his face.

"Your trial and punishment for your crimes," Gardiner said, speaking for the first time. "You are not the only one with connections, and I have been able to speak to the Regent myself. He also does not wish for it to be known that a peer has been involved in smuggling, and he has agreed that, with a full confession, you will be held in the Tower of London for the rest of your life. The viscount will be a separate matter for Parliament to deal with."

"So, I am to rot in prison?"

"Yes, Father," Fitzwilliam replied. "We will let it be known that you are ill, and my brother will take your place both in society and in Parliament. You will have enough funds to ensure that you have food and clothing, but none of us will visit you. Still, it is a better fate than Wickham, who due to his actions, faced a firing squad last week. You sent him to Hertfordshire to spy on Darcy, did you not?"

The earl blanched at the thought of such a punishment, momentarily grateful that he would not be the one to endure it. Yet, as he considered the grim reality of life in the Tower, he could not help but wonder if Wickham had, in some twisted way, escaped the harsher fate.

There was a knock at the door, and Viscount Ashworth strode in. "It is done," he said, nodding towards the others in the room. "Father, you have until tomorrow at noon to present yourself before the Regent. If you do not, there will be no possibility of avoiding a scandal, for he will have a warrant issued for your arrest. There will be no deals, no contacting any of your connections to get you out of it. The Regent has declared you guilty of high treason."

With those few words, the earl sagged in his seat. He did not protest but instead allowed his firstborn to lead him out of the room and into the waiting carriage. His elder son would ensure he arrived at Kensington Palace the next day. Lord Matlock could hardly argue with so many against him.

The others sighed with relief, glad that it had transpired more easily than they might have expected.

"I believe he was genuinely worried about what the viscount may do, and if he approaches any of us, we can repeat what we know about his daughter. My son will ensure his father cannot write to the viscount and that he appears as expected tomorrow," Lady Matlock said after several moments had passed.

"While I cannot celebrate my uncle's actions, or the punishment that will go along with them, I am relieved that this whole episode is finished. Bennet, how long will you remain in London?" Darcy asked.

"A few days longer," he said. "It is hardly worth coming so far if I do not remain for at least a few days, and I have heard much about this library of yours."

The others in the room laughed at his jest, pleased to have cleared the air of at least some of the tension.

"Then we invite you all for dinner on Wednesday night," Darcy said, looking at Elizabeth, who nodded. "Aunt, will you invite Ashworth so he might meet Elizabeth?"

"Of course," she replied. "Would you have me invite others?"

"With your husband so ill?" he asked with a knowing wink.

This drew another laugh, and soon, everyone but Bennet departed, leaving the couple nearly alone.

"I will be in the library," Bennet said with a glance between his daughter and her husband of less than a week. "Show Elizabeth around the house, for I am certain she is eager to see it."

With a grin, Darcy called for a servant to show Bennet to the library. Once he was gone, he turned to Elizabeth. "Come, my dear, and allow me to show you the family rooms."

She accepted his offered hand. "I shall follow you wherever you lead, my dear."

CHAPTER 44

Many Happy Returns

15 NOVEMBER 1811 - LONDON

A fortnight later, the Darcys returned to Netherfield. Bingley's Aunt Horatia had invited them to visit whenever they liked since her nephew would be in the north for several weeks. While they could have stayed at Longbourn, both Darcy and Elizabeth decided that they would prefer a little distance from her parents at this time.

Additionally, Longbourn was full. The Livesays had returned to Hertfordshire with Bennet and planned to stay there for several weeks. Bennet and Livesay had agreed to return together, once the matter with the earl was settled, although Bennet had pleaded for a few extra days to explore his new son's library first. Livesay had granted the request with a laugh, but by Thursday, they all boarded the carriage for the journey back to Hertfordshire.

Lady Matlock had also returned to Hertfordshire with her younger son and Georgiana although she would soon travel north to Matlock under the guise of caring for her husband. When the word of his "sickness" was made public, she would withdraw from society for a time to help her elder son and his wife settle in as master and mistress of the estate.

With their arrival back in the area, Aunt Horatia, together with Mrs. Hurst, Mrs. Bennet, and Lady Matlock, had decided to hold a ball in celebration of the wedding.

"A ball is unnecessary," Darcy complained, sitting in Netherfield's drawing room while they waited for the meal to be announced. It was then that his aunt and Bingley's told them about the plans they had made.

"Elizabeth's neighbours will appreciate the opportunity to celebrate her marriage," Lady Matlock said, her tone scolding as she glared at her nephew.

Elizabeth laughed, laying her hand on her husband's arm. "Surely, Lady Matlock, you realise how little Fitzwilliam enjoys socialising," she teased.

"He is fortunate that my husband's 'illness' will prevent me from spending the Season in town," Lady Matlock retorted. "I would have hosted a grand ball to celebrate your nuptials and to introduce the two of you to all my friends plus many who are not, but who are useful connections."

She pinned her nephew with another glare. "You *must* spend at least a month in London, if not longer, and allow you and your wife to be seen by society. There is enough speculation about your marriage, and you will only add to it if you do not appear. I will insist on this, even if I must drag you from Pemberley myself."

Leaning forward, Elizabeth gave her new aunt a reassuring look. "I will see to it, Aunt," she said with a laugh. "Fitzwilliam knows that I fully intend to enjoy all the amusements the Season has to offer this spring, including visits to the theatre and the museums. I am sure we will attend a few balls, but I will write to you so you may tell me who to befriend and who to avoid."

Their mirth was interrupted by the announcement of several additional guests who had arrived for dinner that evening.

Elizabeth and Darcy, along with the rest of the party, stood to greet her family, who had just arrived with their guests, the Livesays. "Welcome, everyone," Aunt Horatia said.

For several minutes, the entire company remained standing as they exchanged greetings with those they had not seen in several days.

Elizabeth and Jane hugged each other for several long moments before being joined by Mary and Catherine. Mrs. Bennet stood back for a few moments, allowing her daughters several moments to themselves.

Bennet and Livesay approached Darcy, and the three quietly spoke of matters related to the earl and his punishment. While few details had been made public, whispers that several had been arrested in and around Liverpool for smuggling had made their way to London. Likewise, the viscount had withdrawn further from society and apparently was no longer a threat to the earl or his family.

"I do not know much," Darcy admitted, "but Richard paid him a visit and let drop a hint of what we knew. He did not tell me all of what was said, but he was convinced that the viscount would not trouble our family further. The viscount does not have a son, merely a nephew whom he cares little for, and he would not risk word of his daughter's ruin being made public. He fears the nephew, and now I believe he fears Richard as well."

Bennet and Livesay both nodded before turning the conversation. "Amelia believes there will be another match between our families soon," Livesay said, indicating his son, who was standing in the outskirts of the group of Bennet daughters.

In the days between Darcy and Elizabeth's wedding and their departure to London, Jane had spent a great deal of time with Amelia Livesay. Often, they were accompanied by her brother Frederick, and the three found much in common.

When Amelia recognised her brother's fledgling interest in the lady, she began to find excuses to leave the two alone for short periods of time. By the time they left on Monday for London, the two had the beginnings of an attachment.

Upon the Livesays' return to Longbourn, Jane and Frederick were able to further their acquaintance, and by the time Darcy and Elizabeth returned, matters were progressing quickly towards something more.

Frederick was twenty-four and had inherited a modest estate of four thousand pounds per annum from his maternal grandfather just a year before; he had travelled south with his father and sister, hopeful of attending at least a few events before the Season started. He was now comfortable with his estate and had desired to find a wife to make it a home.

He had been struck by Jane Bennet's beauty as soon as he saw her, but he soon found that she was also kind, reasonably well read—not surprising, given who her father was—and had the accomplishments necessary to be the mistress of his estate.

"That is an interesting development," Darcy said to Bennet, watching as Jane released her sister and moved to stand next to Frederick while her younger sisters greeted his wife. "Has she forgotten Bingley so soon?"

"I asked her the same question," Bennet admitted. "She appreciated Bingley's interest, but in all the time she and Bingley knew each other, they truly talked very little. Jane said that talking to Frederick was very different for his conversation tended towards things of substance and not merely superficial matters. I do not believe her heart was ever touched by your friend, and while I cannot say for certain she is in love with young Frederick, I think their relationship has progressed much faster because their conversation has been weightier."

"He is not decided yet, either," Livesay added, then laughed at his friend's affronted expression. "They have known each other for a little over a fortnight, old friend. Unlike Darcy here, Frederick needs a little more time to fall in love and to see whether the lady suits him, or whether he suits her. We must allow them to take things at their own pace."

Bennet sighed. "I am turning into my wife, wishing to see all my daughters married before I die," he admitted, laughing ruefully at himself.

Their conversation was interrupted by the butler's announcement that the meal was served. Darcy moved to his wife, taking her hand and placing it on his arm, grinning down at her.

Livesay and Bennet took a moment to watch their families enter, before they, too, turned and joined rest of the party.

As the last to enter, Bennet and Livesay ended up sitting next to each other near the end of the table. From their positions, they could see all of their children in attendance.

Most of the younger girls were seated together near the middle of the table. Mary, Catherine, and Georgiana, with their companions nearby, chatted happily as they had oft done whenever they were in company. Bennet was pleased to see that friendship forming and judged it to have been good for all three girls.

At the far end of the table, Elizabeth and Darcy sat together with Colonel Fitzwilliam at Elizabeth's other side. Across from them were Frederick, Jane, and Amelia, while Horatia Bingley presided from the head of the table. The group conversed easily—sometimes breaking into smaller discussions, but more often engaged in lively debates that drew the attention of everyone at that end. Although Jane and Amelia were the quietest among them, even they found moments to contribute meaningfully to the conversation.

Ever the instigator, Colonel Fitzwilliam set down his glass with a grin as he recalled an incident from the previous week. "As I rode down Bond Street last week, I passed a curious little carriage—something like a chaise, but fitted with wheels unlike any I have seen. Slender spokes of metal, so fine I thought the thing might collapse. I was astonished to see it."

Setting his fork aside, Frederick nodded, "Yes, it is the tension-spoked wheel. It is a relatively new invention, just a few years old and ingeniously simple. The tension in the spokes supports the rim, rather than the wheel relying on the bulk of wood."

Darcy offered a rare smile. "They are surprisingly strong despite their lightness. I read an article suggesting the design may soon be used in more than carriages—perhaps even in personal conveyances. I have invested a little in the project, and I am anxious to see what comes of it. I even saw a prototype at The Royal Institution last year."

Elizabeth, seated beside him, tilted her head thoughtfully. "So, it is not the strength of the material, but how it is arranged that gives it power? There is a certain elegance in that."

"Trust you to find poetry in wheel construction, Mrs. Darcy," Colonel Fitzwilliam teased.

Amelia leant forward, her eyes alight with curiosity. "It sounds revolutionary. If the wheels are so light, perhaps travel might become easier, especially for ladies, and faster, too."

The colonel, who had scarcely taken notice of her until now, found the lively expression in her eyes unexpectedly compelling.

"And likely safer as well—carriages so often falter on poor roads when the wheels are worn," Jane added.

"Perhaps, under the right conditions," Frederick tentatively agreed. "But they remain highly experimental and have yet to be tested on the deeply rutted roads common in the country."

Darcy glanced at Elizabeth, his tone contemplative. "If such improvements become widespread, travel as we know it may change entirely. Imagine something quieter and faster. Someday, it will not be a trip of days to get from Pemberley to London, but mere hours."

Elizabeth gave a soft laugh at this. "Do you mean to suggest a lady might someday be permitted to travel entirely on her own? Such a shocking idea, Mr. Darcy."

Colonel Fitzwilliam grinned. "What a sight it would be—independent young ladies racing about the countryside, giving the gentlemen a run for their money. Aunt Catherine would be aghast"

From the head of the table, Horatia Bingley gave a sharp sniff of disapproval, although she softened it with a slight smile. "Let us hope such nonsense remains in the realm of speculation. I do not trust such modern contraptions."

Darcy suppressed a smirk while Elizabeth lifted her brows and replied, lightly but with unmistakable warmth, "Yet it is often from speculation that the future takes shape. Without innovation, we would not have got as far as we have."

Elizabeth offered her husband a gentle smile. "Our children will see the fruits of this. Just imagine what the world will be like when they reach our age—and again when they have children of their own."

Darcy gave a fond shake of his head and murmured, "Wed less than a month, and already you have us as grandparents, my love?"

Elizabeth laughed softly, her eyes dancing. "Well, someone must plan ahead, Mr. Darcy. I cannot have our grandchildren riding about in carriages with outdated wheels."

Darcy leant closer, his voice low and wry. "Then I shall take it as my sacred duty to ensure the future of transport is properly secured—for their sake, of course. Have you seen the new steam engine, my dear?" he said, in an attempt to turn the conversation.

Colonel Fitzwilliam, who had caught just enough of their exchange to be intrigued, raised a brow. "Are the two of you drawing up a family legacy already? I was under the impression you were newlyweds, not scientists. What is this talk of steam engines?"

Elizabeth turned towards him with mock solemnity. "We like to be efficient, Colonel. If we plan now, then there will be fewer questions later."

"Terrifying," he muttered with a grin, reaching for his glass.

Amelia, amused, leant towards Jane. "I daresay if we remain here much longer, they will have named the grandchildren and plotted their education."

Darcy smirked but said nothing, content to let Elizabeth take the lead in the repartee.

"I believe I shall leave the names to my husband," she said sweetly. "Provided he does not suggest anything too dreadful like Archibald."

"That," Darcy said gravely, "is my uncle's name."

A beat of silence.

"Oh." Elizabeth paused, lips twitching. "Then perhaps a middle name."

That end of the table burst into laughter once again.

Bennet and the elder Mr. Livesay watched their children with amusement. Near to them, Lady Matlock, Mrs. Bennet, and Mrs. Hurst were engaged in quiet conversation about the plans for the Netherfield Ball, but the gentlemen tuned that out.

"I have never seen a couple quite like your Elizabeth and Fitzwilliam Darcy, Bennet," Livesay said after a few moments of watching.

"Nor I," Bennet admitted. "I have rarely seen a couple more suited to each other. I suppose some might laugh at them, but I confess, I envy them."

"Few would not envy such devotion," Livesay replied. He was quiet as he once again watched the exchanges at the other end of the table.

"I know we spoke about one possible marriage, but perhaps there may be two in the future, if my eyes do not deceive me. I doubt my son or the colonel will work as quickly as Darcy though," Livesay said softly.

Bennet turned to his friend, then glanced down the table to see what he had noticed. "The colonel?"

"He is transfixed with my Amelia," Livesay said quietly. "I am not sure what she said, but something has caused him to look at her differently this evening."

Bennet watched the pair for a moment, before nodding. "Perhaps," he said finally.

"Still, I believe he may wait some time before making any decisions," Livesay replied. He was thoughtful for a moment, then he asked, "I know I am not from this area, Bennet, but has much been said about the suddenness of the wedding between Darcy and your Lizzy?"

Bennet shook his head. "I explained to a few the reason for the haste and the secrecy. No one has said anything, and since Elizabeth and Darcy intend to remain for a few weeks longer, they will no doubt convince the neighbourhood that nothing is amiss with their marriage. Besides, *'for what do we live, but to make sport for our neighbours, and laugh at them in our turn?'* It is simply the Bennets' turn."

CHAPTER 45

Epilogue

SUMMER 1813

More than a year and a half after Elizabeth and Darcy's wedding, both of their families gathered at Pemberley. The Darcy family had recently grown with the birth of their infant son, Bennet Alexander Darcy.

Representing the Fitzwilliam family were the new earl and his wife, the Dowager Countess, and Colonel Fitzwilliam (retired) with his bride of six months, the former Amelia Livesay.

The late earl had endured nearly nine months imprisoned in the Tower before refusing food and water, bringing about his own end. Lady Matlock observed a brief mourning period of three months—emerging from her black just in time for her second son's wedding.

Jane had married Frederick Livesay nearly a year earlier, and the couple had journeyed to Pemberley on their way home to Yorkshire after the London Season. James Livesay naturally accompanied them, along with his new bride. He had met the Bennets' neighbour, Charlotte Lucas, during a visit to Longbourn, and their attachment had been swift and sincere. The two married just a few months after Frederick and Jane. Both Charlotte and Jane were expecting children in the late autumn.

The Bennet family, now reduced to only four living at Longbourn, was represented by Mr. and Mrs. Bennet and their youngest daughters, Lydia and Kitty. Mary had joined Georgiana Darcy for her first Season this spring and while Georgiana had yet to find a husband, Mary had found one—a gentleman with a modest estate in Staffordshire. Married less than a month, they were still on their wedding trip in Lyme.

Lydia's last months at school had brought about a remarkable change. When she returned to Longbourn at the end of the Easter term more than a year earlier, it was clear she had finally begun to understand the consequences of her behaviour—not only for herself, but for her entire family. The turning point had been the scandal involving Miss Sedgewick. Lydia, witnessing the fallout, seemed to grasp for the first time the serious repercussions of disregarding propriety.

With the Bennets had come the Gardiners, rounding out the party. The house was fuller and livelier than it had been in many years, filled with sounds of happiness.

Later that evening, as the soft hush of twilight blanketed the estate, Elizabeth and Darcy stepped onto the terrace adjoining their chambers, a warm shawl draped over her shoulders and their son sleeping peacefully in her arms, having sought the escape after so many months without company.

They watched the activity in the garden below, still echoing with faint laughter. Catherine and Georgiana were walking arm in arm while Frederick and James Livesay participated in genial debate. Somewhere, they heard Lydia calling instructions to the younger cousins who were staging an impromptu game on the lawn.

Even the older members of the party had joined in the merriment and were watching the younger generation as they played.

On the terrace, Darcy stood close to his wife, his hand resting at the small of her back as they both looked down upon their son.

"It is strange," he murmured, "to think how much has changed since I first met your family."

"I am eternally grateful to your father," Elizabeth said. "Can you imagine what my family would have been like had your father not inspired mine to change? Lydia would have been unchecked, Catherine would have followed her, and I am uncertain what Mary would have been."

She laughed softly to herself. "And Mama, she would have been insufferable."

"I would have been proud, arrogant even," Darcy admitted. "I met your family with an open mind when I first came to Hertfordshire, and Father's words to me allowed me to even consider you. I had wondered what you were like for all those years before we met."

He paused for a moment. "Did I ever tell you that I stayed in your room when I visited with my father?" he asked, surprising Elizabeth.

She turned to look at him more fully. "You did?"

"Yes, it must have been yours," he said. "I cannot imagine your sister being the one to read Shakespeare, and I distinctly recall seeing *Midsummer* on the nightstand."

"*Love looks not with the eyes, but with the mind, And therefore is wing'd Cupid painted blind,*" Elizabeth quoted softly.

Darcy laughed. "That is certainly true for us. While I cannot claim that I loved you before I arrived in Hertfordshire, the letters you scribed for your father had been full of your personality and wit."

That caused Elizabeth to chuckle. "Yes," she agreed. "Papa told me about your letter to him once you figured out why the tone of his letters had changed. Then, I began writing more faithfully what he dictated but added my own lines at the ending."

Darcy merely shook his head in reply. Looking down at the garden, he smiled. "We have all grown since then."

"We have," Elizabeth agreed.

He looked at her then, with the familiar warmth that made her heart stir. "Pemberley is quite different with so many guests in residence. I never imagined such harmony among so many strong opinions. Nor did I expect to enjoy the lively…sport of family life quite so much."

She tilted her head playfully. "*Sport*, is it? I suppose it is. There was certainly enough of it at the dinner table this evening."

"I heard from Bingley," Darcy said, again surprising his wife.

"Is he in America still?" Elizabeth asked.

"He is. It proved more difficult than he thought to banish his sister, and he has decided that the opportunities are better for him there. She is still with him, however, so I am uncertain what his plans might be," Darcy replied.

Elizabeth nodded. "I am very sorry that Aunt Horatia could not join us. The Hursts are nice enough company, but I much prefer their aunt."

"She has purchased Netherfield," Darcy said after a moment. "We have an open invitation to stay whenever we are in the area."

Elizabeth laughed. "I will need to ask Mama how she feels about that. She was ever so hopeful that it would be purchased by a young man of means who might marry Catherine or Lydia."

"Horatia Bingley is far better company and much more entertaining," Darcy said. "Catherine is old enough to join Georgiana next spring, and perhaps Lydia might come as well."

Nodding, Elizabeth slowly rocked back and forth as their son stirred in her arms.

"Let us take this young man to the nursery and turn him over to the nurse for the evening," Darcy said, watching his wife. "It is time we joined our families again."

She looked up at him with a gentle smile. "Do you suppose anyone will notice if we are gone just a little longer?"

Darcy chuckled softly. "If they do, they will likely assume I have stolen you away for some private moments."

Elizabeth arched an eyebrow, amused. "Would they be wrong?"

"Not entirely," he replied, offering his arm as they turned towards the house. "I will admit, as much as I enjoy our usual peace, it is rather pleasant to have so many under one roof—pleasant chaos, perhaps, but still welcome."

They walked slowly through the corridor, the soft glow of candlelight guiding their steps. From the drawing room ahead, the sound of a pianoforte drifted through the halls—Georgiana and Amelia playing a duet, accompanied by the distant hum of conversation and laughter as their guests returned inside.

Reaching the nursery, Elizabeth pressed a kiss to Bennet's forehead before handing him over to the nurse. The child stirred once, then settled with a contented sigh.

Darcy paused at the door, his gaze on his sleeping son. "It is a strange thing," he said quietly. "To love someone so small so completely."

Elizabeth slipped her hand into his. "He is everything good from both of us."

Darcy turned to her, his expression soft. "And we—" He stopped, his eyes searching hers. "We are everything I once worried may be beyond my reach."

They lingered a moment more before returning to their guests, hand in hand—ready to rejoin the laughter, the music, and the unpredictable, spirited joy that came with family and friendship.

Acknowledgments

I have an incredible group of people who support me and my writing. Of course, my family allows me to spend far too much of my time sitting in front of my computer. But others provide their assistance in so many ways. I thank you all. Whether it is pointing out what I did wrong, or just encouraging me by sending me an email, sharing on social media, or commenting on Substack telling me that you enjoy my writing, I am so appreciative for all that you do.

Specifically, I'd like to thank Debbie Allen and Cathy Earle who helped so much by being both a sounding board, along with pointing out all my errors, not only in mechanics, but also the inconsistencies and other mistakes I made along the way.

Others, such as Caroline Cartier, Debra McMaster, Lis Batten, Rebecca McBrayer, Ruth, and dozens of others who are happy to receive advance copies and give me feedback, encouragement, and share kind words on social media and other sites. I cannot express how much I appreciate the help you provide!

To my readers—thank you for taking this journey with me. Your enthusiasm and love for these characters inspire me to keep writing.

I love your feedback. Please feel free to email me or contact me on social media if you'd like to share your thoughts about the book.

About the Author

Melissa Anne first read Pride and Prejudice in high school and discovered the world of JAFF a few years ago. After reading quite a few, she thought perhaps she could do that and began writing, first on fan fiction sites, and then published as an independent author. Melissa Anne is a pen name.

She began her career as a newspaper reporter before becoming a middle school English teacher and then a high school English teacher. She lives and works in Georgia, although she grew up in East Tennessee and claims that as home. Melissa has been married to a rather wonderful man (something of a cross between a Darcy and a Bingley) for two decades, and together they have three children.

Contact her at melissa.anne.author@gmail.com

Be the first to know when Melissa Anne's next book is available! Follow her at https://www.bookbub.com/authors/melissa-anne *to get an alert whenever she has a new release, preorder, or discount!*

Want to read snippets of Melissa's Works in Progress? Check out her Substack here: https://melissaanneauthor.substack.com/

You can also listen to samples of her audiobooks on her YouTube channel: youtube.com/@MelissaAnneAuthor

Occassionally, I will share bonus materials on my new website https://melissaanneauthor.com/. Be sure to check it out!

Also by Melissa Anne

Regency Pride and Prejudice Variations

The Bennet Heir

In Spite of All

When Love is True

Darcy & Elizabeth's Dreams of Redemption

Worthy of Her Trust

Hearts Entwined

Responsibility and Resentment

A Different Impression

What Happened After Lambton

The Accidental Letter (novella)

Holidays With Darcy and Elizabeth

A Return at Christmas (short story)

Darcy and Elizabeth's Valentine's Meet Cute (short story)

Darcy's Redemption: Easter at Hunsford (short story)

Modern Variations

Finding Love at Loch Ness

Coming Soon

THE VERY BEST OF FRIENDS

Chapter 1: An Incident at Netherfield

"Thank you for your help, Miss Elizabeth."

"You are welcome, Mrs. Nicholls. I still think she needs to be seen by the apothecary, but I have patched up the injury as best I can."

"Miss Bingley refused to allow us to call for Mr. Jones."

Elizabeth pursed her lips. "No doubt because she did not want others to know she caused such an injury to the maid. She will need this evening off, probably the morning as well, and she will need to be careful of that hand for a time. If she begins to run a fever or red streaks begin to show from the wound, that will indicate an infection, and Mr. Jones will definitely need to see her then. I know the cook has a good poultice that will help, but still…"

"I will do what I can. Perhaps if I approach the master instead…" Mrs.

Nicholls trailed off as she heard the floor creak outside the library where Elizabeth was treating the maid.

"Pardon me," came the deep, solemn voice of Mr. Darcy. He looked between the three women and noted the bandages around the maid's wrist and the evidence that Elizabeth had been helping to care for her. "Is the apothecary needed? I can send a footman to town if needed. One of my servants would not mind going if Netherfield cannot spare anyone."

"Miss Bingley refused to send for one," Elizabeth said tartly.

Darcy frowned at that. "What happened?"

"Apparently…" The startled glance from the maid and Mrs. Nicholls caused Elizabeth to stop. "Never mind that. She had a shard of porcelain embedded in her wrist. I helped Mrs. Nicholls pluck it out and then cleaned and bandaged it. I believe she may need a stitch or two, but I am not equipped to do that, and Miss Bingley refused the request to have the apothecary called to do it. I did what I could, but I worry it will not be enough."

His frown deepened. "Did the shard come from some *objet d'art* thrown by Miss Bingley in a fit of temper? Honestly, that woman…" he trailed off as his cheeks reddened as he realised what he had said. "Forgive me. I should not criticise my hostess. Please send for the apothecary, and *I* will pay for the girl's care. I will also cover her wages if Miss Bingley objects; she will likely need several days to recover from her injury, and someone will need to be certain she does not take a fever."

Elizabeth looked at him with her mouth agape for a second. He quirked his brow at her, and it caused her to recover her wits. "I was just saying that. We used alcohol to clean the injury, though Mr. Jones may desire to do it again before he sews the cut. If she takes a fever or if the wound becomes infected, she will need to be seen again."

"I will arrange for it. Mrs. Nicholls, will you inform me if the apothecary needs to visit again or if Miss Bingley gives you any trouble."

"Of course, sir. Also, Mr. Smith asked me to thank you for the assistance you arranged for him and his wife. They are growing older, and since the manor has not had an interested master in some time…" The look on Mr Darcy's face made her trail off.

"It was nothing. Bingley is the master here, although he knows little about how to care for the tenants yet. The tenants have been cared for well; is it typically you who does that?"

"No, sir; it is mainly Miss Elizabeth. I think Miss Jane and Miss Mary help some, but ever since the Pattinsons' closed the house five years ago, Miss Elizabeth had tended to the tenants as she does at Longbourn."

This time, it was Elizabeth's cheeks that flamed. "Mrs. Nicholls, you know I do very little. It is simple to do the same for Netherfield's tenants as *my family* does for ours at Longbourn."

Darcy gave her a searching look at that comment but did not say anything. Mrs. Nicholls finished gathering the supplies, and she and the maid both curtsied as they left the room.

"Why am I not surprised to learn that *you* visit not only your own tenants but those on the neighbouring estate as well?" Darcy asked after a moment.

Elizabeth looked at him quizzically. "You are an enigma, sir."

He arched that eyebrow again, which made Elizabeth grin. "What does that mean?"

"Mrs. Nicholls has said much about the way you have," she cleared her throat, "*assisted* Mr. Bingley as he learnt to manage this estate. You appear to be very helpful and interested in estate matters despite the fact it is not yours, and from what I have heard of you, ensuring Molly has the care she needs is not outside of the norm for you."

"Why do I hear a 'but' in there, Miss Elizabeth?"

"You care for the tenants and servants of an estate your friend has merely leased, yet you disdain those of the gentry who live here. You appear friendly and at ease in speaking with those who serve you, yet nearly every family who lives here has felt the sting of your scorn."

He looked stunned by her comment. "Scorn? Disdain? How have I demonstrated these?"

Elizabeth cleared her throat and deepened her voice. "She is tolerable, I suppose, but not handsome enough to tempt me," she replied.

Darcy's mouth fell open. "Who said that?"

She let out a small laugh. "You did, sir. It was nearly the first thing most of our neighbours heard you say. At the assembly, you barely spoke to anyone at the assembly, and when your friend encouraged you to dance, that is what you said. You continued to stalk the edge of the room for the rest of the night and spoke to no one outside your party."

"I did not know anyone," he defended.

"Neither did your friend before he allowed himself to be introduced to those in attendance."

"I feel awkward in company. I heard the whispers of my estate and my income on everyone's tongues, and it added to my unease."

"I can understand that, Mr. Darcy, but your words were hateful. They formed many in the area's first impression of you, and quite frankly, your actions today seem to contradict the man I thought you were."

"I need to apologise to the woman. Do you know who she is?"

She laughed nearly hysterically. Briefly, he worried she would stumble until she finally plopped down on an armchair.

"I do," she said when she finally regained her composure.

"Then will you tell me who she is so I can make my apologies? Obviously, I did not bother to look at her. Bingley was prodding me to dance, and I simply wanted to be left alone."

Elizabeth stood and faced him. "Think back for a moment, Mr. Darcy. What else do you remember Mr. Bingley saying to you?"

He did as she asked and pondered. "He was dancing with Miss Bennet, I think, and he stopped to speak with me between dances. He, uhh, said it was one of her sisters..." he trailed off, his face becoming pale. "Please tell me it was not you who sat there," he begged.

She looked him directly in the eyes. "It was," she replied, and after a moment, her eyes dropped. "Can you imagine how it felt to have the most handsome man I had ever encountered speak of me as 'tolerable' and 'not handsome'? Is it not enough that my mother has told me my entire life that I am 'nothing to Jane' only to have it confirmed immediately by some arrogant man? Granted, you are wealthy and have all sorts of connections and are no doubt pursued by many for those two attributes, but to have Mama's words confirmed by you was incredibly hurtful."

"I am sorry, Elizabeth, so very sorry. Obviously, I scarcely looked at the woman before I spoke. You are extraordinarily tempting, and I have had to remind myself frequently in the last month that it is my duty to my family to marry for wealth and connections. If not for my sister, I would have been tempted to make you an offer already." Both noticed his slip in calling her by her Christian name, and their cheeks flushed a little, though neither commented on it.

Ducking her head slightly to cover her blush, Elizabeth retorted: "Sir, there is no need to flatter me now. I know what you think of me, and it is pointless trying to convince me otherwise. I would prefer the blunt truth."

"The blunt truth, Elizabeth, is I would have asked you to marry me when you arrived at Netherfield two days ago if I had only myself to consider. You are enchanting, and I have rarely seen you as beautiful as you appeared when you arrived that day to enquire about your sister. While Miss Bingley and Mrs Hurst laughed about the little bit of dirt on your petticoats, all I could think of was how the exercise brightened your eyes and made your cheeks flow. It took great restraint to remain a gentleman at that moment."

She blushed, recognising the implication in his statement, even if she did not fully understand it. "What does your sister have to do with your not making me an offer? Not that I would be inclined to accept one from you at this moment since both Jane and I have always sworn to marry only for the deepest love. I am not even certain I like you at this moment."

Darcy gulped. "Forgive me for stating the matter so baldly. Since childhood, my parents impressed upon me that my duty was to marry to increase my family's wealth and status by choosing a woman with dowry and connections. My aunt likes to tell me that she and my mother spoke of marriage to her daughter, the heiress of Rosings Park in Kent, but I know that is not true. Mother would not have objected to the idea of joining the two estates but would not have forced me to marry against my will. However, she did impress upon me the importance of marrying well.

"When she passed away, my father took up the refrain. My duty to my family was to care for Pemberley, its staff, its tenants, and all the hundreds of other people who rely on the estate by marrying well, fathering a son or two, and keeping the accounts of Pemberley flush. Nearly his last words emphasised this and reminded me of my responsibility to care for and protect Georgiana. He also did not favour the match with my cousin since, by then, she was known to be sickly and frail, and he doubted her ability to carry a child."

He sighed deeply. "I broached with him once during my university years the idea of marrying for love, and he mocked me for it. He said love is what you feel for mistresses and courtesans; 'a Darcy marries for duty.' *My* duty was to raise the family's status by marrying someone who would add to our wealth or connections – though preferably, she would bring both. He married with those considerations in mind; my mother was the daughter of an earl and brought a substantial dowry with her. My uncle, Lord Matlock, has reinforced these ideas in my mind. Each year, he and my aunt identify a few debutantes they would like to match me with, and I grudgingly complied and allowed myself to be introduced to them."

Darcy shook his head as though clearing it. "However, they are all the same; they can speak of the weather, a novel or two, the latest fashion and gossip, but they can speak of nothing of substance. That is why I have refused to marry any of them. I do not want a marriage that would require me to seek someone or something outside my marriage to find…well, anything. I want a marriage with a woman who is an equal partner, one who shares my interests, and one with whom I can debate. I have enjoyed my conversations with you tremendously, even when we debate, since you have made me reconsider my thoughts on several matters, and have even bested me a time or two. You do not defer to me or merely agree with whatever I say to make yourself agreeable. I like that you are willing to challenge me."

Elizabeth grinned at him. "You like me because I am impertinent. You would grow tired of that over time, if you could overcome your objections to my lack of wealth and connections," Elizabeth said, her tone sounding a little wounded as she finished her speech.

"I would not. I adore your kindness towards others; for example, how many others would walk three miles to tend to an ill sister? You would make a magnificent mistress of an estate, even one so large as Pemberley. I have heard much good spoken of you as I visited the tenants here." He sighed deeply. "For the first time, I have considered throwing over all my lessons regarding my duty to my family and allowing my heart to lead. Perhaps it is best that you would not accept me anyway."

"You never answered the question of why your sister prevents you?"

"If I marry as I desire, would it limit my sister's ability to make a good match? She has had a…a troubling summer and has unfortunately learnt a lesson I would have rather she not had to learn just yet. A…a rake, a former friend even, attempted to importune her and convince her to elope to Gretna Green. I was able to prevent it, but her heart was injured in the process. He only wanted her for her thirty thousand pound dowry. As you can imagine, as a young, sensitive girl, she was terribly distressed at this realisation and still believes no one would ever want her for any other reason. You…you would be very good for her, I think. If anyone could cajole her out of her doldrums, it would be you."

She flushed scarlet again. "Why is that?"

"I cannot imagine you remaining sad for very long. You would tease her and prod her into being happy. You would know the right thing to say to her to convince her that I am not disappointed in her and that she is worthless. I am angry about what occurred, but mainly at myself. It never occurred to me to warn her that our former friend, my father's godson, was a rake who might attempt to injure her someday. Clearly, I should have done a better job of preparing her for the world, but how do I speak to my innocent, much younger sister about such things? Do you know how difficult it was for me to speak to her when she began her courses?"

This time, he flushed brightly, though the blush that had faded on her cheeks burned once more.

She choked back a laugh. "I cannot imagine. It was painful enough to have that conversation with my mother; it would be impossible with a brother."

"I had not even given thought to her mortification on the subject, only my own. It was terrifying."

Elizabeth could not hold back her laughter this time, and after a moment, he joined in. "You would be good for me as well, Elizabeth. I have never felt this at ease with anyone else."

"Well then, sir, you must decide whether your duty or your heart will have the highest place. Should you choose to court me, I think I would be inclined to let you, but, as I have said, I will not marry without love. However, before you ask, you must decide whether duty will take the highest place in your choice. If you decide against your heart, I will have a pleasant memory of an interesting conversation with a friend. Perhaps if your friend and my sister come to an agreement to bind themselves together, we will continue to encounter each other as friends. If you decide otherwise, well, then I do not know what the result will be. Perhaps none of these considerations will matter as when we know each other better, we will decide we do not suit, and we will remain as friends.

"I will only ask you this: what do you want? I think you know what your family expects, but what do those whose opinion matters most think? Would your sister want you to marry for duty and be miserable? Or would she want you to seek out someone who touches your heart? Are there others you care about who might give an opinion?"

Darcy sighed profoundly and stood silent for several long minutes. "I know what I want. But perhaps I should speak to Georgiana about what she wants. I would bring her here – she would adore you, and I think you would adore her in return — but she is a little afraid of Miss Bingley and would prefer not to share a residence with her right now."

"Perhaps I can ask my aunt and uncle, and they will permit me to return to London with them in January. If you are in town, we could meet. I have four sisters and am quite used to cajoling them out of their doldrums."

"How would I know?"

"How would you know what?"

"If you were in London?"

She furrowed her brow. "I am not certain. I suppose I could have my uncle write to you."

"I do not know him."

"He is a tradesman named Edward Gardiner. He has several warehouses in Cheapside, but he and my aunt have probably been my greatest influences. He attended Cambridge and then married a gentleman's daughter from Lambton, which is somewhere in the north. They are both well-educated and have had a significant influence on me and my elder sister."

"Lambton, you say. That is but five miles from Pemberley."

"Then perhaps you know her family. Her father was, oh, I think his name was Mr. Wright, but I cannot remember the name of his estate."

"I recall the family, but they moved away quite a few years ago. I do not recall why, but it was more than a decade ago."

"Then perhaps you can renew the connection with my aunt, which will give you a reason to call on my uncle and learn when I am to come, if I am to come to Town."

"You will let me court you then?" Darcy asked.

"Have you decided to ask?" she returned.

"I am willing to try. I am uncertain of the result, but I would like to see what this between us might be. I have rarely enjoyed a conversation with a woman more than I have this last half hour, and, well, I think I would like to have a lifetime of conversations like this. If Georgiana can learn to have some of your poise and confidence, then perhaps my marrying with my heart will affect her prospects less than I fear. Not to mention, I suddenly realised I would not want to condemn Georgiana to the type of marriage I am proposing for myself."

"Perhaps it is time to listen to your heart then?"

"I think it is."

She smiled broadly at him. Then she laughed. "I would have never imagined having this sort of conversation with you of all people. You are very different from what I believed. You will need to show me this side of yourself often, that is, if you want to make me fall in love with you."

"Might I confess something?" At her nod, he continued. "Before you, I had never imagined having this sort of conversation with anyone. I have never spoken this openly to anyone before – not Bingley, nor even Richard. I share guardianship of Georgiana with my cousin, Colonel Richard Fitzwilliam, and before this moment, would have considered him my greatest friend."

"Before this moment?"

"After such a conversation as this, can we be anything other than the best of friends, Elizabeth?"

She scowled at him. "It is unfair, sir."

"What is?" he asked, confused at her sudden change.

"You have already begun to address me informally, but I do not know what else to call you other than Mr. Darcy. What is your Christian name? And can I assume I have your permission to address you as such, at least in private?"

"My name is Fitzwilliam; I was named for my mother's family. Most people call me Darcy, but my mother used to call me William. Georgiana had begun to adopt that name as well. I would be honoured if you would refer to me by that name."

The smile she gave him was beatific and transformed her face into an almost ethereal beauty. "I would be delighted, William. Now, we are in a library; tell me, what think you of books?"

The two continued their conversation for another half hour complete before Miss Bingley discovered them together and interrupted them. Both were

COMING SOON

displeased at the interruption, but the smile they exchanged led them to believe much had changed in their lives and hearts. It was the first of many diverting conversations, for the two would become the very best of friends, and before too long, far, far more.

This is unedited and is subject to change.

Printed in Dunstable, United Kingdom